THIEF OF THIEVES™

CREATED BY ROBERT KIRKMAN

ROBERT KIRKMAN
JAMES ASMUS
ANDY DIGGLE
STORY

ANDY DIGGLE
WRITER

SHAWN MARTINBROUGH
ARTIST

FELIX SERRANO
COLORIST

RUS WOOTON
LETTERER

SEAN MACKIEWICZ
EDITOR

SHAWN MARTINBROUGH
FELIX SERRANO
COVER

THIEF OF THIEVES, VOL. 3: "VENICE."
ISBN: 978-1-60706-844-0
PRINTED IN U.S.A.
First Printing

IMAGE COMICS, INC.
Robert Kirkman - Chief Operating Officer
Erik Larsen - Chief Financial Officer
Todd McFarlane - President
Marc Silvestri - Chief Executive Officer
Jim Valentino - Vice-President

Eric Stephenson - Publisher
Ron Richards - Director of Business Development
Jennifer de Guzman - Director of Trade Book Sales
Kat Salazar - Director of PR & Marketing
Jeremy Sullivan - Director of Digital Sales
Emilio Bautista - Sales Assistant
Branwyn Bigglestone - Senior Accounts Manager
Emily Miller - Accounts Manager
Jessica Ambriz - Administrative Assistant
Tyler Shainline - Events Coordinator
David Brothers - Content Manager
Jonathan Chan - Production Manager
Drew Gill - Art Director
Meredith Wallace - Print Manager
Monica Garcia - Senior Production Artist
Jenna Savage - Production Artist
Addison Duke - Production Artist
IMAGECOMICS.COM

For SKYBOUND ENTERTAINMENT

Robert Kirkman - CEO
J.J. Didde - President
Sean Mackiewicz - Editorial Director
Shawn Kirkham - Director of Business Development
Brian Huntington - Online Editorial Director
Helen Leigh - Office Manager
Lizzy Iverson - Administrative Assistant

For international rights inquiries,
please contact: foreign@skybound.com
WWW.SKYBOUND.COM

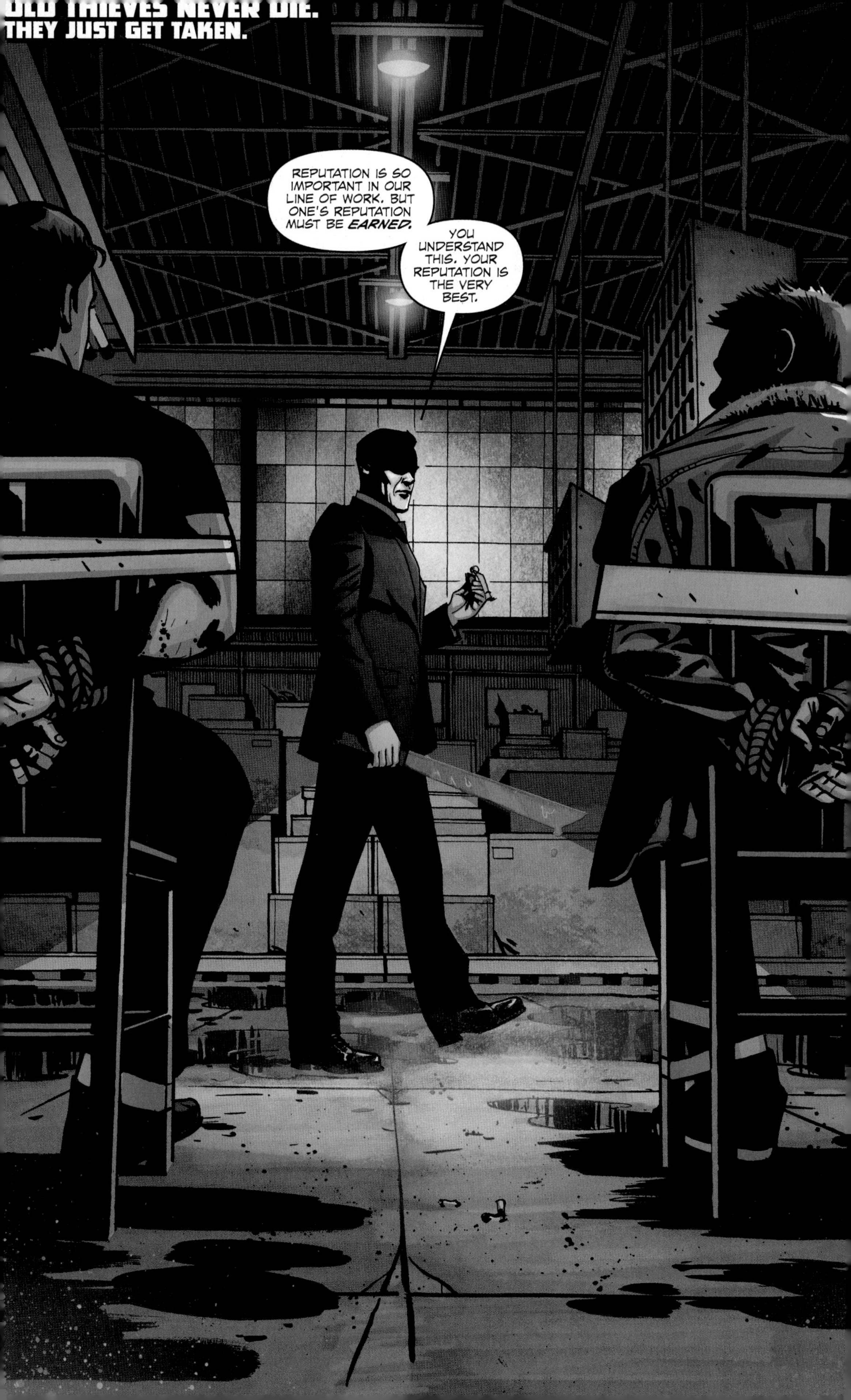
OLD THIEVES NEVER DIE.
THEY JUST GET TAKEN.
REPUTATION IS SO IMPORTANT IN OUR LINE OF WORK. BUT ONE'S REPUTATION MUST BE *EARNED.*
YOU UNDERSTAND THIS. YOUR REPUTATION IS THE VERY BEST.

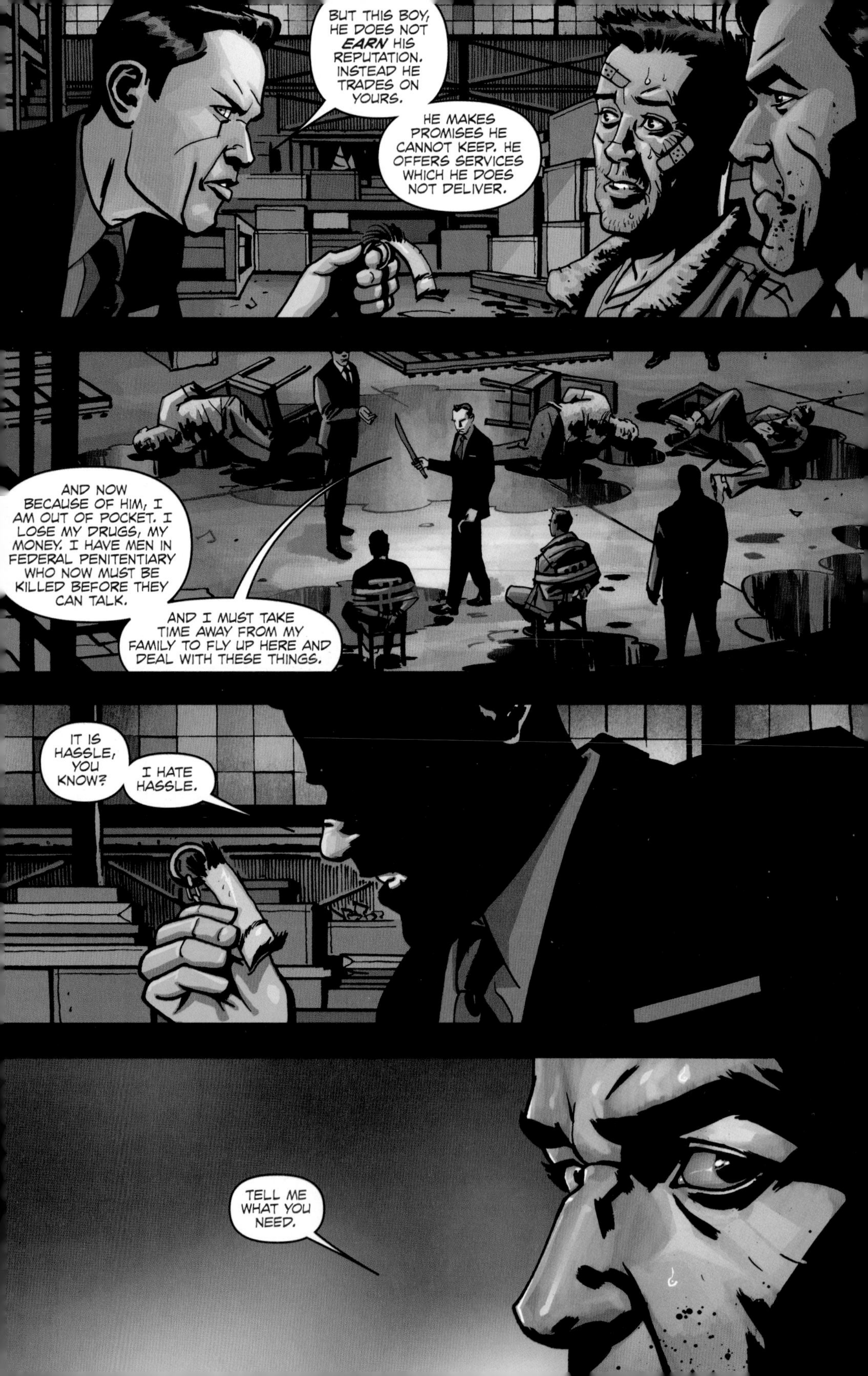
BUT THIS BOY, HE DOES NOT EARN HIS REPUTATION. INSTEAD HE TRADES ON YOURS.
HE MAKES PROMISES HE CANNOT KEEP. HE OFFERS SERVICES WHICH HE DOES NOT DELIVER.
AND NOW BECAUSE OF HIM, I AM OUT OF POCKET. I LOSE MY DRUGS, MY MONEY. I HAVE MEN IN FEDERAL PENITENTIARY WHO NOW MUST BE KILLED BEFORE THEY CAN TALK.
AND I MUST TAKE TIME AWAY FROM MY FAMILY TO FLY UP HERE AND DEAL WITH THESE THINGS.
IT IS HASSLE, YOU KNOW?
I HATE HASSLE.
TELL ME WHAT YOU NEED.

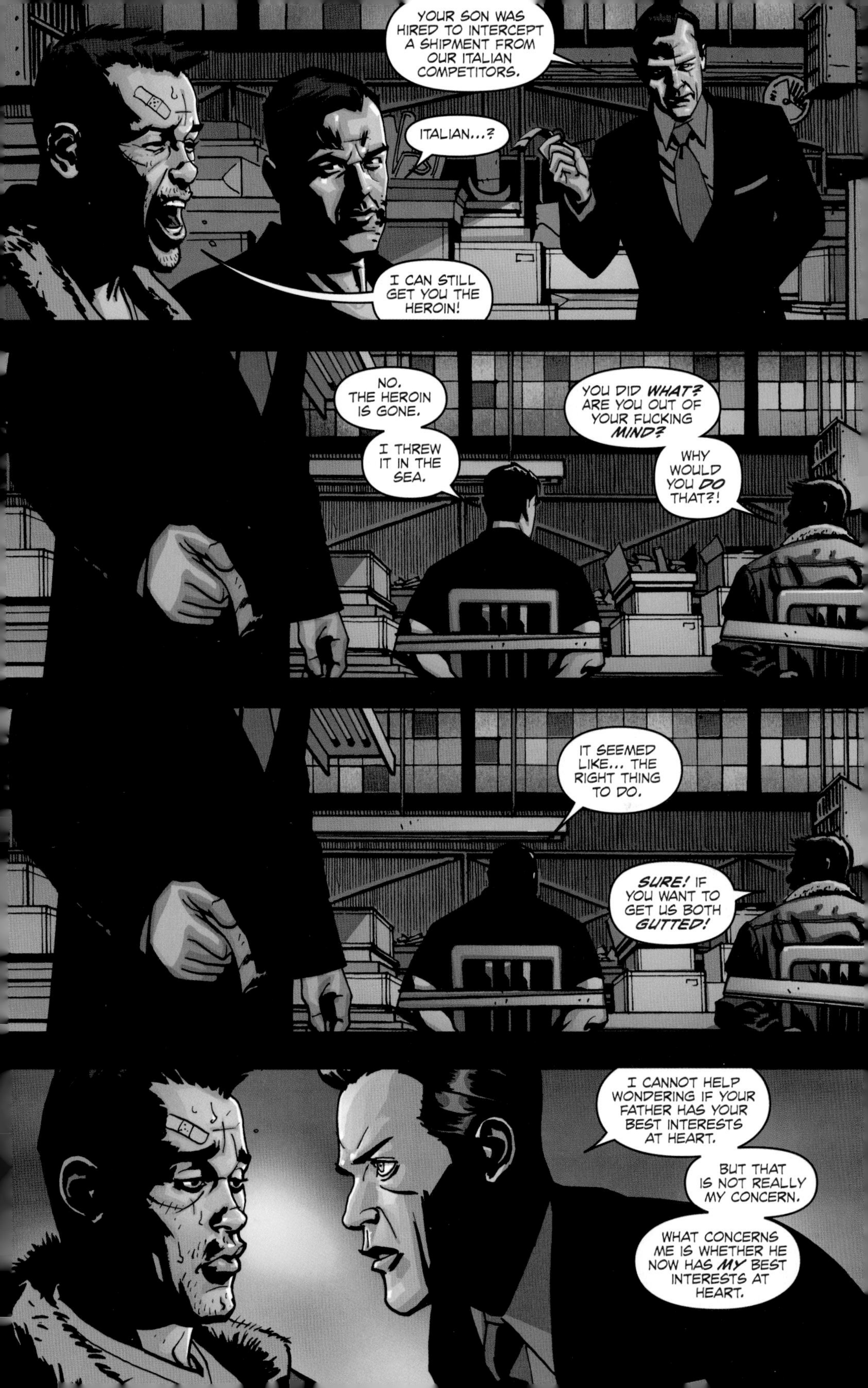
YOUR SON WAS HIRED TO INTERCEPT A SHIPMENT FROM OUR ITALIAN COMPETITORS.
ITALIAN...?
I CAN STILL GET YOU THE HEROIN!
NO. THE HEROIN IS GONE.
I THREW IT IN THE SEA.
YOU DID WHAT? ARE YOU OUT OF YOUR FUCKING MIND?
WHY WOULD YOU DO THAT?!
IT SEEMED LIKE... THE RIGHT THING TO DO.
SURE! IF YOU WANT TO GET US BOTH GUTTED!
I CANNOT HELP WONDERING IF YOUR FATHER HAS YOUR BEST INTERESTS AT HEART.
BUT THAT IS NOT REALLY MY CONCERN.
WHAT CONCERNS ME IS WHETHER HE NOW HAS MY BEST INTERESTS AT HEART.

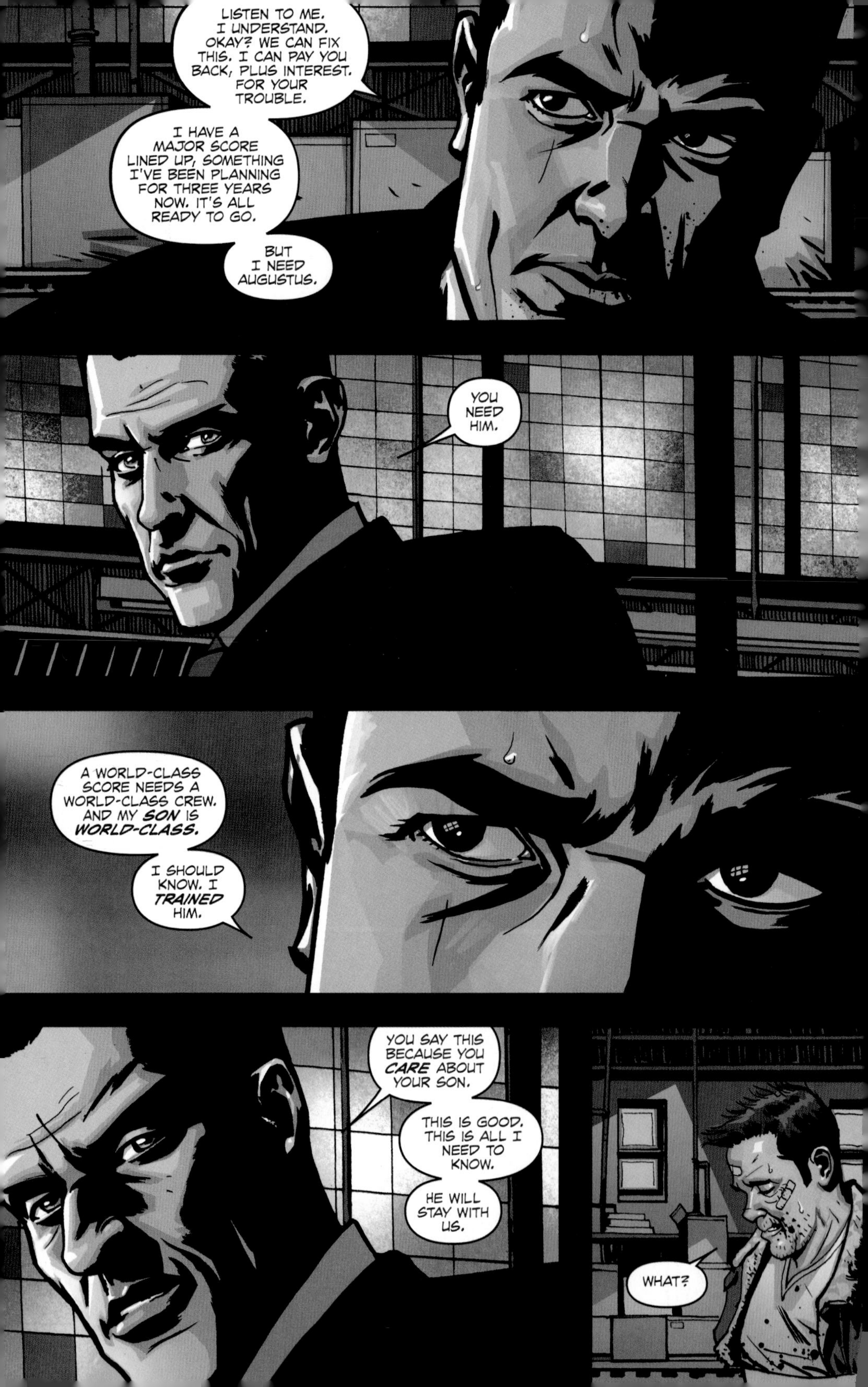
LISTEN TO ME. I UNDERSTAND. OKAY? WE CAN FIX THIS. I CAN PAY YOU BACK, PLUS INTEREST. FOR YOUR TROUBLE.
I HAVE A MAJOR SCORE LINED UP, SOMETHING I'VE BEEN PLANNING FOR THREE YEARS NOW. IT'S ALL READY TO GO.
BUT I NEED AUGUSTUS.
YOU NEED HIM.
A WORLD-CLASS SCORE NEEDS A WORLD-CLASS CREW. AND MY SON IS WORLD-CLASS.
I SHOULD KNOW. I TRAINED HIM.
YOU SAY THIS BECAUSE YOU CARE ABOUT YOUR SON.
THIS IS GOOD. THIS IS ALL I NEED TO KNOW.
HE WILL STAY WITH US.
WHAT?

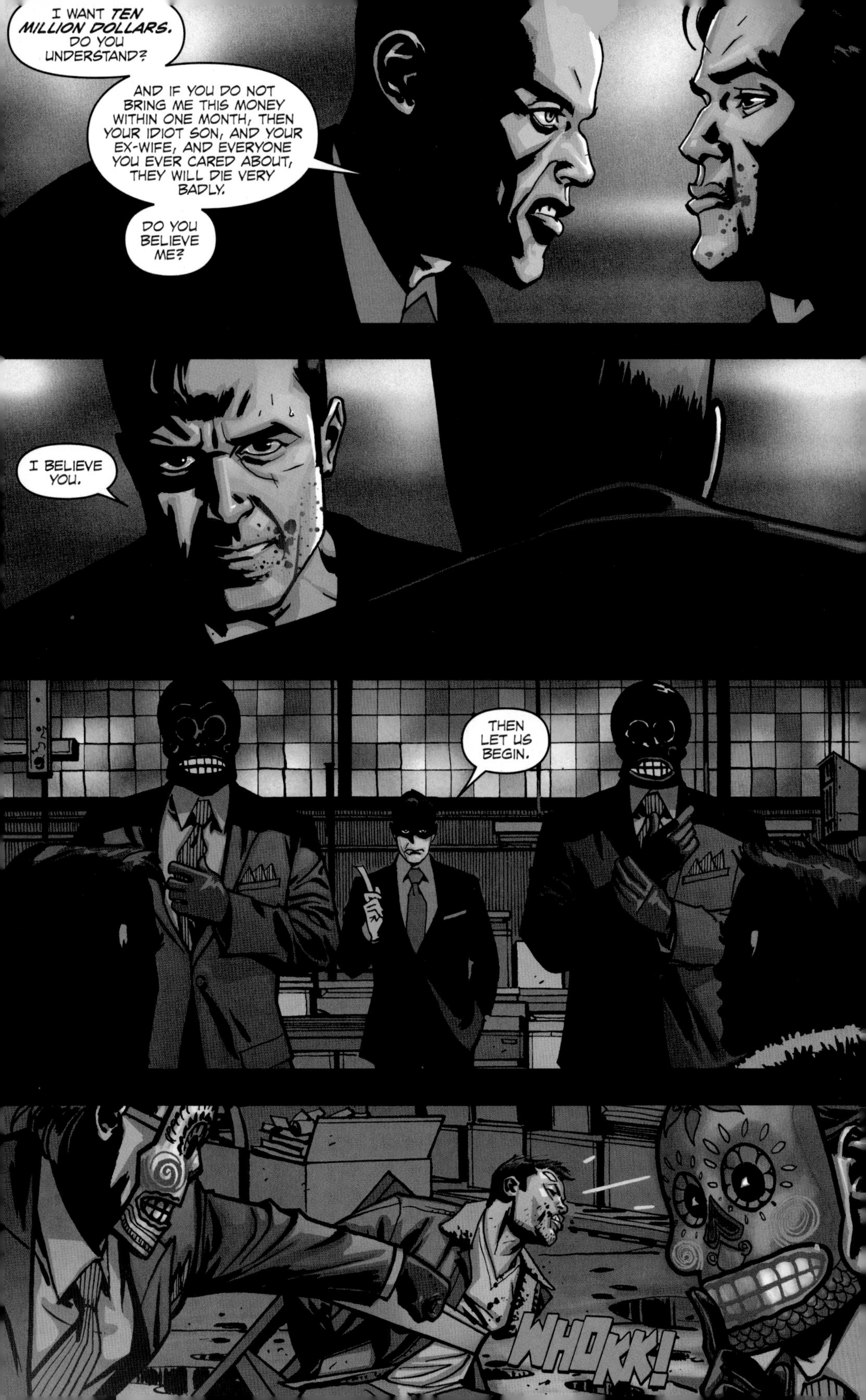
I WANT *TEN MILLION DOLLARS.* DO YOU UNDERSTAND?
AND IF YOU DO NOT BRING ME THIS MONEY WITHIN ONE MONTH, THEN YOUR IDIOT SON, AND YOUR EX-WIFE, AND EVERYONE YOU EVER CARED ABOUT, THEY WILL DIE VERY BADLY.
DO YOU BELIEVE ME?
I BELIEVE YOU.
THEN LET US BEGIN.
WHOKK!

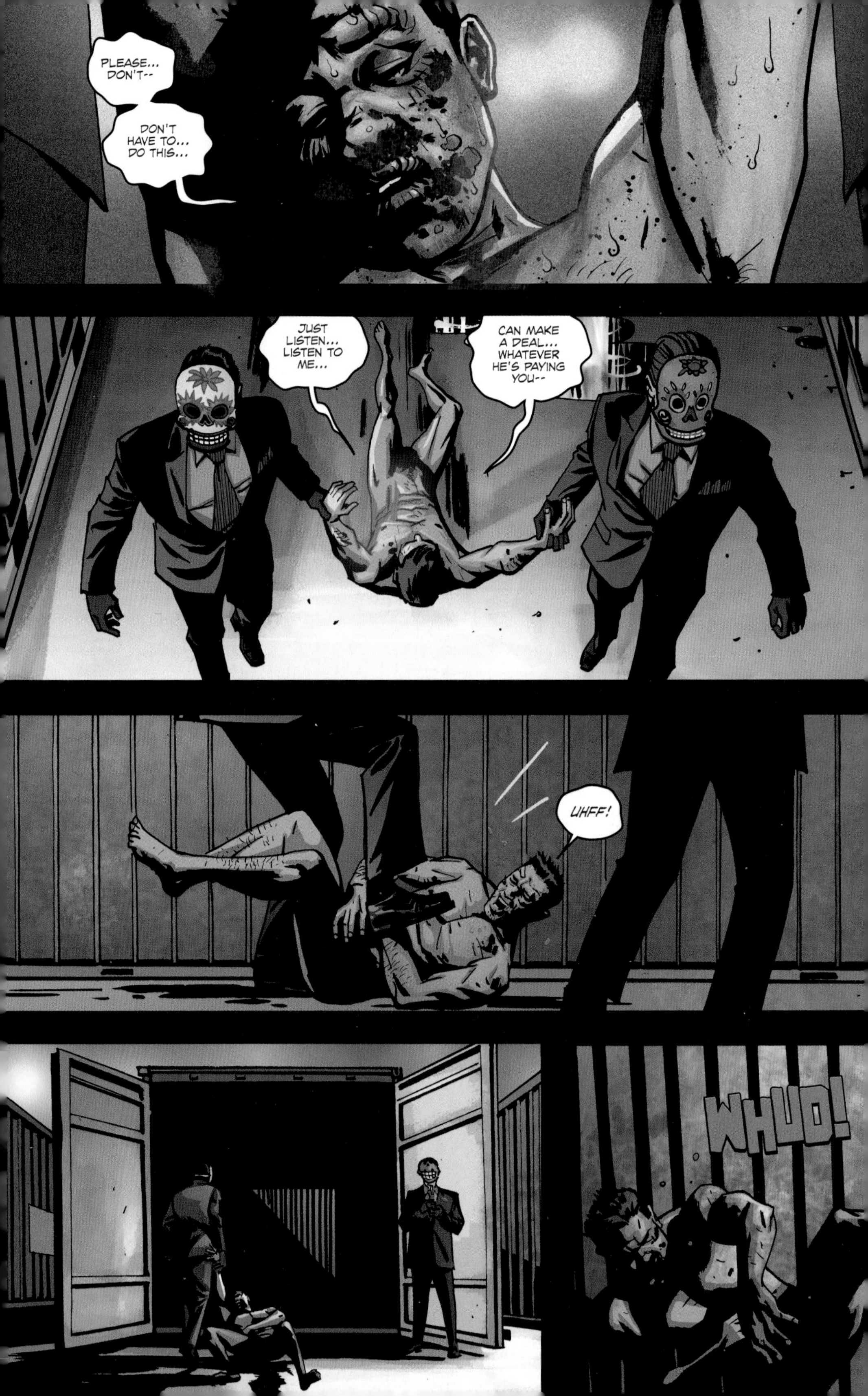
PLEASE... DON'T--
DON'T HAVE TO... DO THIS...
JUST LISTEN... LISTEN TO ME...
CAN MAKE A DEAL... WHATEVER HE'S PAYING YOU--
UHFF!
WHUD!

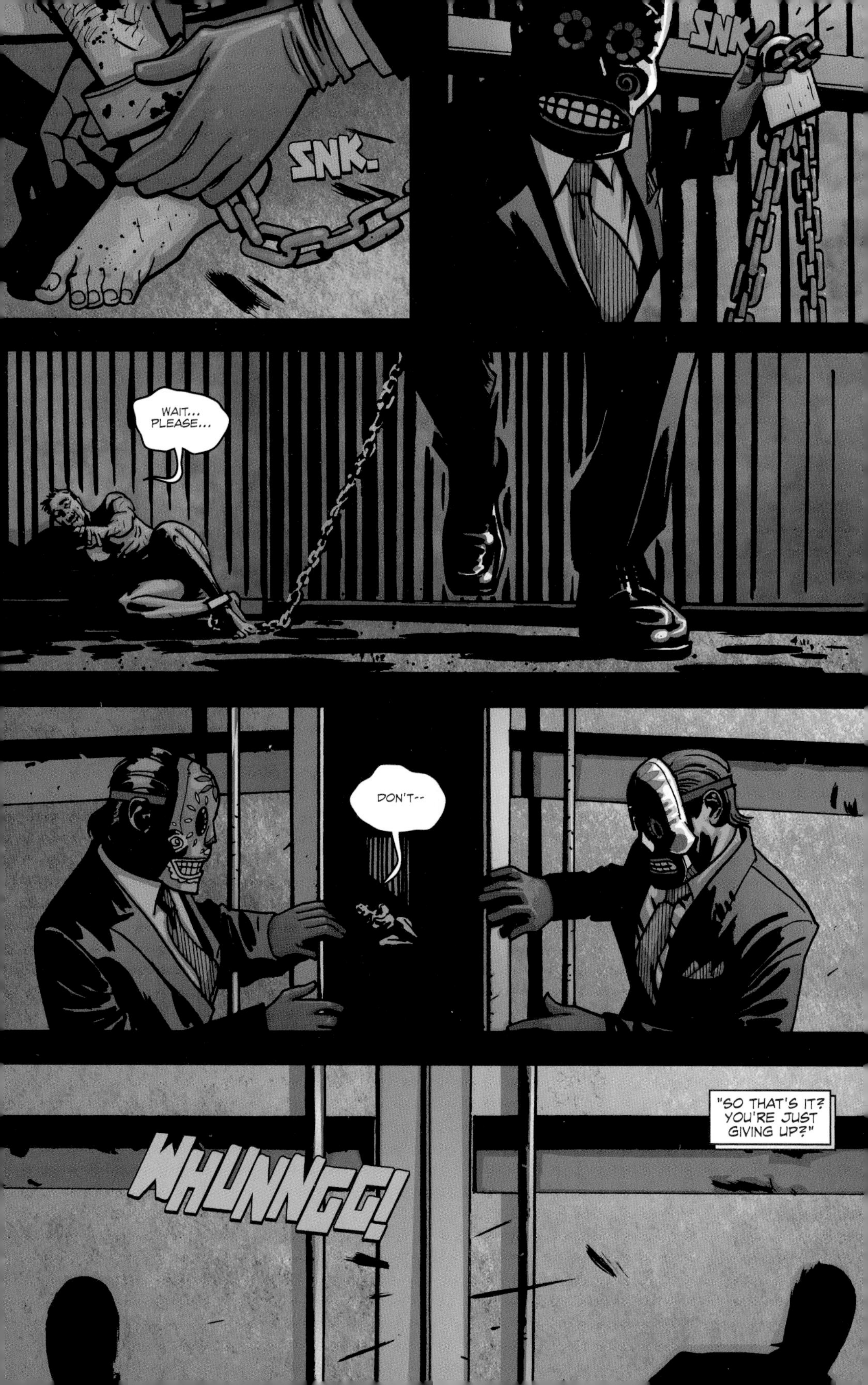
SNK.
SNK
WAIT... PLEASE...
DON'T--
"SO THAT'S IT? YOU'RE JUST GIVING UP?"
WHUNNGG!

SCHOOL'S OUT.
OR, THE FRESHMAN SWAPS MAJORS.

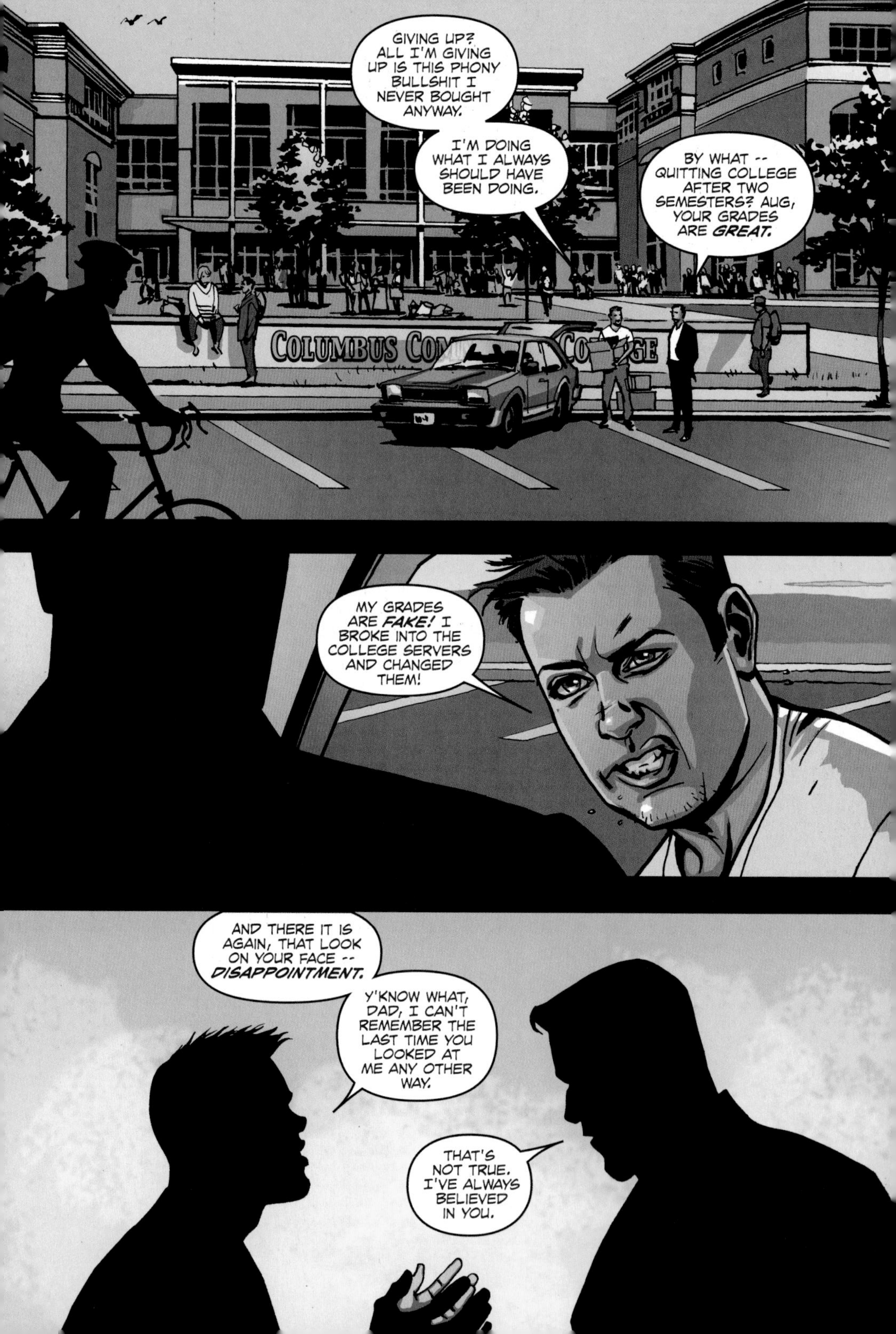
GIVING UP? ALL I'M GIVING UP IS THIS PHONY BULLSHIT I NEVER BOUGHT ANYWAY.
I'M DOING WHAT I ALWAYS SHOULD HAVE BEEN DOING.
BY WHAT -- QUITTING COLLEGE AFTER TWO SEMESTERS? AUG, YOUR GRADES ARE *GREAT.*
MY GRADES ARE *FAKE!* I BROKE INTO THE COLLEGE SERVERS AND CHANGED THEM!
AND THERE IT IS AGAIN, THAT LOOK ON YOUR FACE -- *DISAPPOINTMENT.*
Y'KNOW WHAT, DAD, I CAN'T REMEMBER THE LAST TIME YOU LOOKED AT ME ANY OTHER WAY.
THAT'S NOT TRUE. I'VE ALWAYS BELIEVED IN YOU.

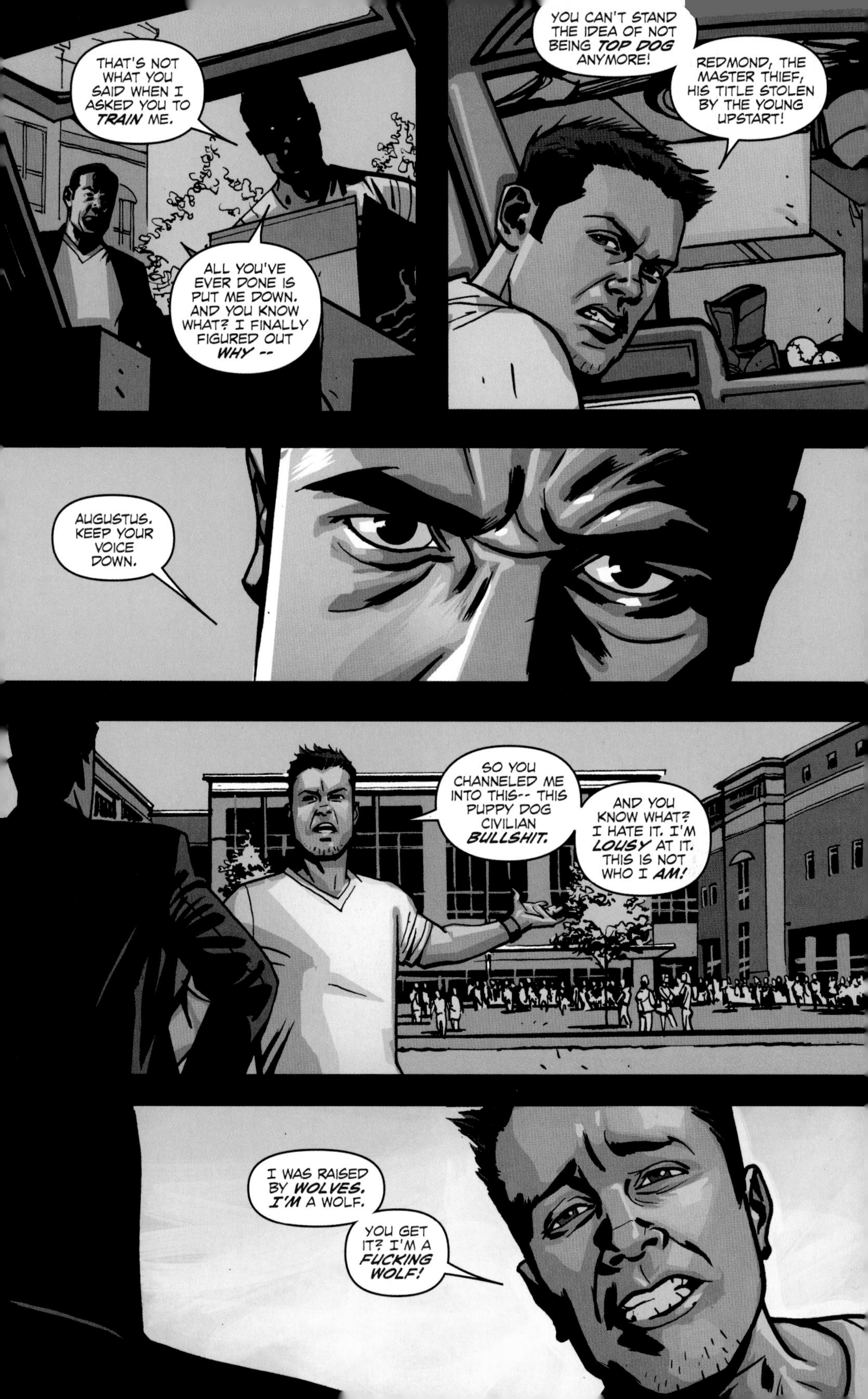
THAT'S NOT WHAT YOU SAID WHEN I ASKED YOU TO *TRAIN* ME.
ALL YOU'VE EVER DONE IS PUT ME DOWN. AND YOU KNOW WHAT? I FINALLY FIGURED OUT *WHY* --
YOU CAN'T STAND THE IDEA OF NOT BEING *TOP DOG* ANYMORE!
REDMOND, THE MASTER THIEF, HIS TITLE STOLEN BY THE YOUNG UPSTART!
AUGUSTUS. KEEP YOUR VOICE DOWN.
SO YOU CHANNELED ME INTO THIS-- THIS PUPPY DOG CIVILIAN *BULLSHIT.*
AND YOU KNOW WHAT? I HATE IT. I'M *LOUSY* AT IT. THIS IS NOT WHO I *AM!*
I WAS RAISED BY *WOLVES. I'M* A WOLF.
YOU GET IT? I'M A *FUCKING WOLF!*

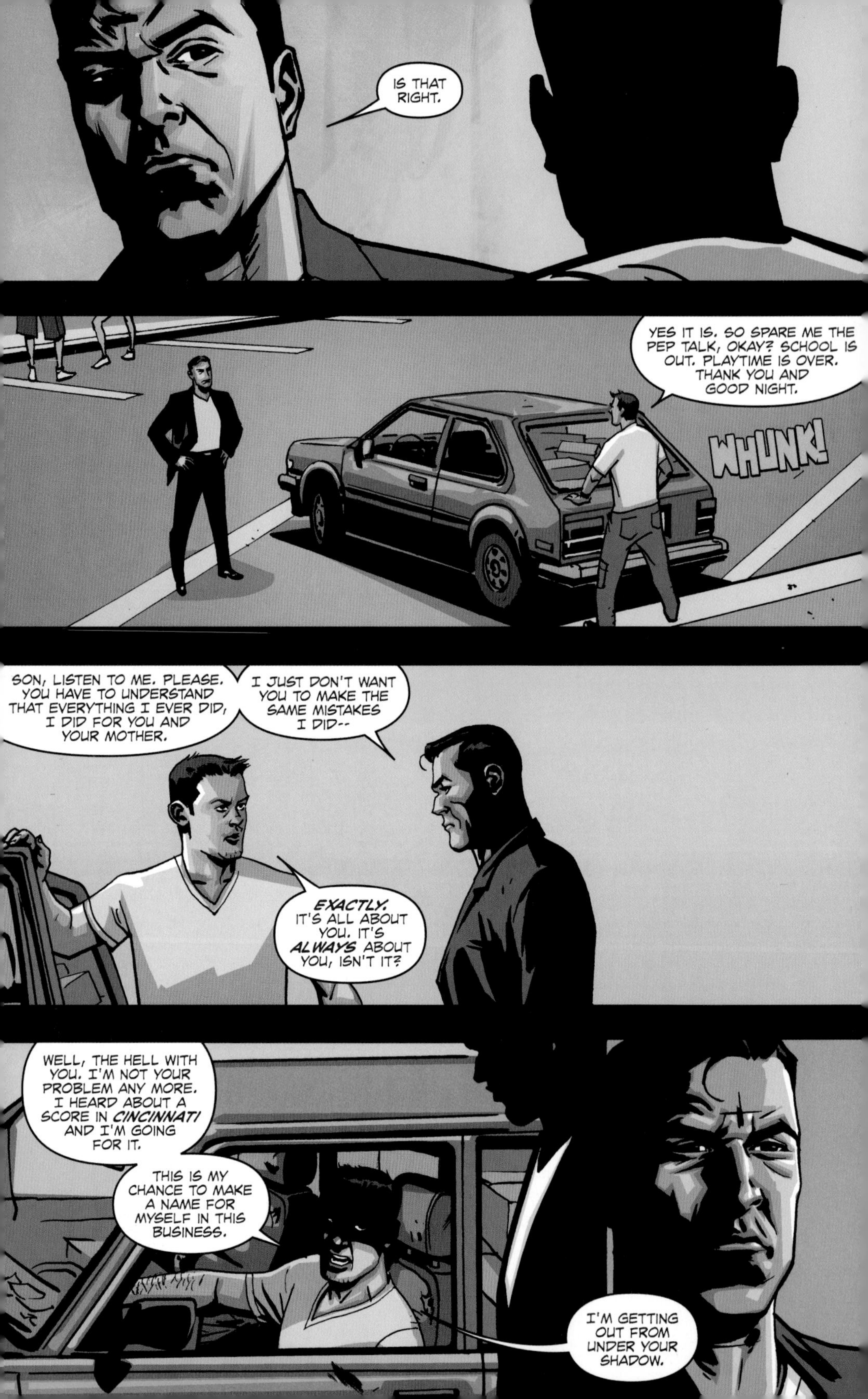
IS THAT RIGHT.
YES IT IS. SO SPARE ME THE PEP TALK, OKAY? SCHOOL IS OUT. PLAYTIME IS OVER. THANK YOU AND GOOD NIGHT.
WHUNK!
SON, LISTEN TO ME. PLEASE. YOU HAVE TO UNDERSTAND THAT EVERYTHING I EVER DID, I DID FOR YOU AND YOUR MOTHER.
I JUST DON'T WANT YOU TO MAKE THE SAME MISTAKES I DID--
EXACTLY. IT'S ALL ABOUT YOU. IT'S ALWAYS ABOUT YOU, ISN'T IT?
WELL, THE HELL WITH YOU. I'M NOT YOUR PROBLEM ANY MORE. I HEARD ABOUT A SCORE IN CINCINNATI AND I'M GOING FOR IT.
THIS IS MY CHANCE TO MAKE A NAME FOR MYSELF IN THIS BUSINESS.
I'M GETTING OUT FROM UNDER YOUR SHADOW.

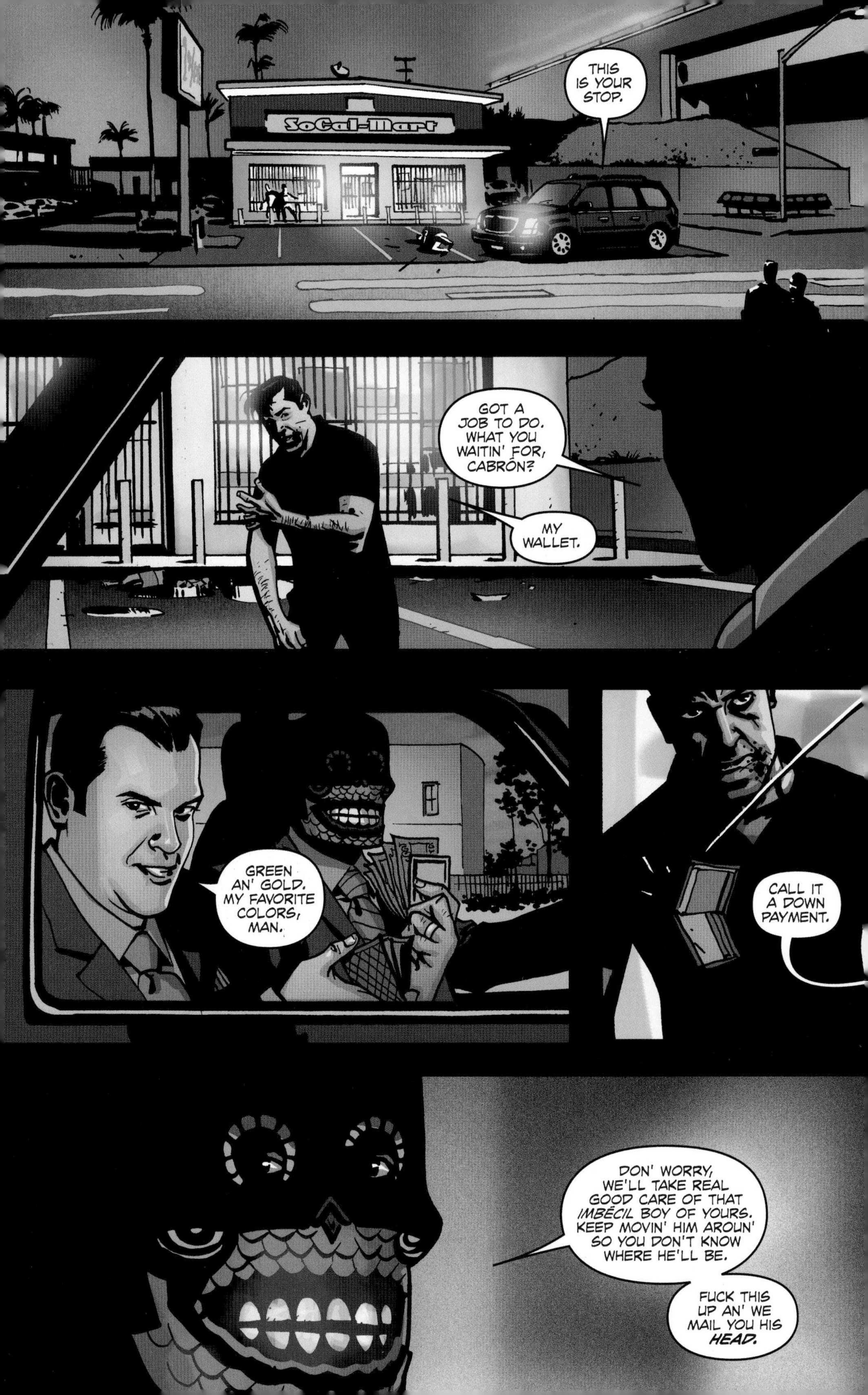
SoCal-Mart
THIS IS YOUR STOP.
GOT A JOB TO DO. WHAT YOU WAITIN' FOR, CABRÓN?
MY WALLET.
GREEN AN' GOLD. MY FAVORITE COLORS, MAN.
CALL IT A DOWN PAYMENT.
DON' WORRY, WE'LL TAKE REAL GOOD CARE OF THAT *IMBÉCIL* BOY OF YOURS. KEEP MOVIN' HIM AROUN' SO YOU DON'T KNOW WHERE HE'LL BE.
FUCK THIS UP AN' WE MAIL YOU HIS ***HEAD.***

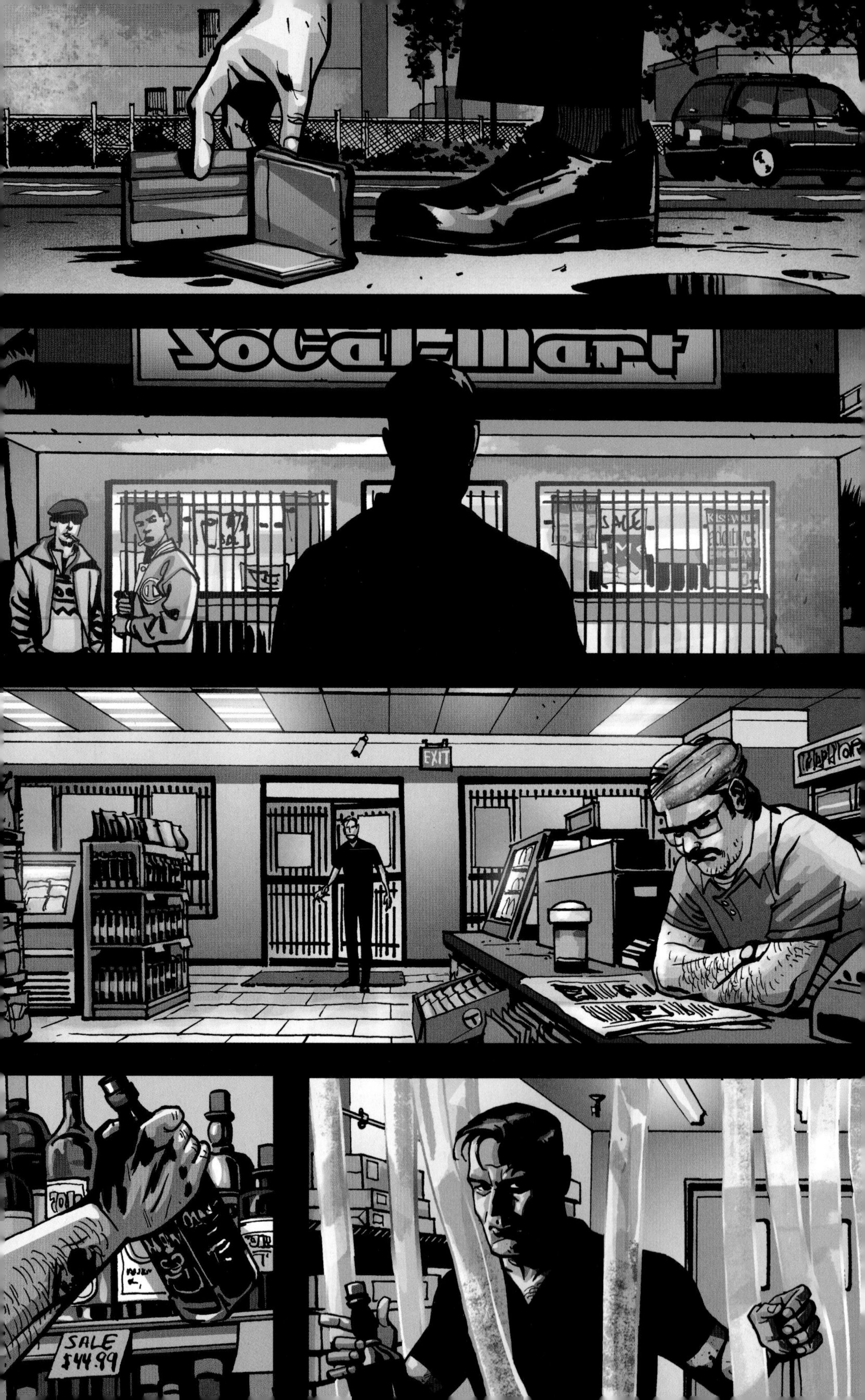
SoCal-Mart
EXIT
SALE
$44.99

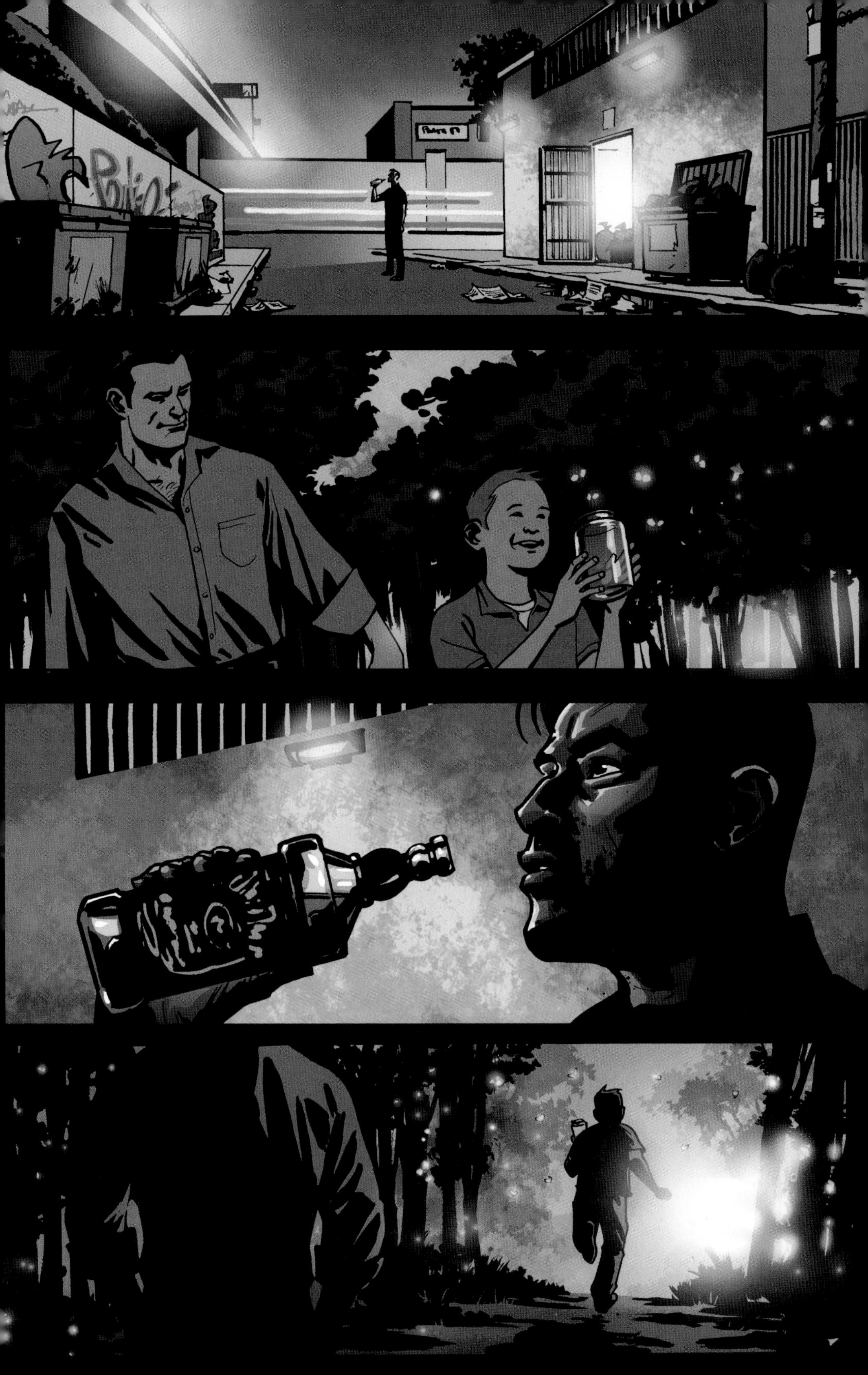

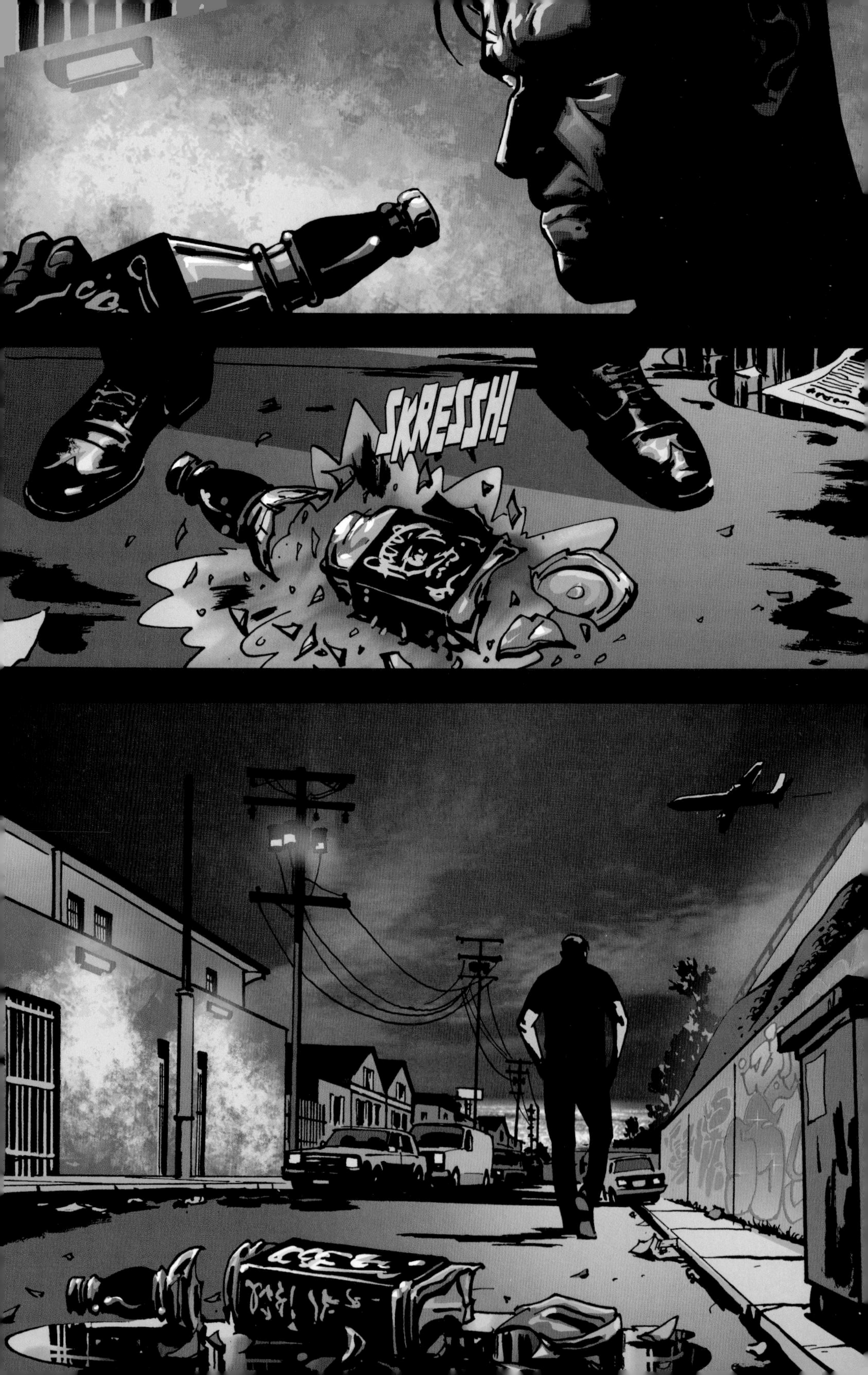
SKRESSH!

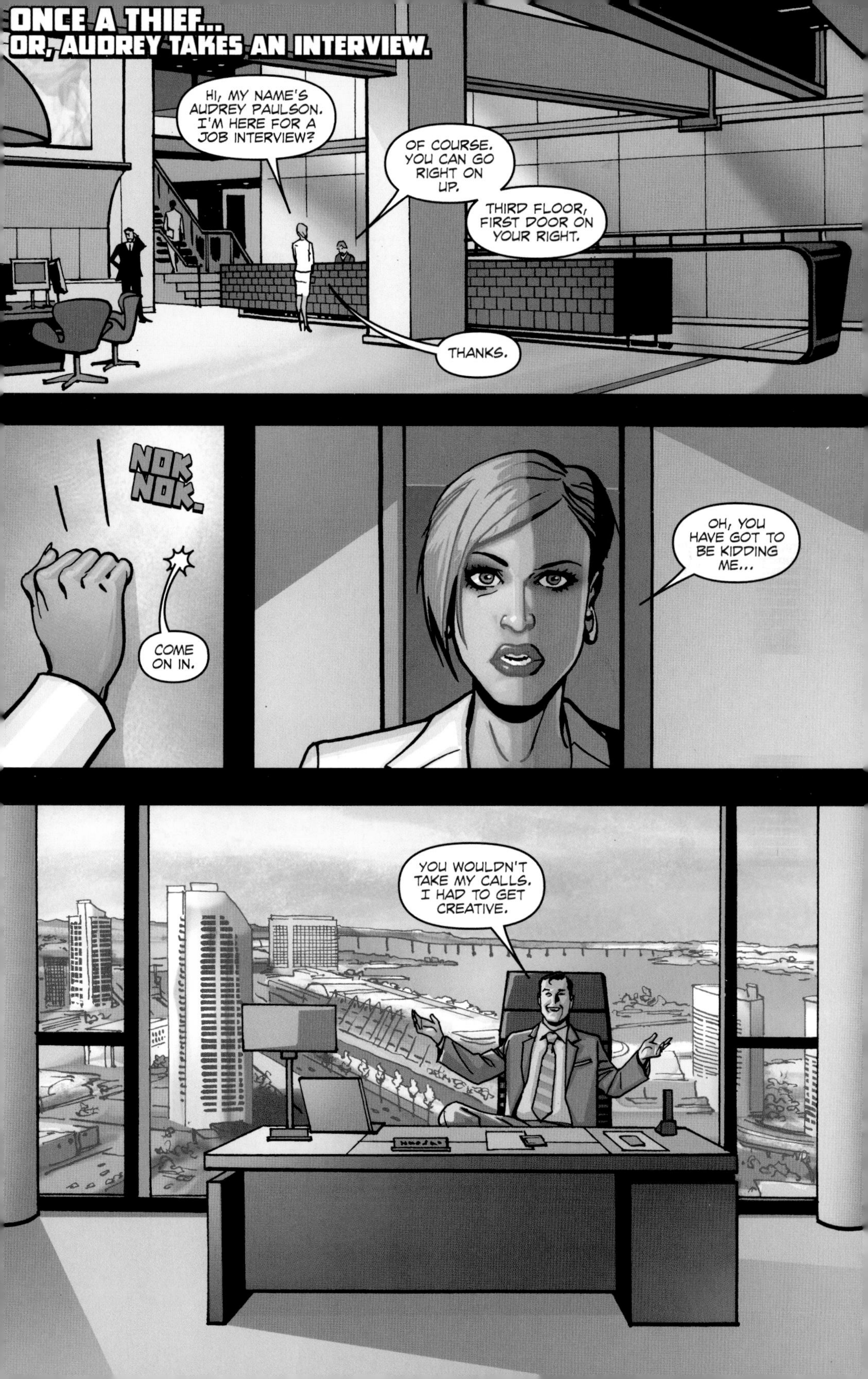
ONCE A THIEF...
OR, AUDREY TAKES AN INTERVIEW.
HI, MY NAME'S AUDREY PAULSON. I'M HERE FOR A JOB INTERVIEW?
OF COURSE. YOU CAN GO RIGHT ON UP.
THIRD FLOOR, FIRST DOOR ON YOUR RIGHT.
THANKS.
NOK NOK.
COME ON IN.
OH, YOU HAVE GOT TO BE KIDDING ME...
YOU WOULDN'T TAKE MY CALLS. I HAD TO GET CREATIVE.

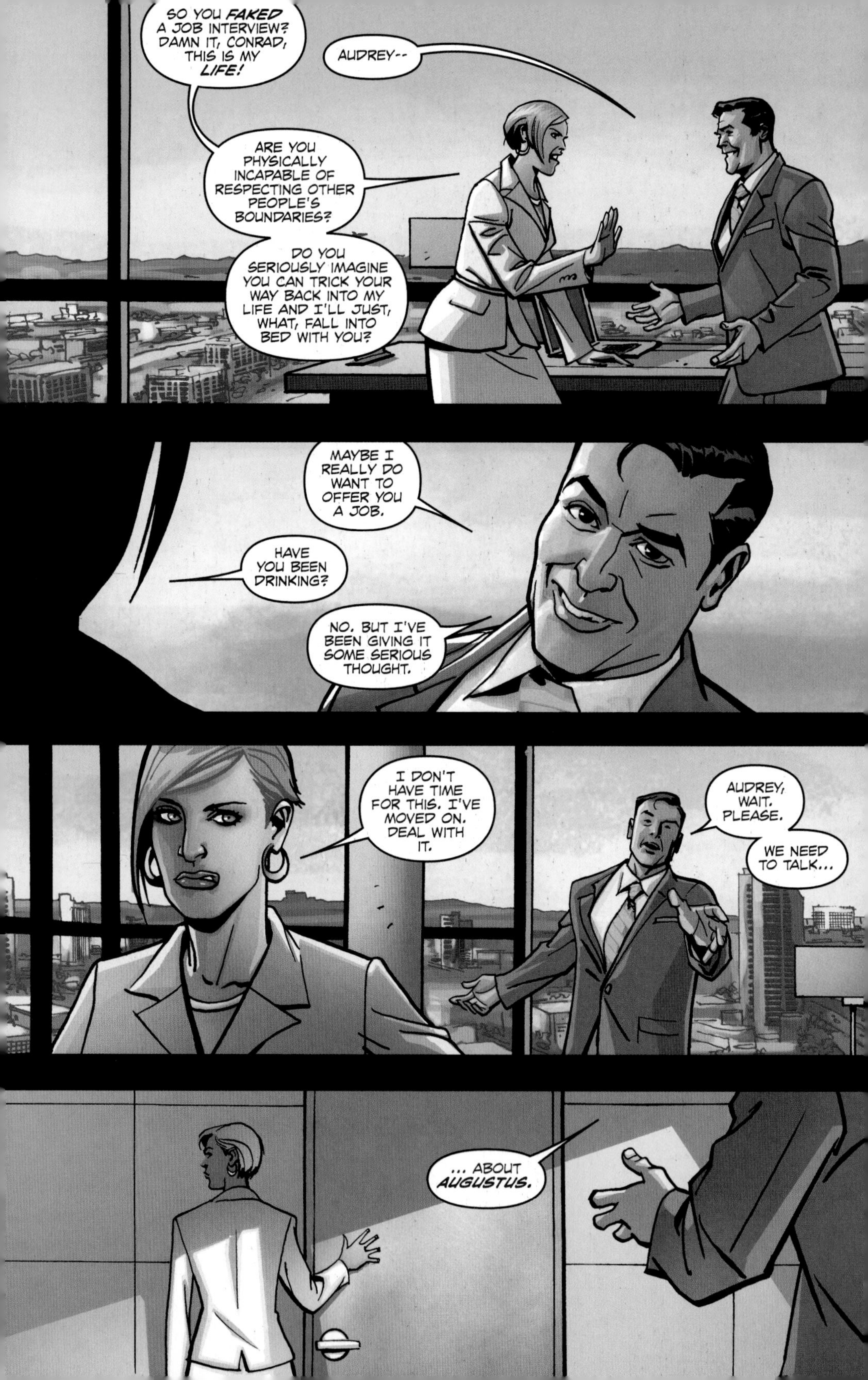
SO YOU FAKED A JOB INTERVIEW? DAMN IT, CONRAD, THIS IS MY LIFE!
AUDREY--
ARE YOU PHYSICALLY INCAPABLE OF RESPECTING OTHER PEOPLE'S BOUNDARIES?
DO YOU SERIOUSLY IMAGINE YOU CAN TRICK YOUR WAY BACK INTO MY LIFE AND I'LL JUST, WHAT, FALL INTO BED WITH YOU?
MAYBE I REALLY DO WANT TO OFFER YOU A JOB.
HAVE YOU BEEN DRINKING?
NO. BUT I'VE BEEN GIVING IT SOME SERIOUS THOUGHT.
I DON'T HAVE TIME FOR THIS. I'VE MOVED ON. DEAL WITH IT.
AUDREY, WAIT. PLEASE.
WE NEED TO TALK...
... ABOUT AUGUSTUS.

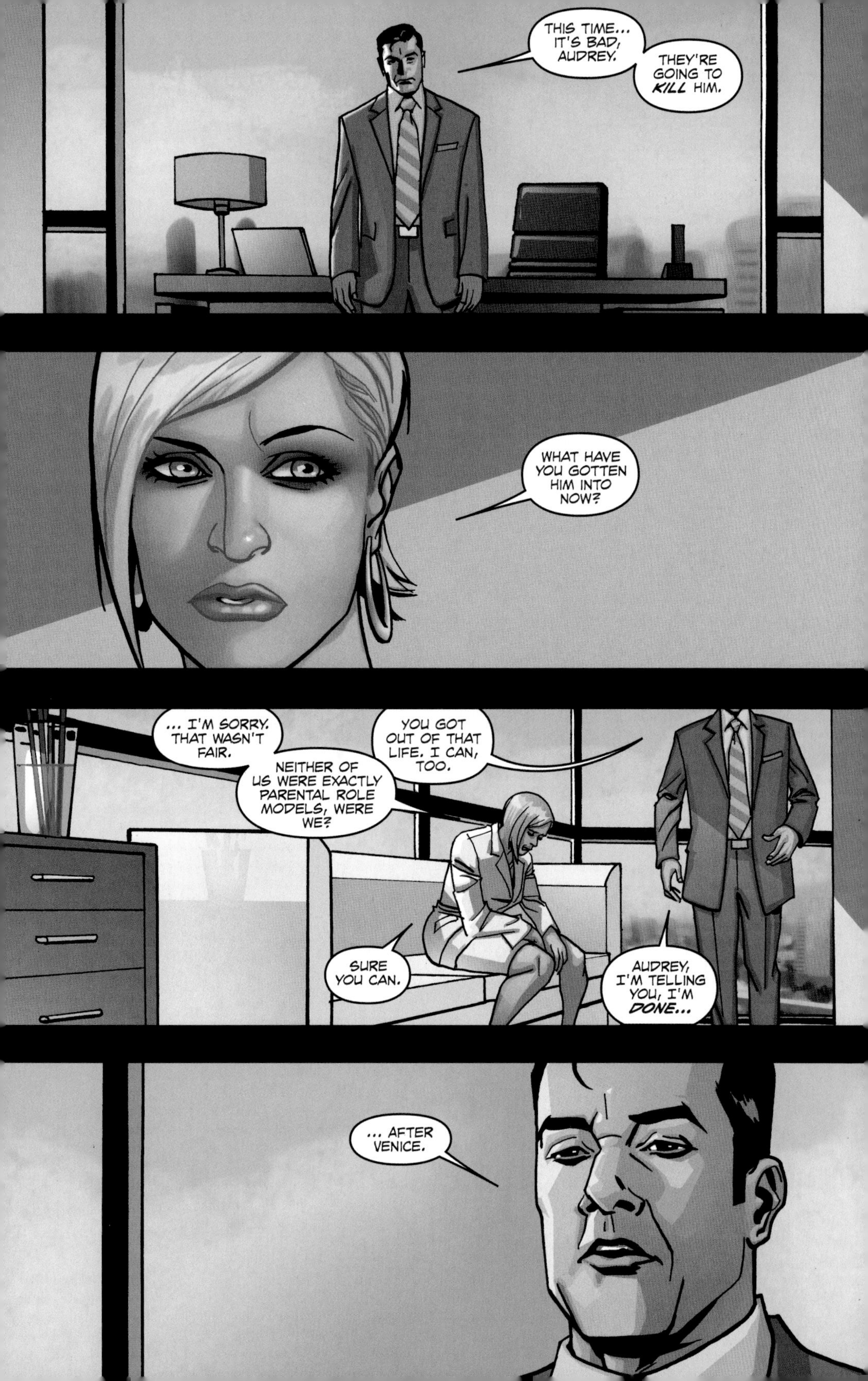

THIS TIME... IT'S BAD, AUDREY.
THEY'RE GOING TO *KILL* HIM.
WHAT HAVE YOU GOTTEN HIM INTO NOW?
... I'M SORRY. THAT WASN'T FAIR.
NEITHER OF US WERE EXACTLY PARENTAL ROLE MODELS, WERE WE?
YOU GOT OUT OF THAT LIFE. I CAN, TOO.
SURE YOU CAN.
AUDREY, I'M TELLING YOU, I'M *DONE...*
... AFTER VENICE.

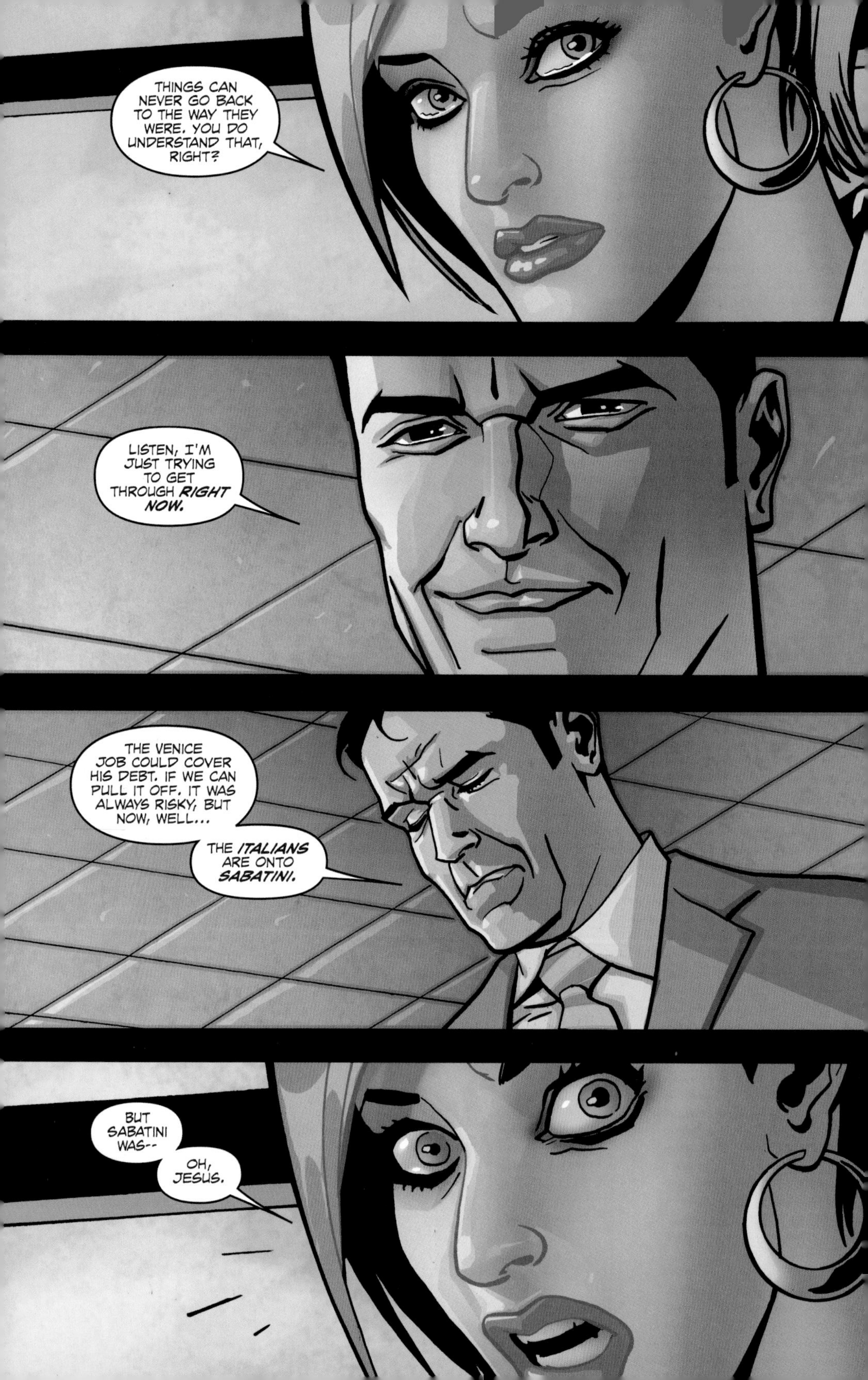
THINGS CAN NEVER GO BACK TO THE WAY THEY WERE. YOU DO UNDERSTAND THAT, RIGHT?
LISTEN, I'M JUST TRYING TO GET THROUGH **RIGHT NOW.**
THE VENICE JOB COULD COVER HIS DEBT. IF WE CAN PULL IT OFF. IT WAS ALWAYS RISKY, BUT NOW, WELL...
THE ***ITALIANS*** ARE ONTO ***SABATINI.***
BUT SABATINI WAS--
OH, JESUS.

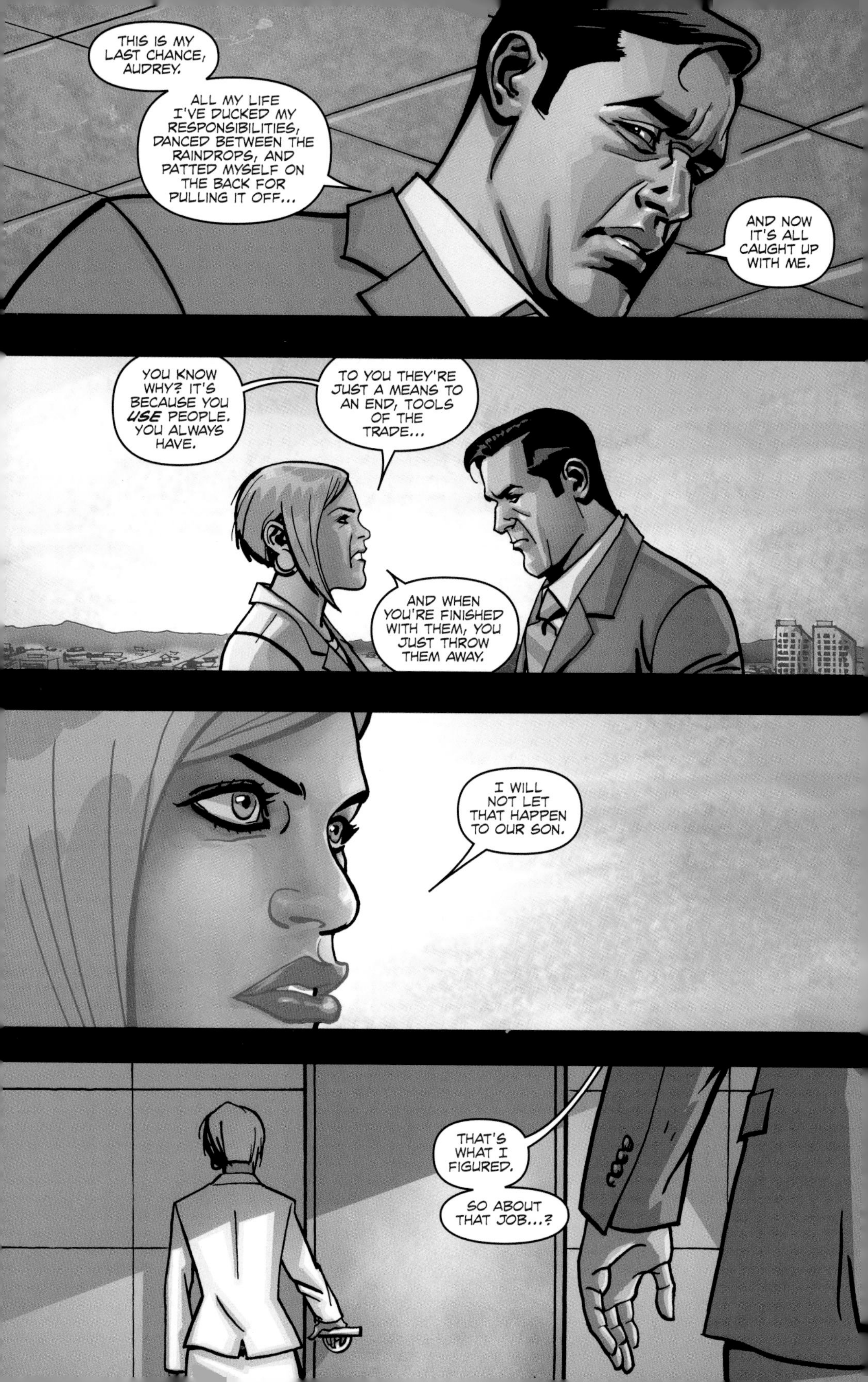

THIS IS MY LAST CHANCE, AUDREY.
ALL MY LIFE I'VE DUCKED MY RESPONSIBILITIES, DANCED BETWEEN THE RAINDROPS, AND PATTED MYSELF ON THE BACK FOR PULLING IT OFF...
AND NOW IT'S ALL CAUGHT UP WITH ME.
YOU KNOW WHY? IT'S BECAUSE YOU *USE* PEOPLE. YOU ALWAYS HAVE.
TO YOU THEY'RE JUST A MEANS TO AN END, TOOLS OF THE TRADE...
AND WHEN YOU'RE FINISHED WITH THEM, YOU JUST THROW THEM AWAY.
I WILL NOT LET THAT HAPPEN TO OUR SON.
THAT'S WHAT I FIGURED.
SO ABOUT THAT JOB...?

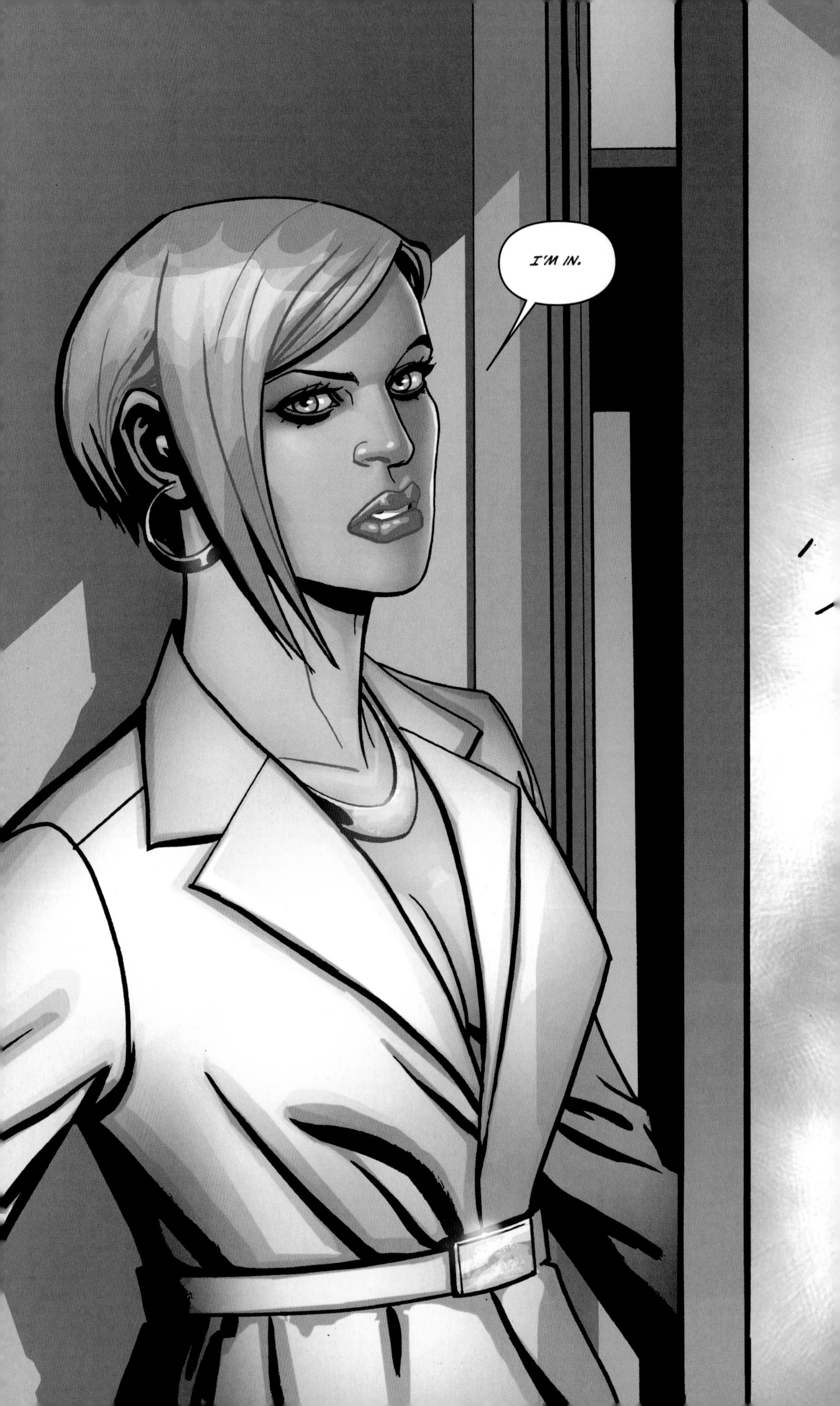
I'M IN.

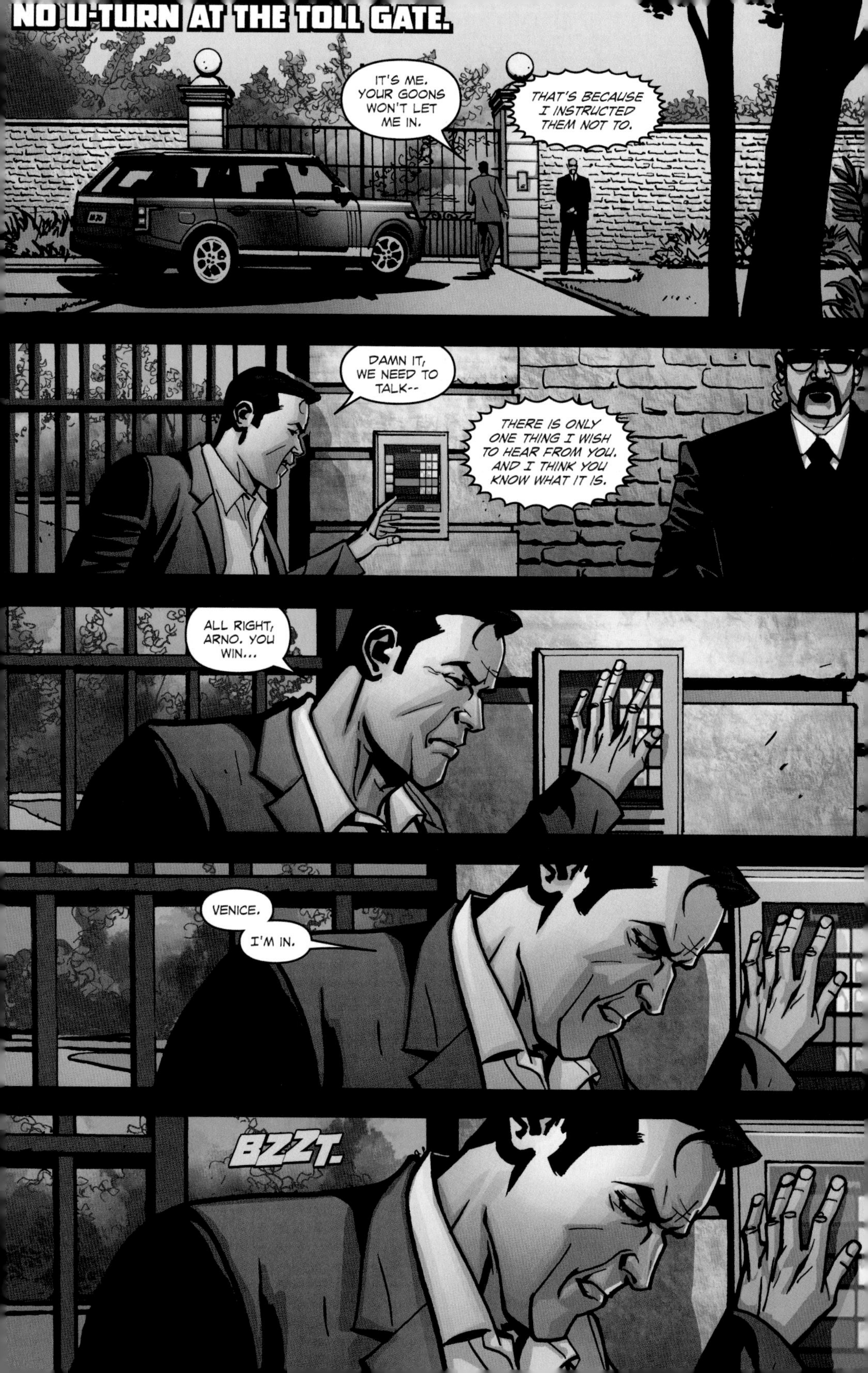
NO U-TURN AT THE TOLL GATE.
IT'S ME. YOUR GOONS WON'T LET ME IN.
THAT'S BECAUSE I INSTRUCTED THEM NOT TO.
DAMN IT, WE NEED TO TALK--
THERE IS ONLY ONE THING I WISH TO HEAR FROM YOU. AND I THINK YOU KNOW WHAT IT IS.
ALL RIGHT, ARNO. YOU WIN...
VENICE.
I'M IN.
BZZT.

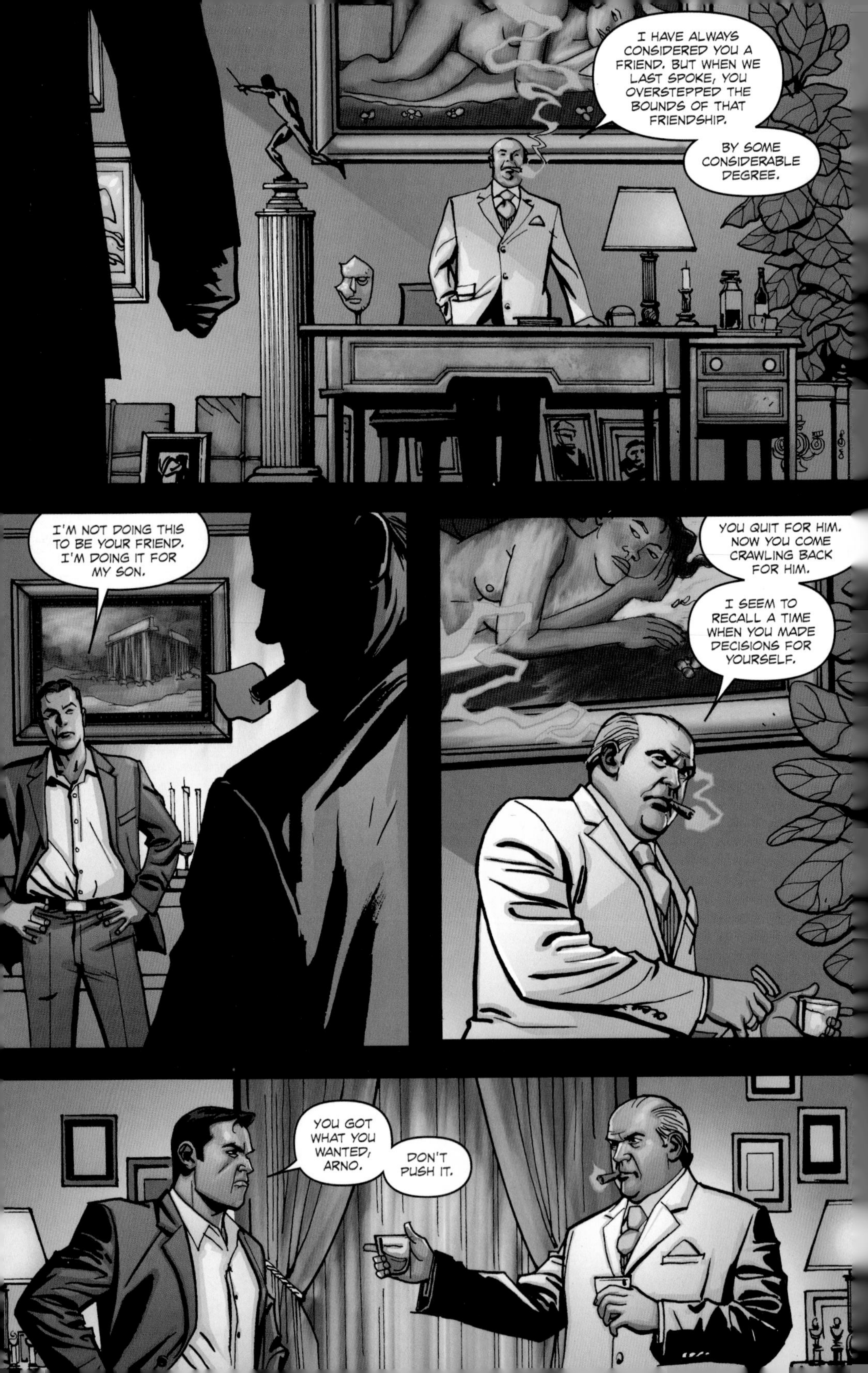
I HAVE ALWAYS CONSIDERED YOU A FRIEND. BUT WHEN WE LAST SPOKE, YOU OVERSTEPPED THE BOUNDS OF THAT FRIENDSHIP.
BY SOME CONSIDERABLE DEGREE.
I'M NOT DOING THIS TO BE YOUR FRIEND. I'M DOING IT FOR MY SON.
YOU QUIT FOR HIM. NOW YOU COME CRAWLING BACK FOR HIM.
I SEEM TO RECALL A TIME WHEN YOU MADE DECISIONS FOR YOURSELF.
YOU GOT WHAT YOU WANTED, ARNO.
DON'T PUSH IT.

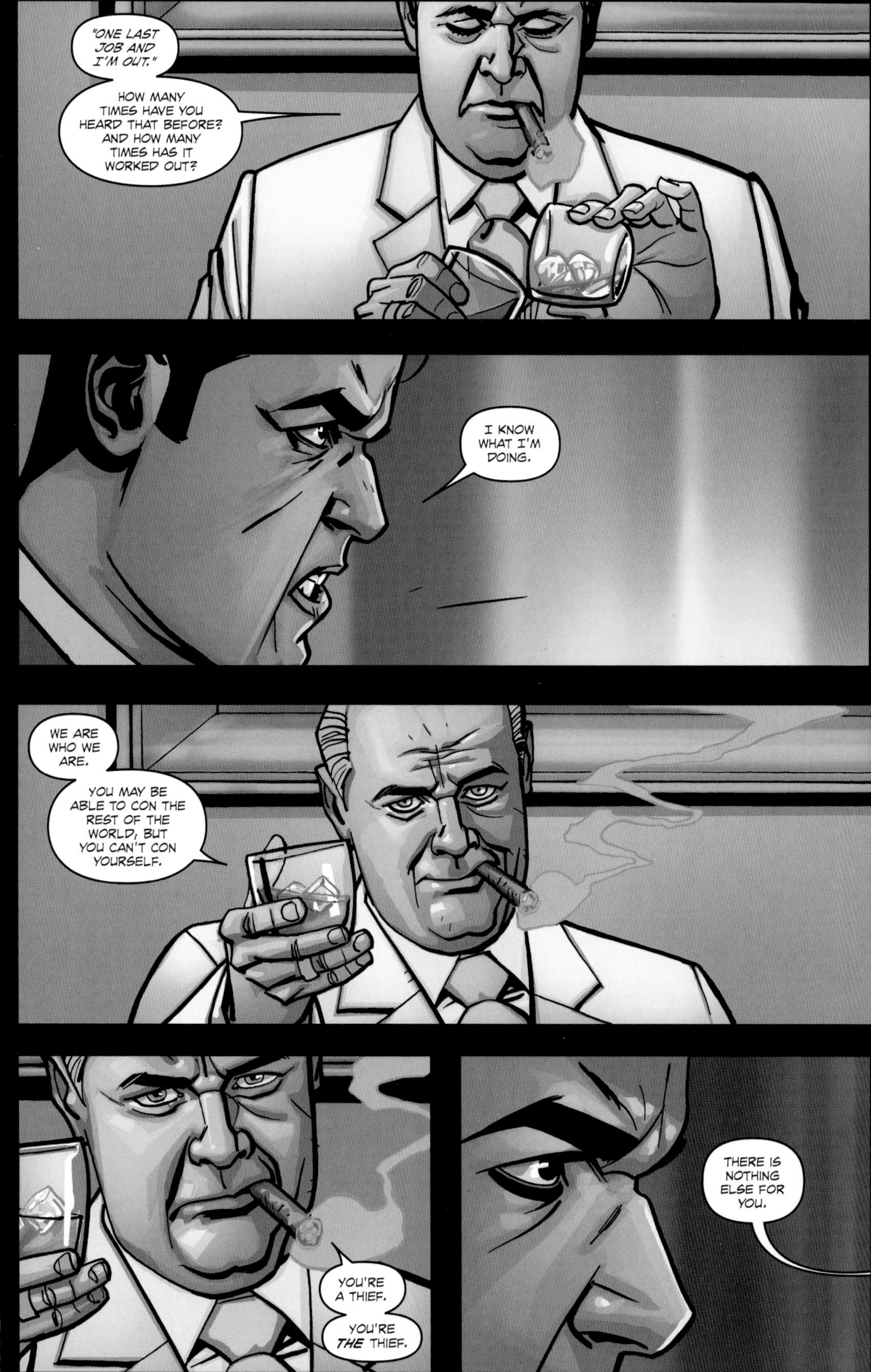
"ONE LAST JOB AND I'M OUT."
HOW MANY TIMES HAVE YOU HEARD THAT BEFORE? AND HOW MANY TIMES HAS IT WORKED OUT?
I KNOW WHAT I'M DOING.
WE ARE WHO WE ARE.
YOU MAY BE ABLE TO CON THE REST OF THE WORLD, BUT YOU CAN'T CON YOURSELF.
YOU'RE A THIEF.
YOU'RE *THE* THIEF.
THERE IS NOTHING ELSE FOR YOU.

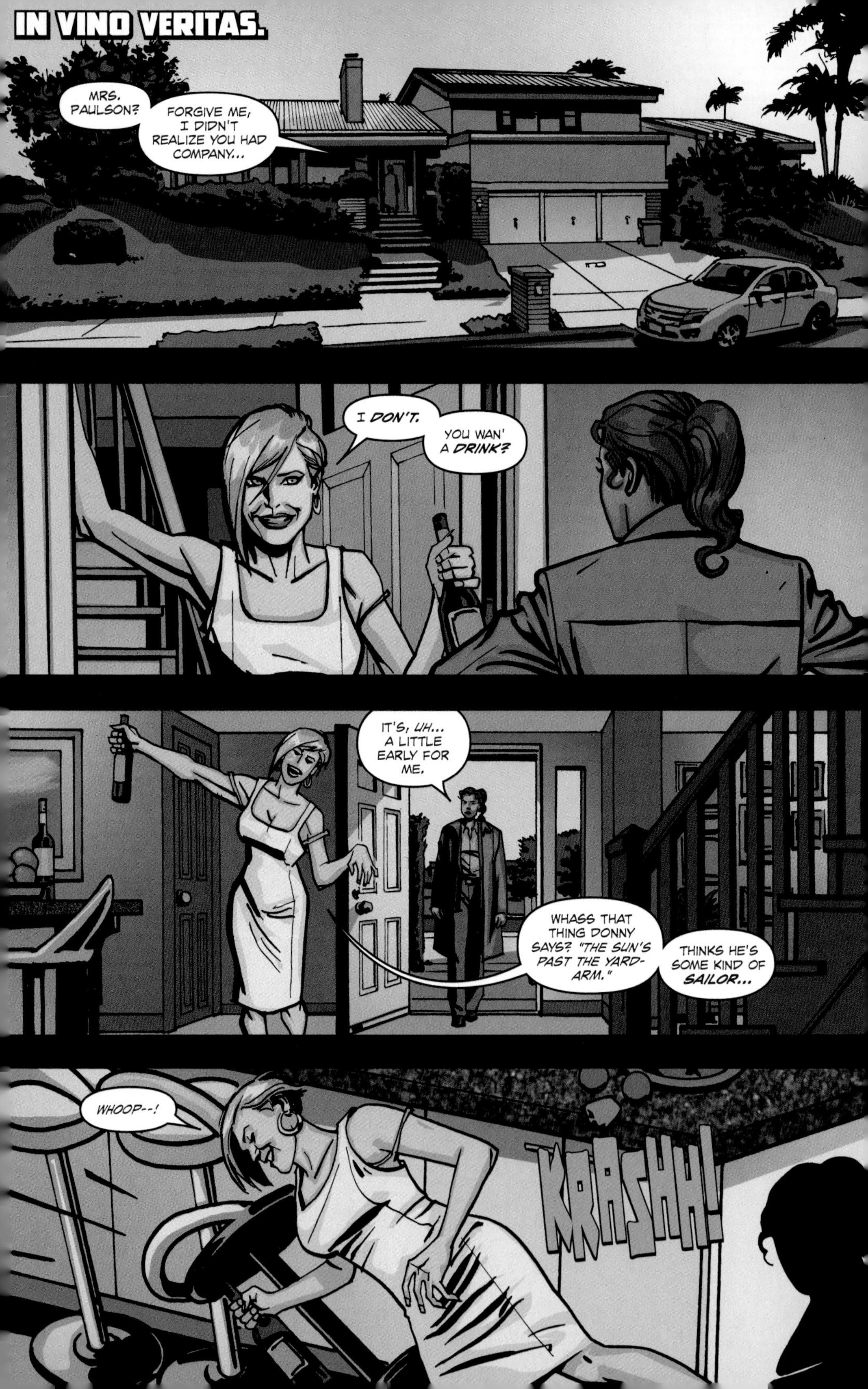
IN VINO VERITAS.
MRS. PAULSON?
FORGIVE ME, I DIDN'T REALIZE YOU HAD COMPANY...
I DON'T.
YOU WAN' A DRINK?
IT'S, UH... A LITTLE EARLY FOR ME.
WHASS THAT THING DONNY SAYS? "THE SUN'S PAST THE YARD-ARM."
THINKS HE'S SOME KIND OF SAILOR...
WHOOP--!
KRASHH!

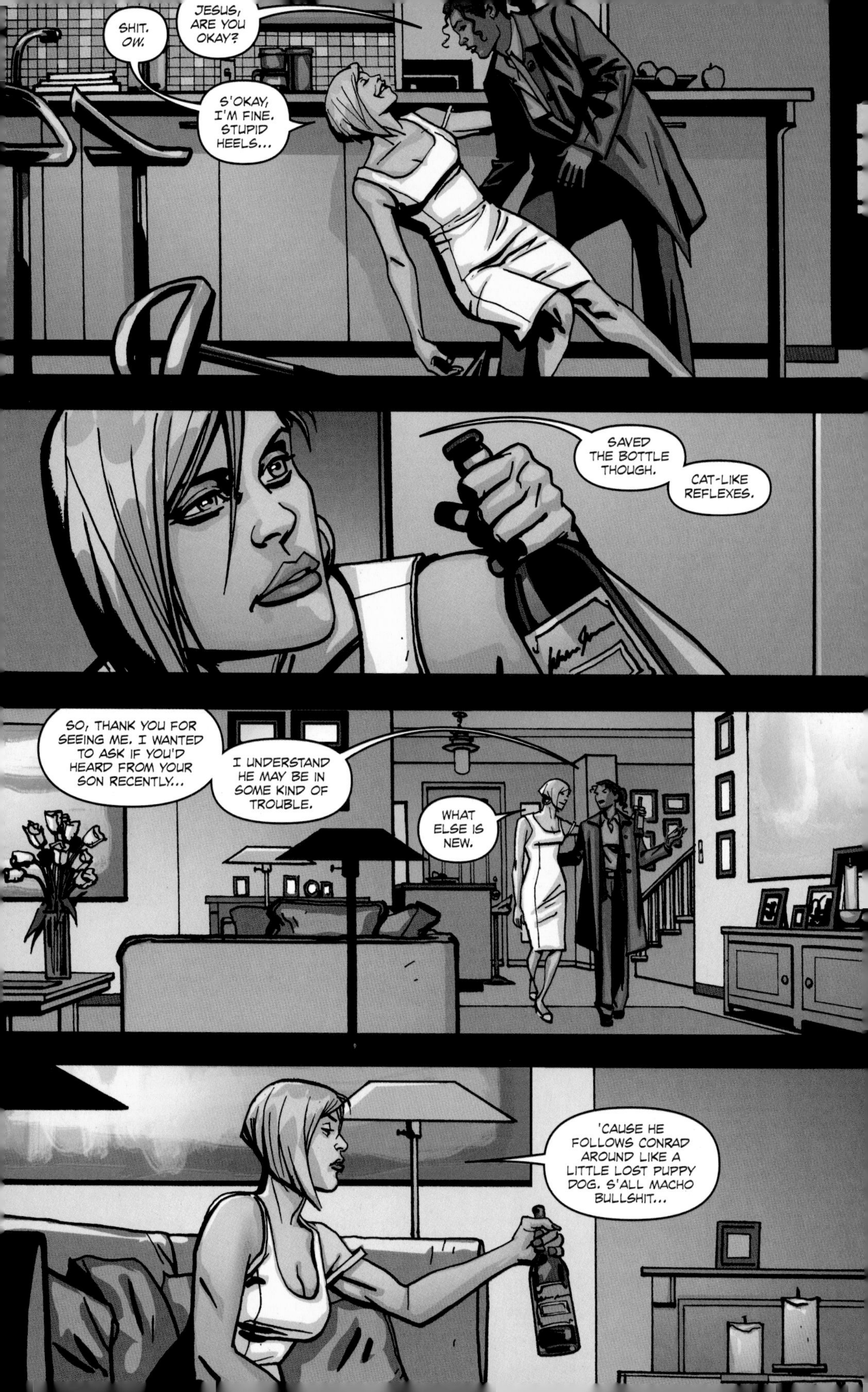
SHIT. OW.
JESUS, ARE YOU OKAY?
S'OKAY, I'M FINE. STUPID HEELS...
SAVED THE BOTTLE THOUGH.
CAT-LIKE REFLEXES.
SO, THANK YOU FOR SEEING ME. I WANTED TO ASK IF YOU'D HEARD FROM YOUR SON RECENTLY...
I UNDERSTAND HE MAY BE IN SOME KIND OF TROUBLE.
WHAT ELSE IS NEW.
'CAUSE HE FOLLOWS CONRAD AROUND LIKE A LITTLE LOST PUPPY DOG. S'ALL MACHO BULLSHIT...

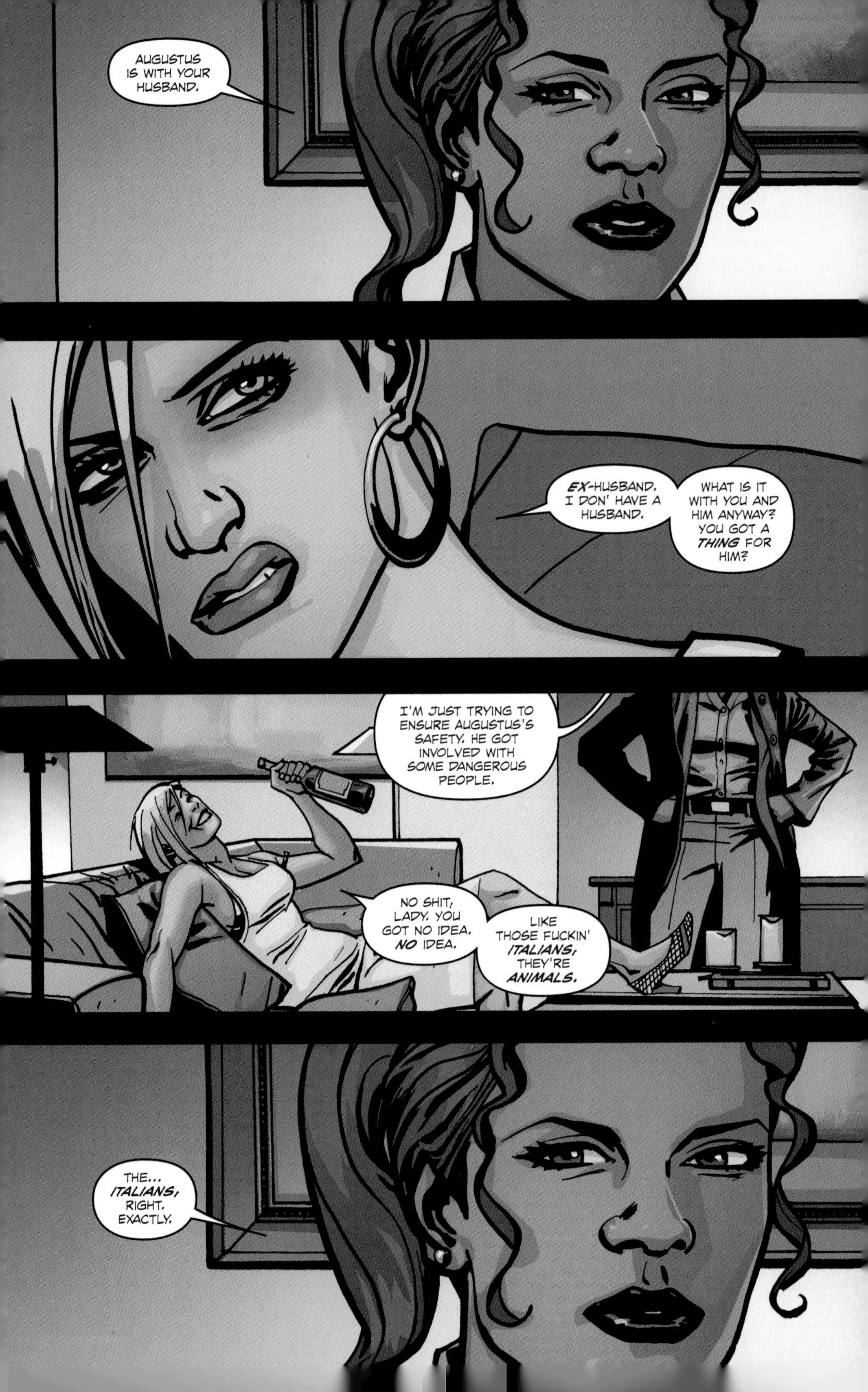
AUGUSTUS IS WITH YOUR HUSBAND.
EX-HUSBAND. I DON' HAVE A HUSBAND.
WHAT IS IT WITH YOU AND HIM ANYWAY? YOU GOT A THING FOR HIM?
I'M JUST TRYING TO ENSURE AUGUSTUS'S SAFETY. HE GOT INVOLVED WITH SOME DANGEROUS PEOPLE.
NO SHIT, LADY. YOU GOT NO IDEA. NO IDEA.
LIKE THOSE FUCKIN' ITALIANS, THEY'RE ANIMALS.
THE... ITALIANS, RIGHT. EXACTLY.

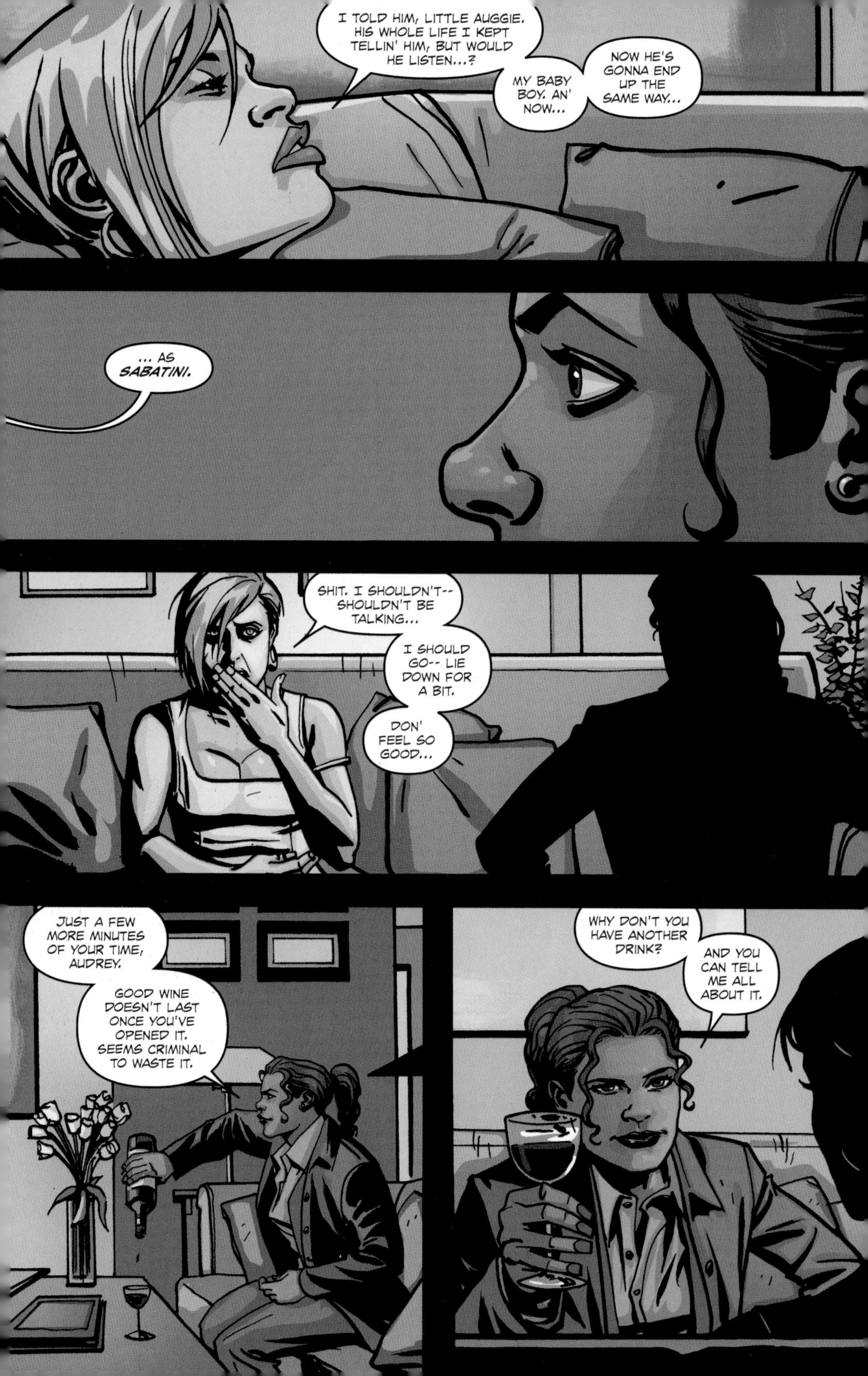
I TOLD HIM, LITTLE AUGGIE. HIS WHOLE LIFE I KEPT TELLIN' HIM, BUT WOULD HE LISTEN...?
MY BABY BOY. AN' NOW...
NOW HE'S GONNA END UP THE SAME WAY...
... AS SABATINI.
SHIT. I SHOULDN'T-- SHOULDN'T BE TALKING...
I SHOULD GO-- LIE DOWN FOR A BIT.
DON' FEEL SO GOOD...
JUST A FEW MORE MINUTES OF YOUR TIME, AUDREY.
GOOD WINE DOESN'T LAST ONCE YOU'VE OPENED IT. SEEMS CRIMINAL TO WASTE IT.
WHY DON'T YOU HAVE ANOTHER DRINK?
AND YOU CAN TELL ME ALL ABOUT IT.

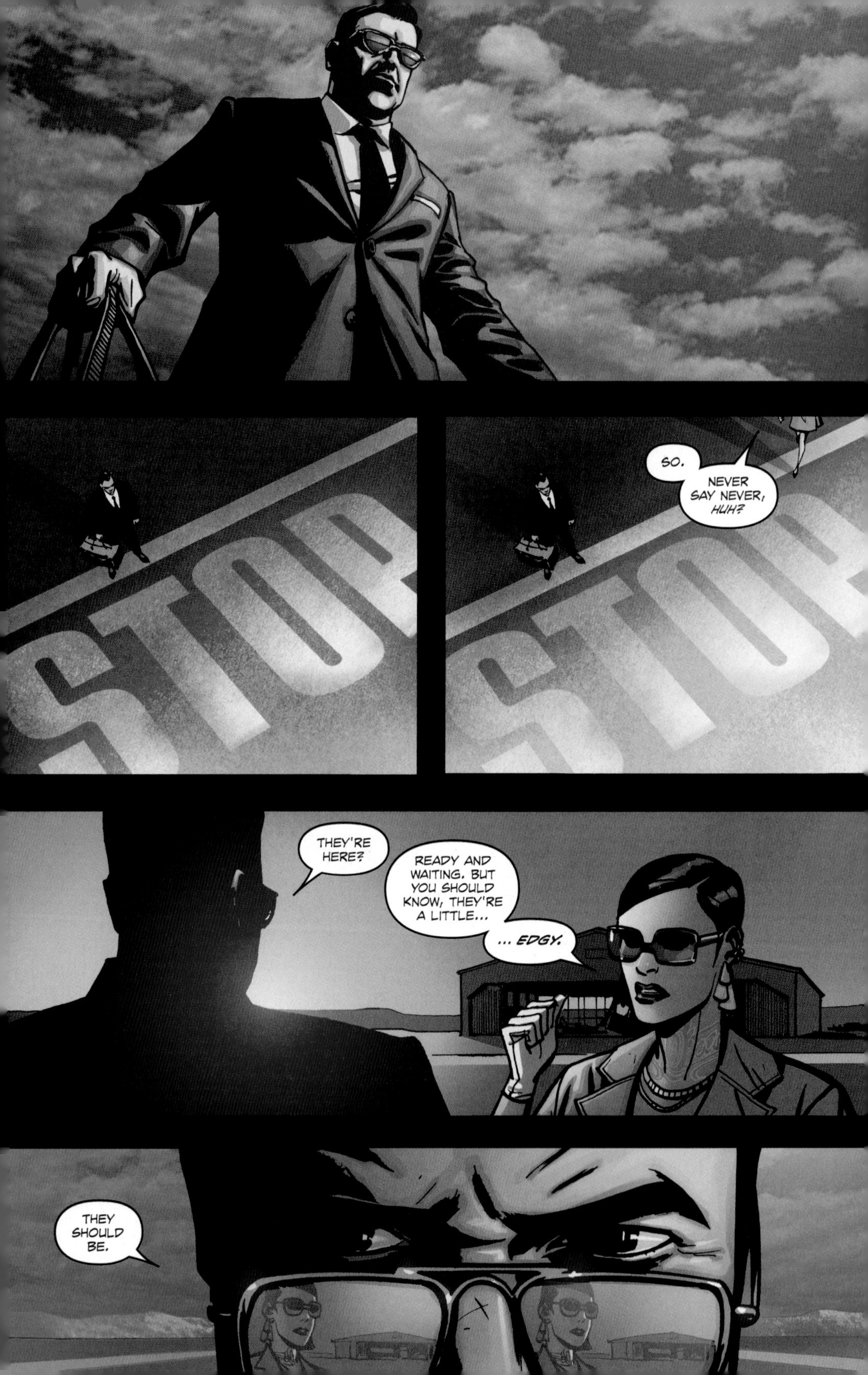
STOP
STOP
SO.
NEVER SAY NEVER, *HUH?*
THEY'RE HERE?
READY AND WAITING. BUT YOU SHOULD KNOW, THEY'RE A LITTLE...
... *EDGY.*
THEY SHOULD BE.

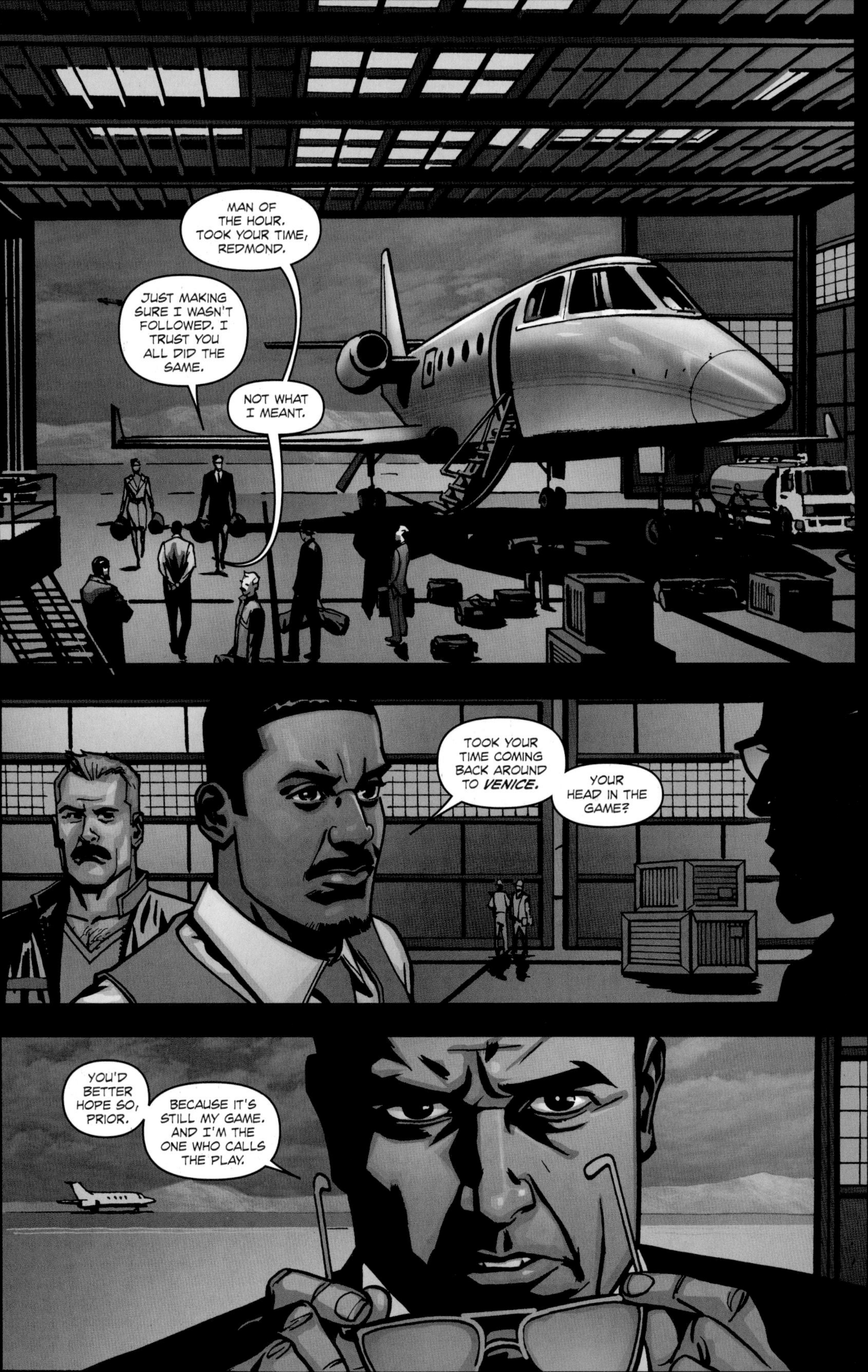
MAN OF THE HOUR. TOOK YOUR TIME, REDMOND.
JUST MAKING SURE I WASN'T FOLLOWED. I TRUST YOU ALL DID THE SAME.
NOT WHAT I MEANT.
TOOK YOUR TIME COMING BACK AROUND TO *VENICE.*
YOUR HEAD IN THE GAME?
YOU'D BETTER HOPE SO, PRIOR.
BECAUSE IT'S STILL MY GAME. AND I'M THE ONE WHO CALLS THE PLAY.

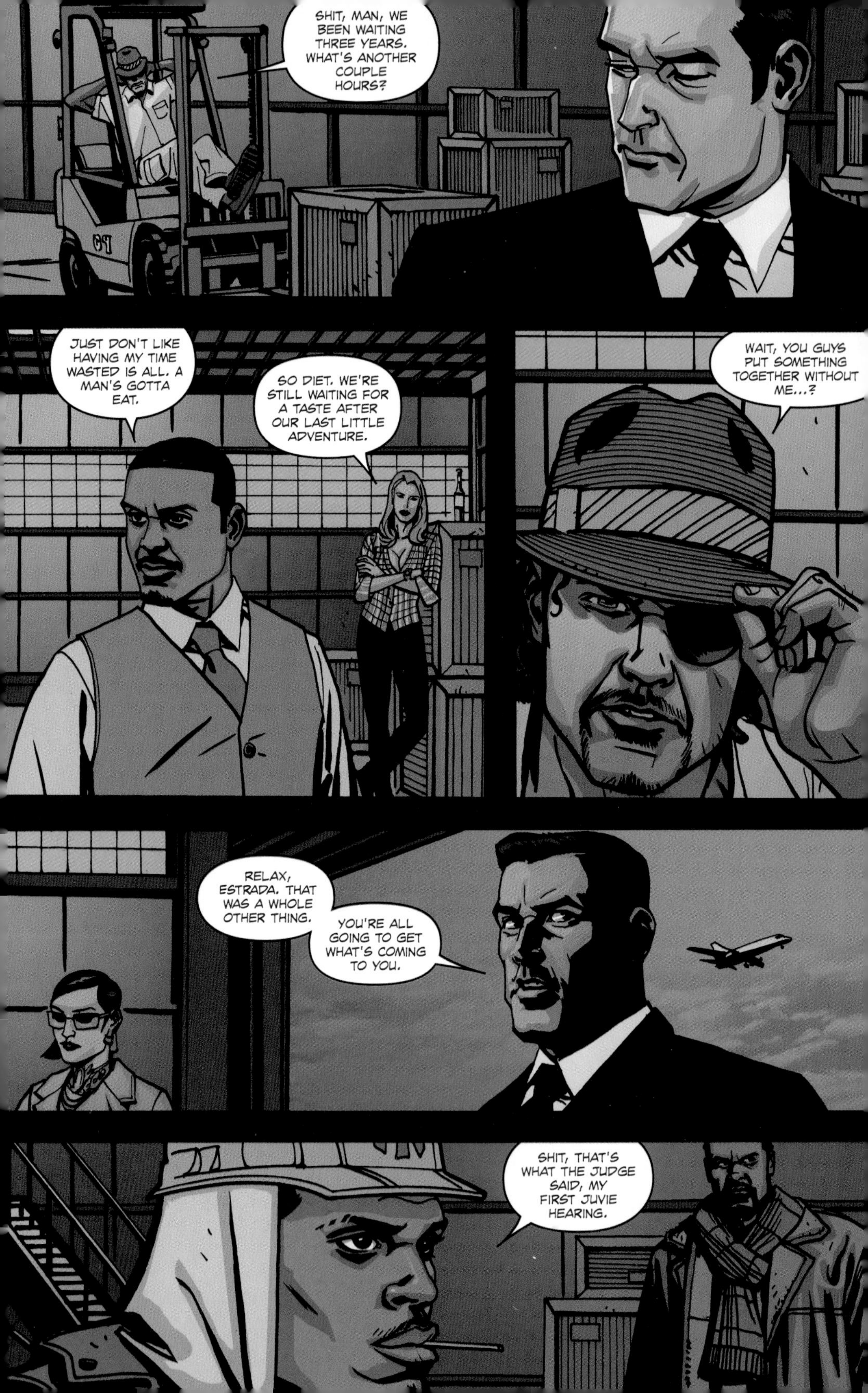
SHIT, MAN, WE BEEN WAITING THREE YEARS. WHAT'S ANOTHER COUPLE HOURS?
JUST DON'T LIKE HAVING MY TIME WASTED IS ALL. A MAN'S GOTTA EAT.
SO DIET. WE'RE STILL WAITING FOR A TASTE AFTER OUR LAST LITTLE ADVENTURE.
WAIT, YOU GUYS PUT SOMETHING TOGETHER WITHOUT ME...?
RELAX, ESTRADA. THAT WAS A WHOLE OTHER THING.
YOU'RE ALL GOING TO GET WHAT'S COMING TO YOU.
SHIT, THAT'S WHAT THE JUDGE SAID, MY FIRST JUVIE HEARING.

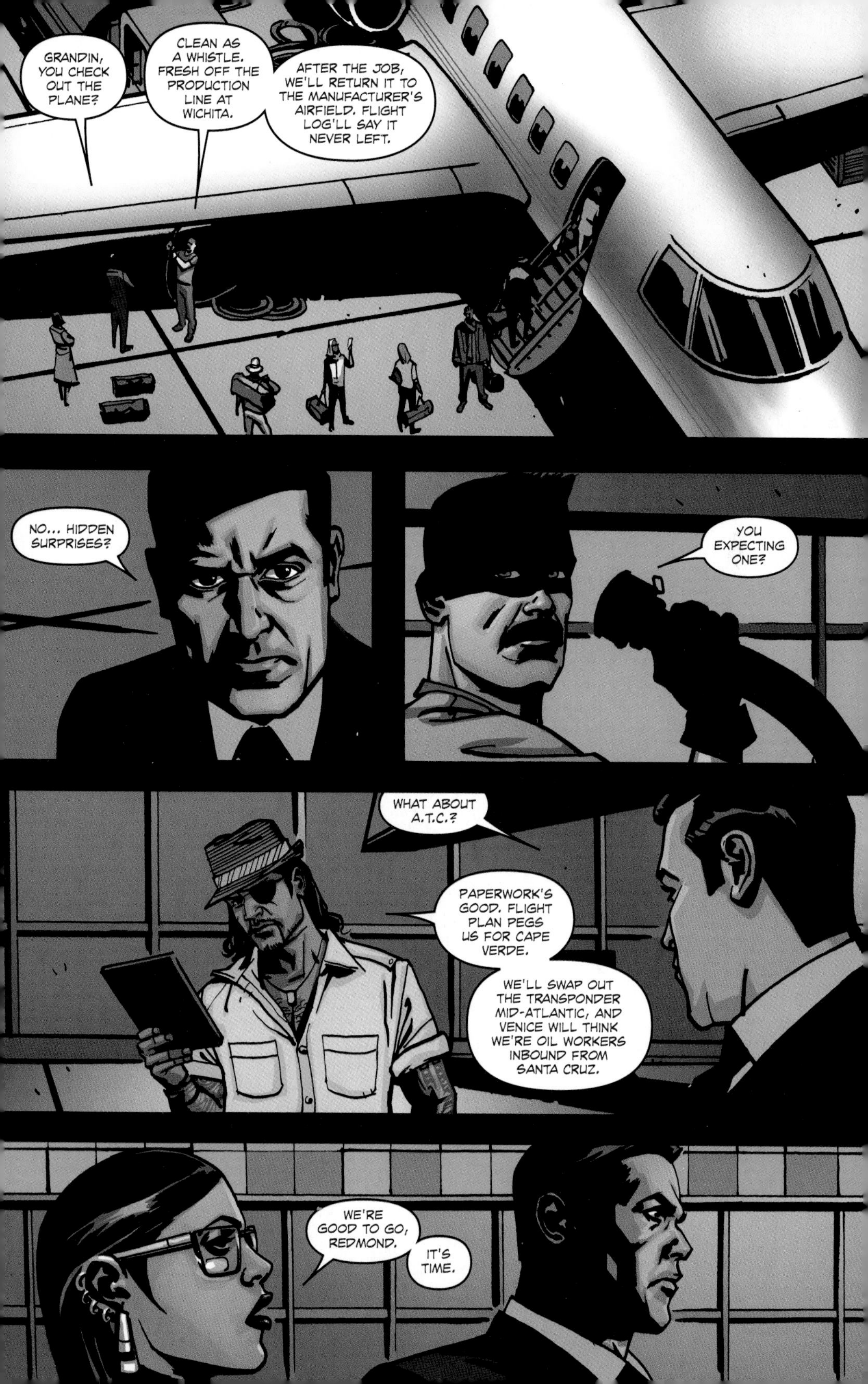
GRANDIN, YOU CHECK OUT THE PLANE?
CLEAN AS A WHISTLE. FRESH OFF THE PRODUCTION LINE AT WICHITA.
AFTER THE JOB, WE'LL RETURN IT TO THE MANUFACTURER'S AIRFIELD. FLIGHT LOG'LL SAY IT NEVER LEFT.
NO... HIDDEN SURPRISES?
YOU EXPECTING ONE?
WHAT ABOUT A.T.C.?
PAPERWORK'S GOOD. FLIGHT PLAN PEGS US FOR CAPE VERDE.
WE'LL SWAP OUT THE TRANSPONDER MID-ATLANTIC, AND VENICE WILL THINK WE'RE OIL WORKERS INBOUND FROM SANTA CRUZ.
WE'RE GOOD TO GO, REDMOND.
IT'S TIME.

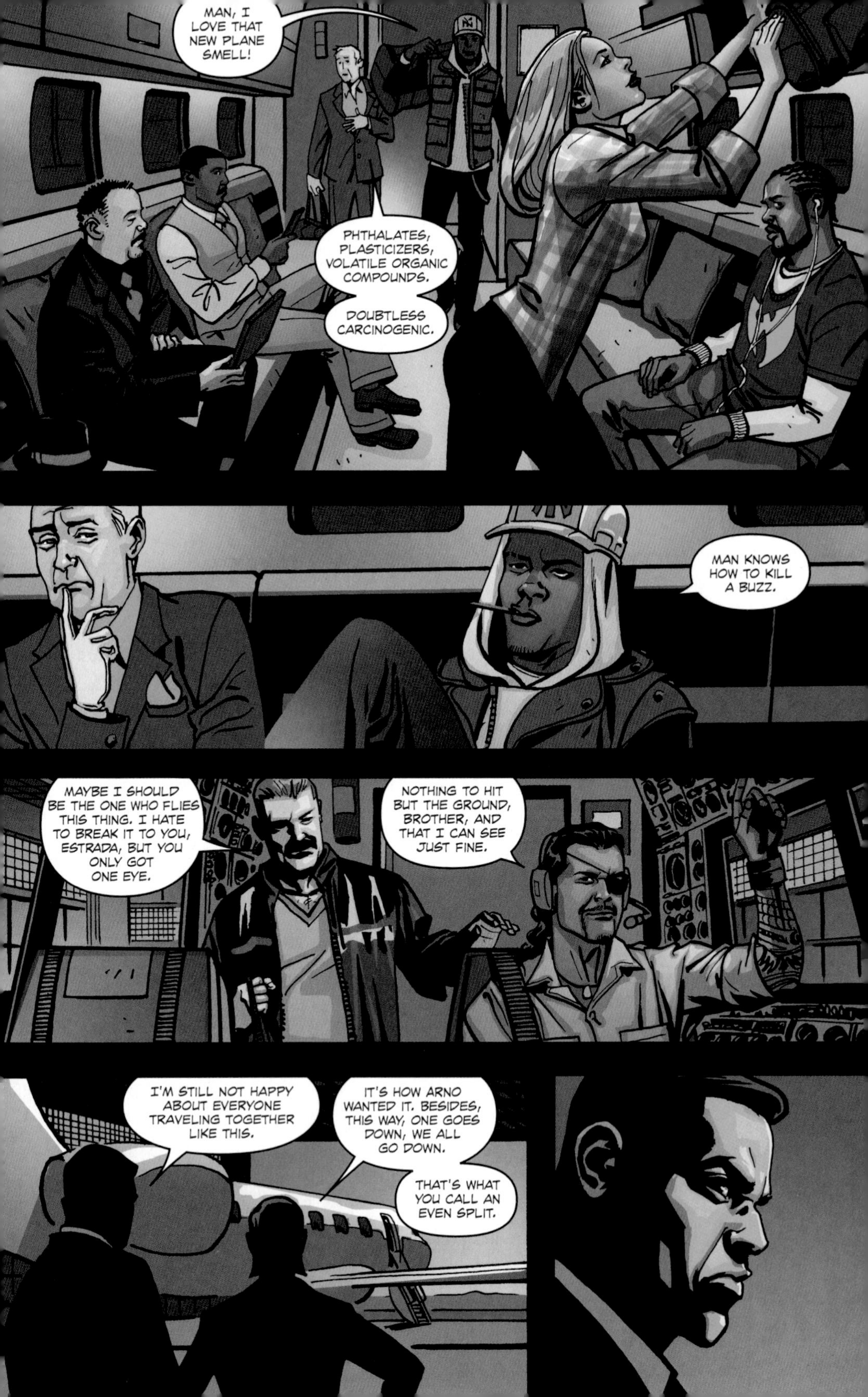
MAN, I LOVE THAT NEW PLANE SMELL!
PHTHALATES, PLASTICIZERS, VOLATILE ORGANIC COMPOUNDS.
DOUBTLESS CARCINOGENIC.
MAN KNOWS HOW TO KILL A BUZZ.
MAYBE I SHOULD BE THE ONE WHO FLIES THIS THING. I HATE TO BREAK IT TO YOU, ESTRADA, BUT YOU ONLY GOT ONE EYE.
NOTHING TO HIT BUT THE GROUND, BROTHER, AND THAT I CAN SEE JUST FINE.
I'M STILL NOT HAPPY ABOUT EVERYONE TRAVELING TOGETHER LIKE THIS.
IT'S HOW ARNO WANTED IT. BESIDES, THIS WAY, ONE GOES DOWN, WE ALL GO DOWN.
THAT'S WHAT YOU CALL AN EVEN SPLIT.

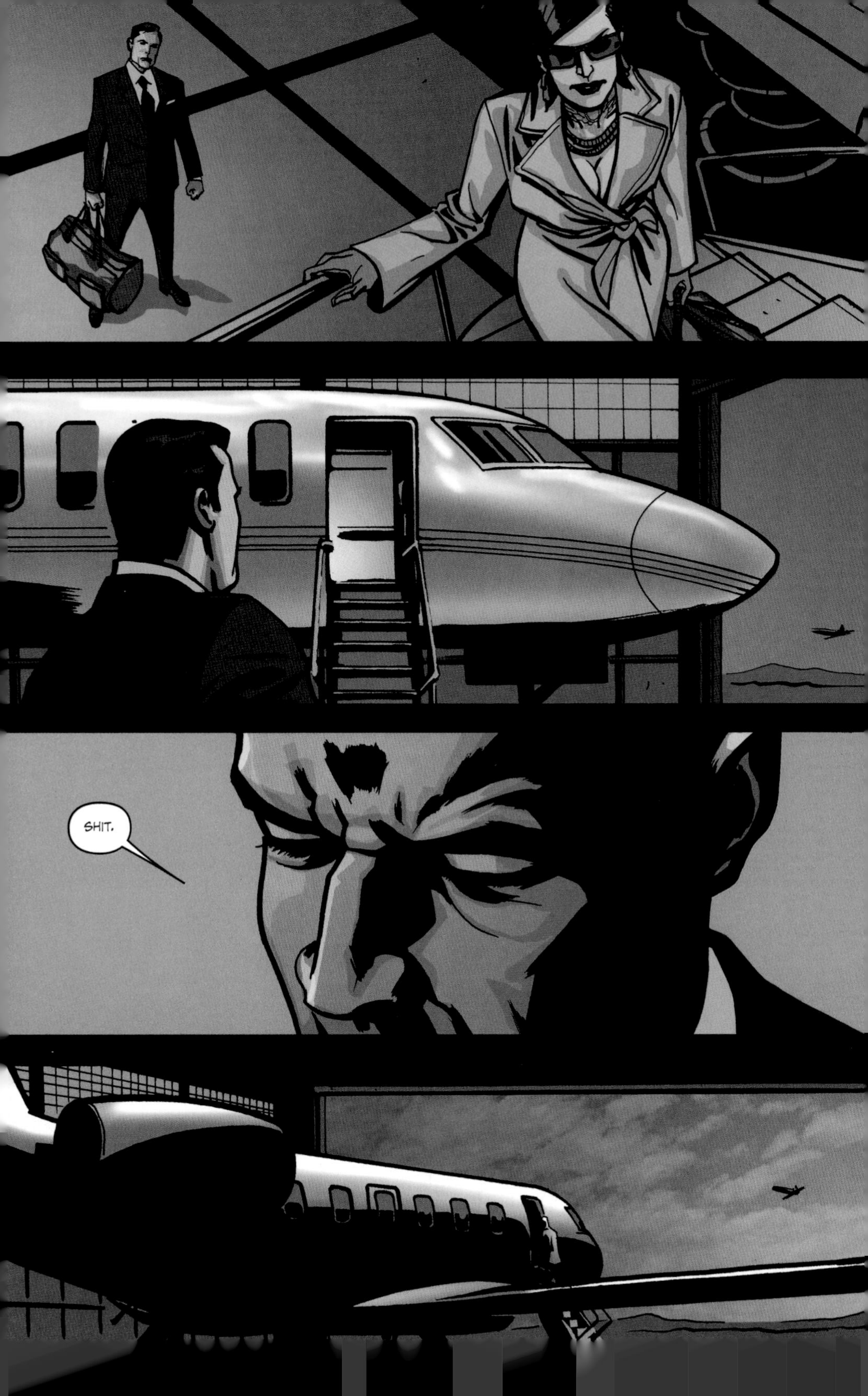
SHIT.

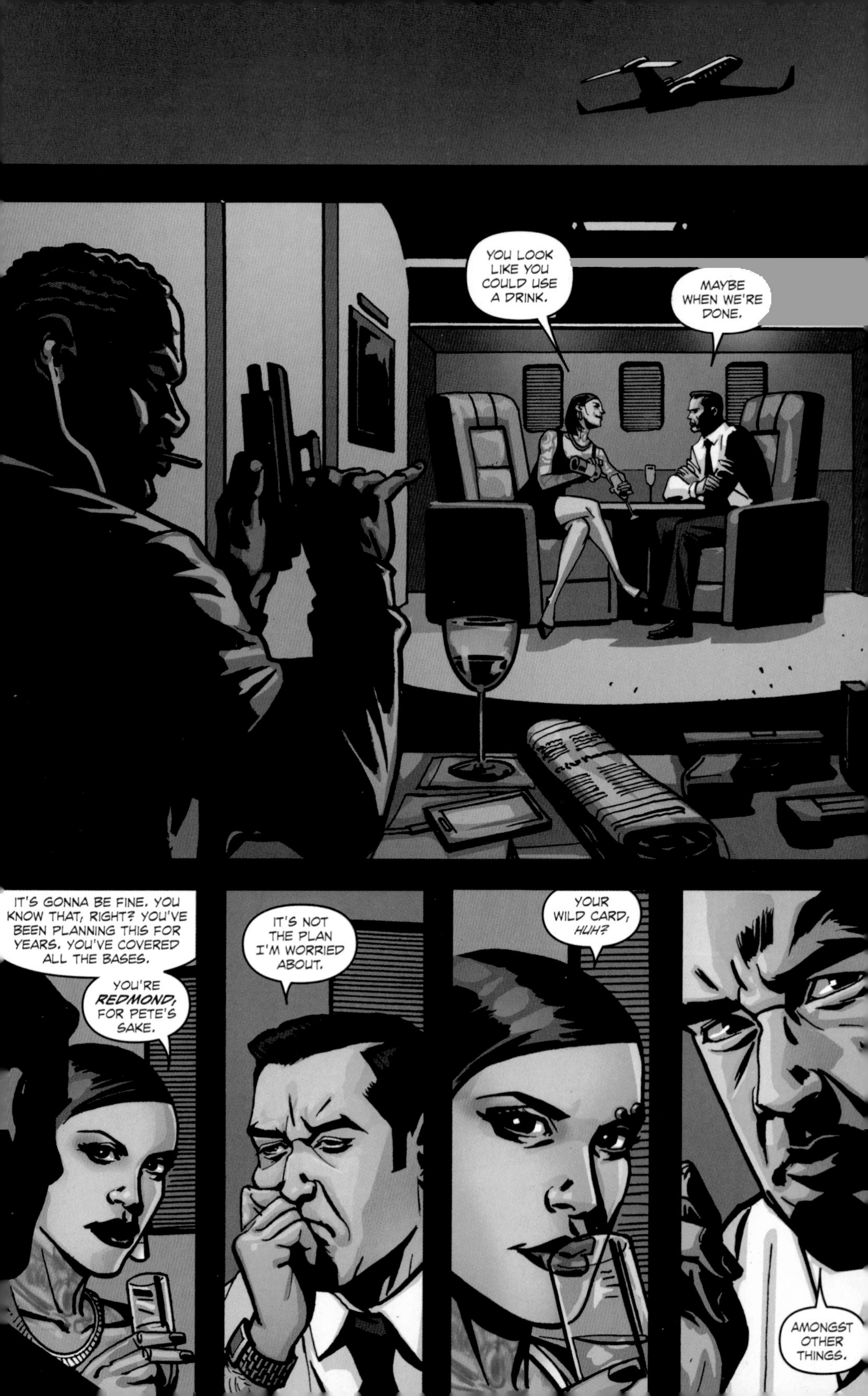
YOU LOOK LIKE YOU COULD USE A DRINK.
MAYBE WHEN WE'RE DONE.
IT'S GONNA BE FINE. YOU KNOW THAT, RIGHT? YOU'VE BEEN PLANNING THIS FOR YEARS. YOU'VE COVERED ALL THE BASES.
YOU'RE *REDMOND*, FOR PETE'S SAKE.
IT'S NOT THE PLAN I'M WORRIED ABOUT.
YOUR WILD CARD, *HUH?*
AMONGST OTHER THINGS.

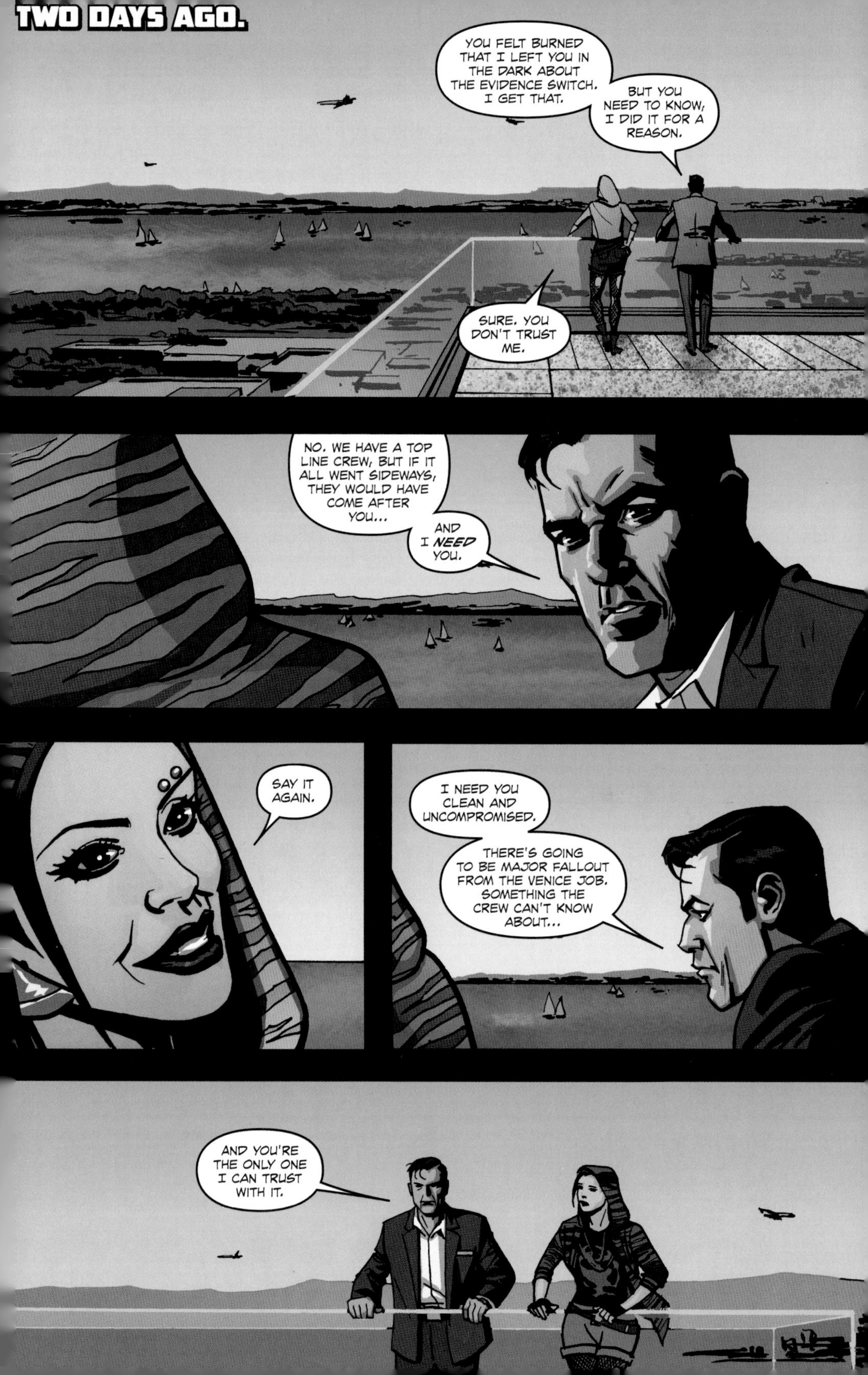
TWO DAYS AGO.
YOU FELT BURNED THAT I LEFT YOU IN THE DARK ABOUT THE EVIDENCE SWITCH. I GET THAT.
BUT YOU NEED TO KNOW, I DID IT FOR A REASON.
SURE. YOU DON'T TRUST ME.
NO. WE HAVE A TOP LINE CREW, BUT IF IT ALL WENT SIDEWAYS, THEY WOULD HAVE COME AFTER YOU...
AND I NEED YOU.
SAY IT AGAIN.
I NEED YOU CLEAN AND UNCOMPROMISED.
THERE'S GOING TO BE MAJOR FALLOUT FROM THE VENICE JOB. SOMETHING THE CREW CAN'T KNOW ABOUT...
AND YOU'RE THE ONLY ONE I CAN TRUST WITH IT.

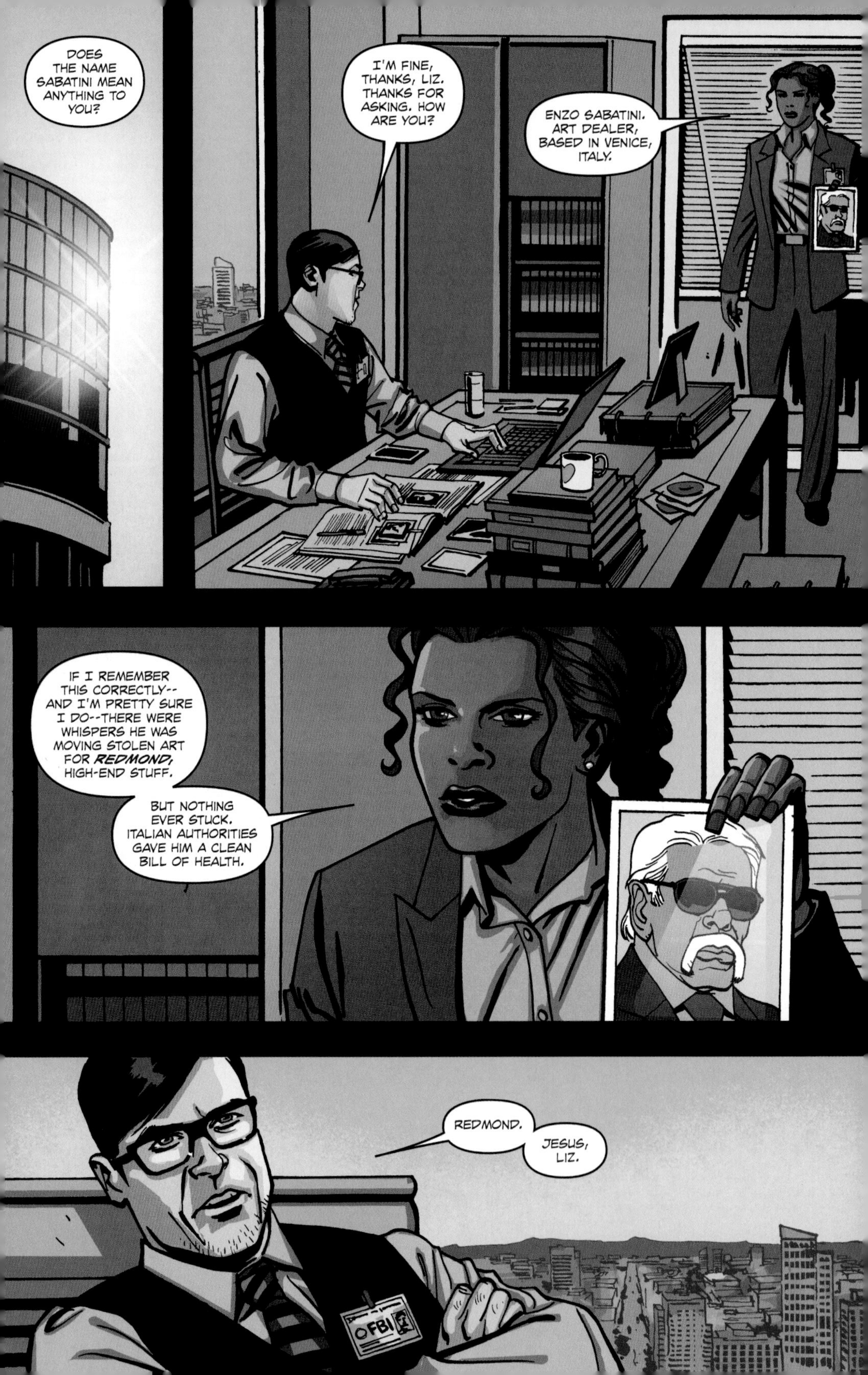
DOES THE NAME SABATINI MEAN ANYTHING TO YOU?
I'M FINE, THANKS, LIZ. THANKS FOR ASKING. HOW ARE YOU?
ENZO SABATINI. ART DEALER, BASED IN VENICE, ITALY.
IF I REMEMBER THIS CORRECTLY--AND I'M PRETTY SURE I DO--THERE WERE WHISPERS HE WAS MOVING STOLEN ART FOR REDMOND, HIGH-END STUFF.
BUT NOTHING EVER STUCK. ITALIAN AUTHORITIES GAVE HIM A CLEAN BILL OF HEALTH.
REDMOND.
JESUS, LIZ.
FBI

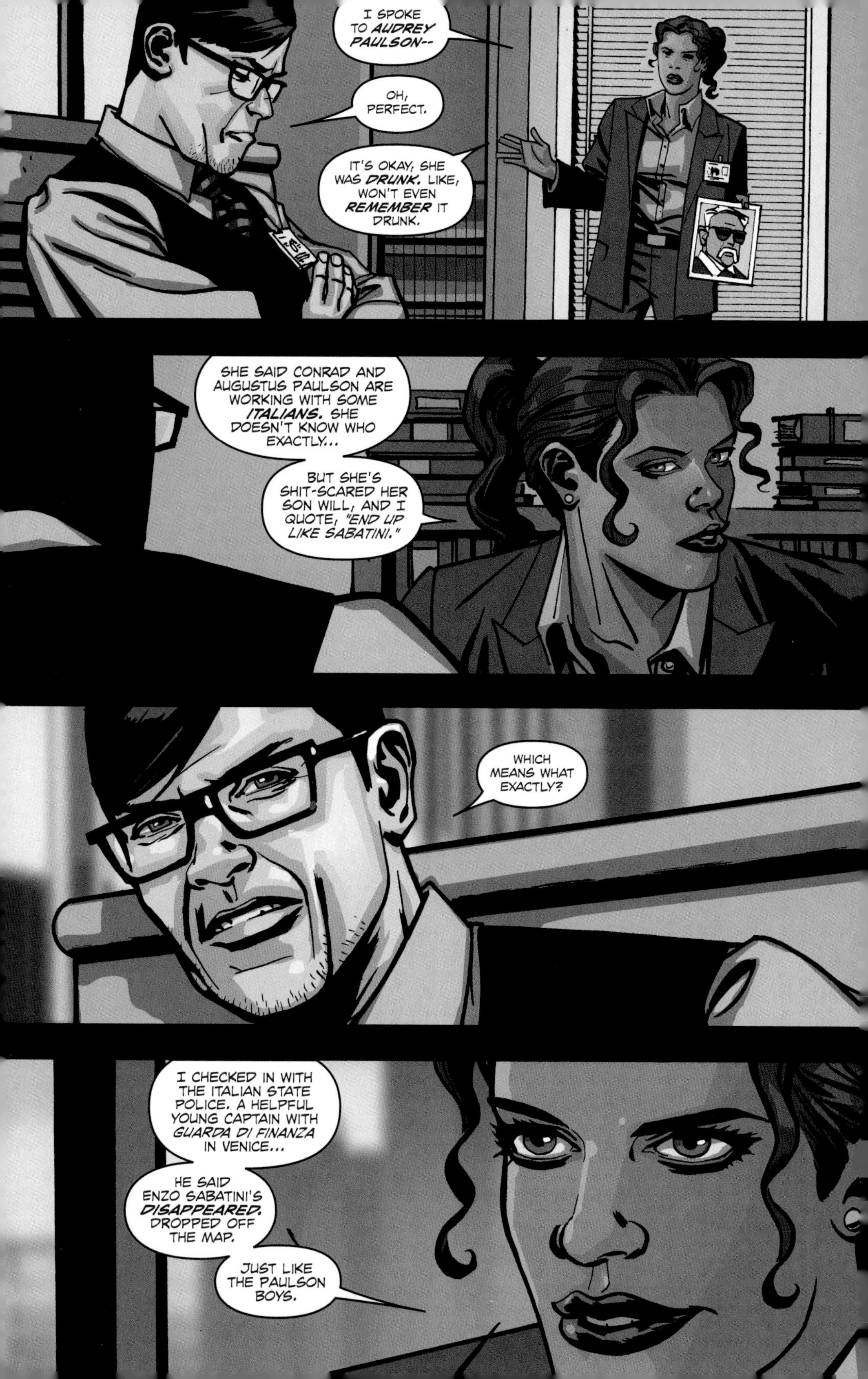
I SPOKE TO *AUDREY PAULSON*--
OH, PERFECT.
IT'S OKAY, SHE WAS *DRUNK.* LIKE, WON'T EVEN *REMEMBER* IT DRUNK.
SHE SAID CONRAD AND AUGUSTUS PAULSON ARE WORKING WITH SOME *ITALIANS.* SHE DOESN'T KNOW WHO EXACTLY...
BUT SHE'S SHIT-SCARED HER SON WILL, AND I QUOTE, *"END UP LIKE SABATINI."*
WHICH MEANS WHAT EXACTLY?
I CHECKED IN WITH THE ITALIAN STATE POLICE. A HELPFUL YOUNG CAPTAIN WITH *GUARDA DI FINANZA* IN VENICE...
HE SAID ENZO SABATINI'S *DISAPPEARED.* DROPPED OFF THE MAP.
JUST LIKE THE PAULSON BOYS.

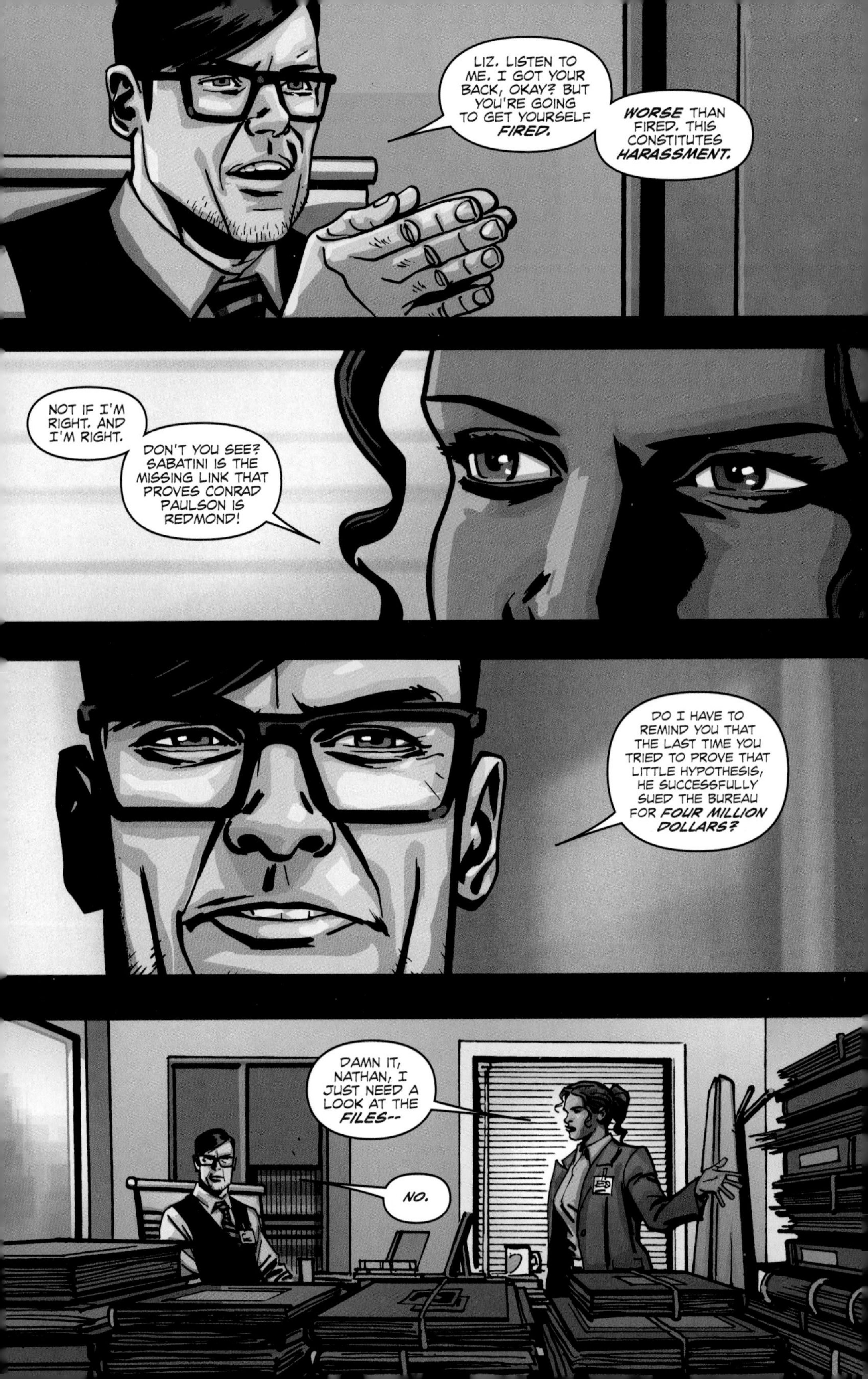
LIZ. LISTEN TO ME. I GOT YOUR BACK, OKAY? BUT YOU'RE GOING TO GET YOURSELF FIRED.
WORSE THAN FIRED. THIS CONSTITUTES HARASSMENT.
NOT IF I'M RIGHT. AND I'M RIGHT.
DON'T YOU SEE? SABATINI IS THE MISSING LINK THAT PROVES CONRAD PAULSON IS REDMOND!
DO I HAVE TO REMIND YOU THAT THE LAST TIME YOU TRIED TO PROVE THAT LITTLE HYPOTHESIS, HE SUCCESSFULLY SUED THE BUREAU FOR FOUR MILLION DOLLARS?
DAMN IT, NATHAN, I JUST NEED A LOOK AT THE FILES--
NO.

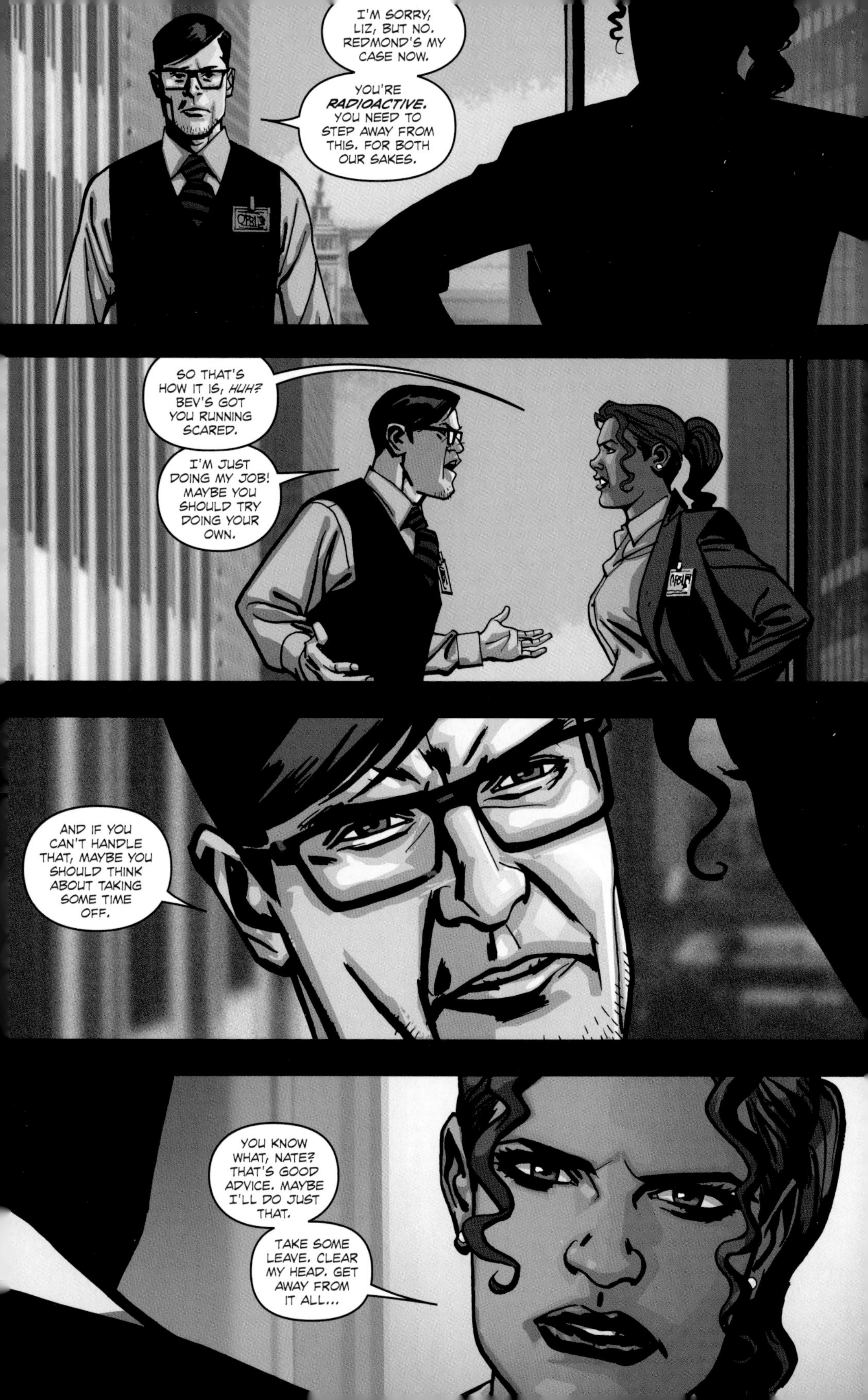
I'M SORRY, LIZ, BUT NO. REDMOND'S MY CASE NOW.
YOU'RE **RADIOACTIVE.** YOU NEED TO STEP AWAY FROM THIS. FOR BOTH OUR SAKES.
SO THAT'S HOW IT IS, *HUH?* BEV'S GOT YOU RUNNING SCARED.
I'M JUST DOING MY JOB! MAYBE YOU SHOULD TRY DOING YOUR OWN.
AND IF YOU CAN'T HANDLE THAT, MAYBE YOU SHOULD THINK ABOUT TAKING SOME TIME OFF.
YOU KNOW WHAT, NATE? THAT'S GOOD ADVICE. MAYBE I'LL DO JUST THAT.
TAKE SOME LEAVE. CLEAR MY HEAD. GET AWAY FROM IT ALL...

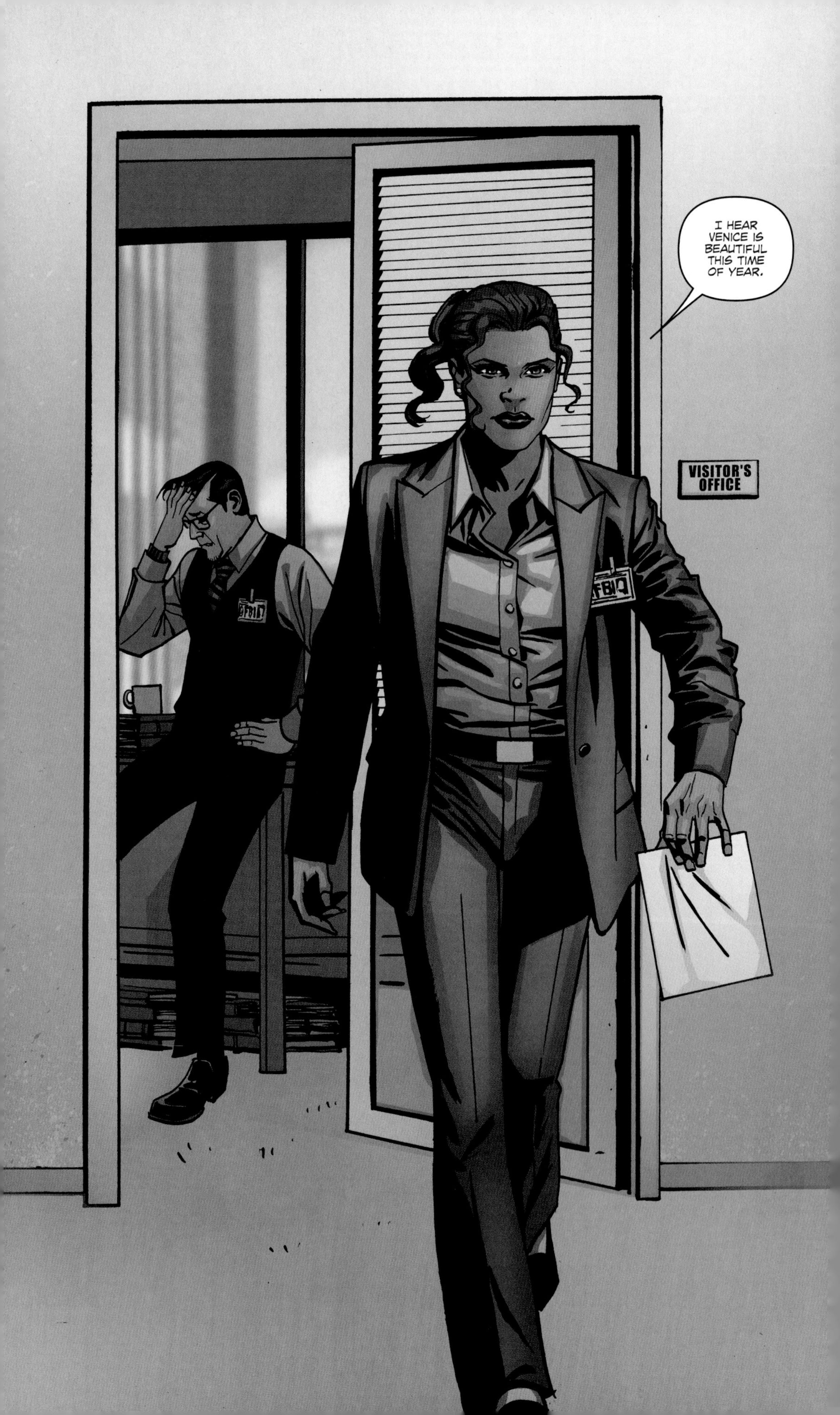
I HEAR VENICE IS BEAUTIFUL THIS TIME OF YEAR.
VISITOR'S OFFICE
FBI
FBI

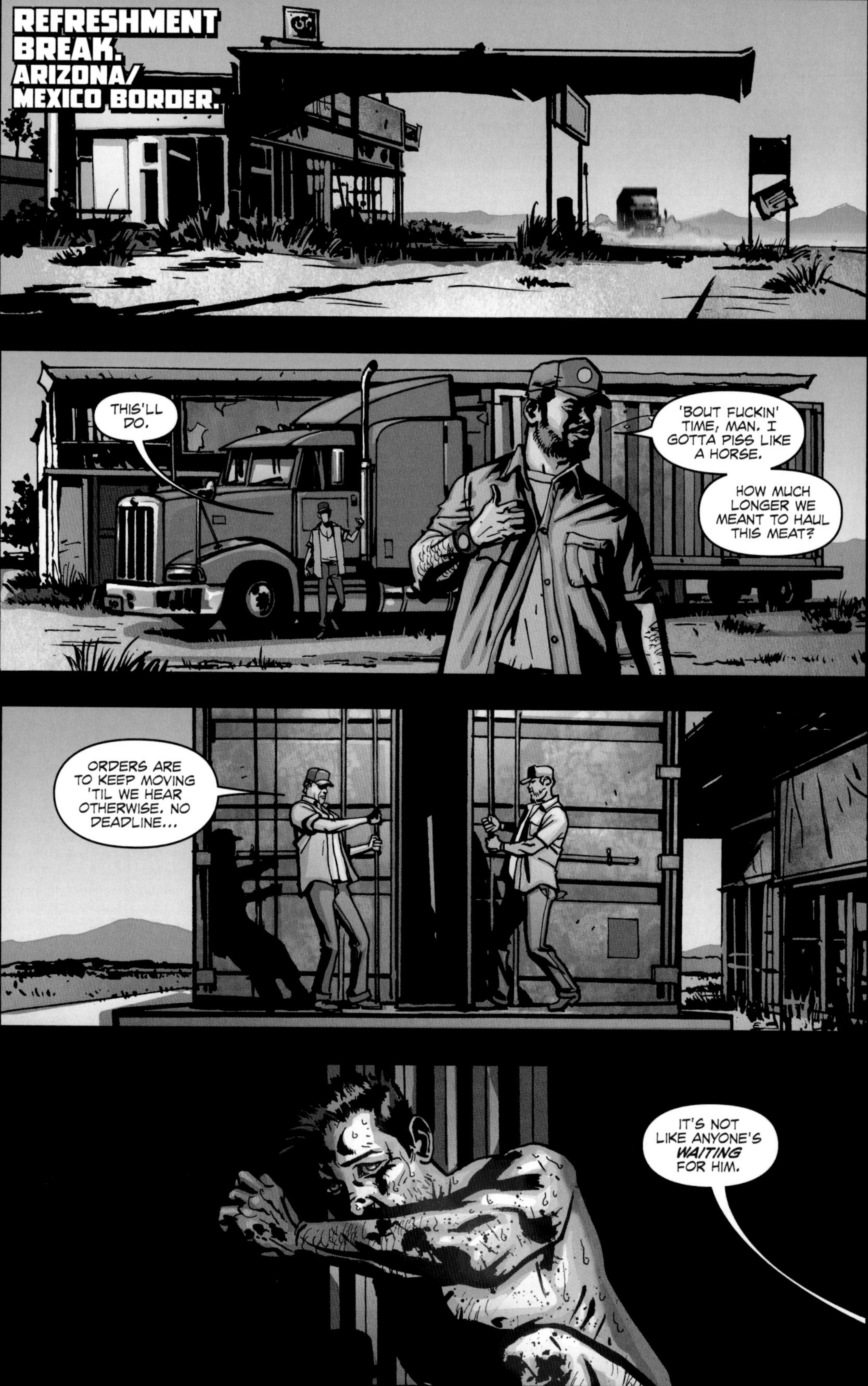
REFRESHMENT BREAK. ARIZONA/ MEXICO BORDER.
THIS'LL DO.
'BOUT FUCKIN' TIME, MAN. I GOTTA PISS LIKE A HORSE.
HOW MUCH LONGER WE MEANT TO HAUL THIS MEAT?
ORDERS ARE TO KEEP MOVING 'TIL WE HEAR OTHERWISE. NO DEADLINE...
IT'S NOT LIKE ANYONE'S *WAITING* FOR HIM.

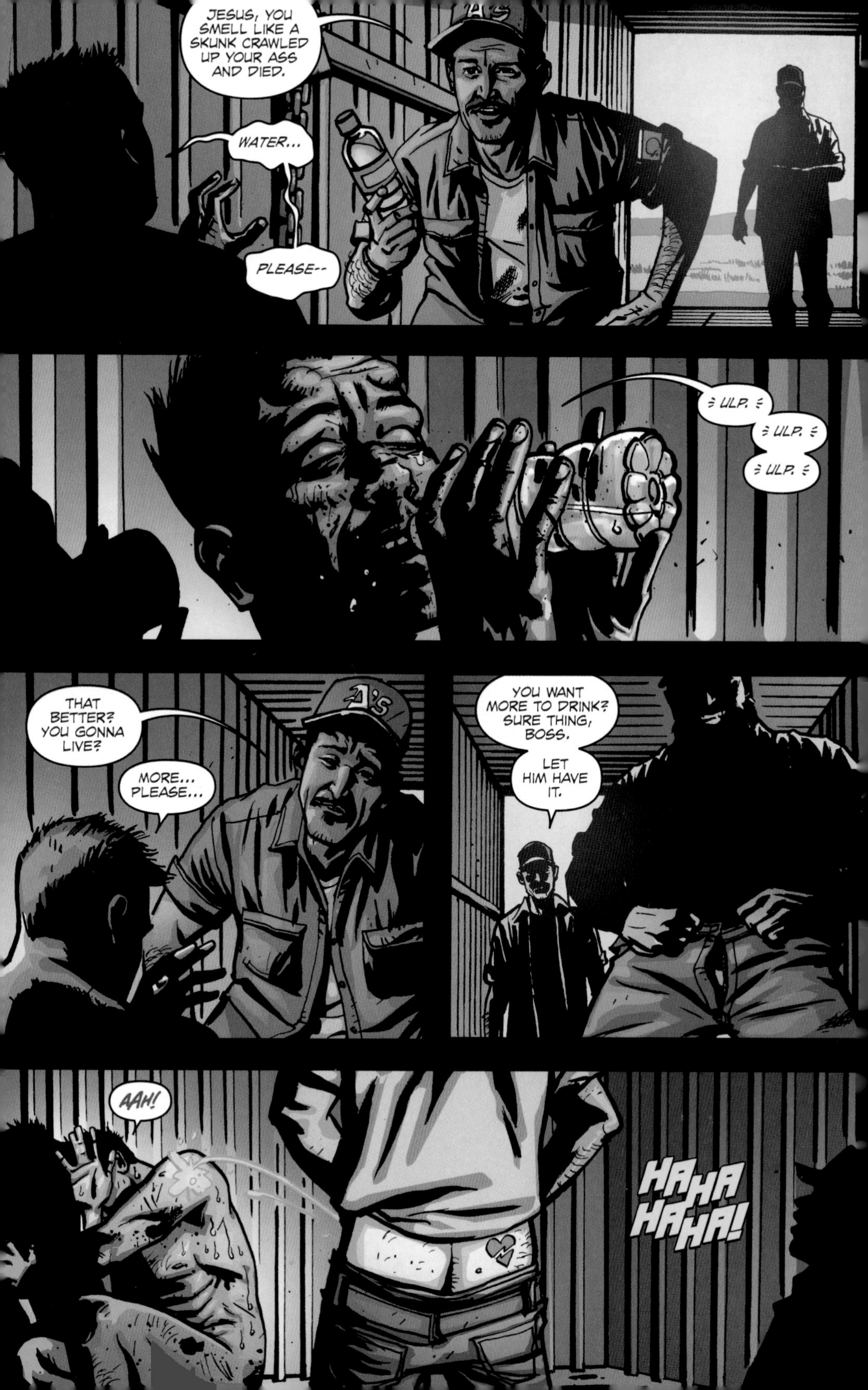
JESUS, YOU SMELL LIKE A SKUNK CRAWLED UP YOUR ASS AND DIED.
WATER...
PLEASE--
ULP.
ULP.
ULP.
THAT BETTER? YOU GONNA LIVE?
MORE... PLEASE...
YOU WANT MORE TO DRINK? SURE THING, BOSS.
LET HIM HAVE IT.
AAH!
HAHA HAHA!

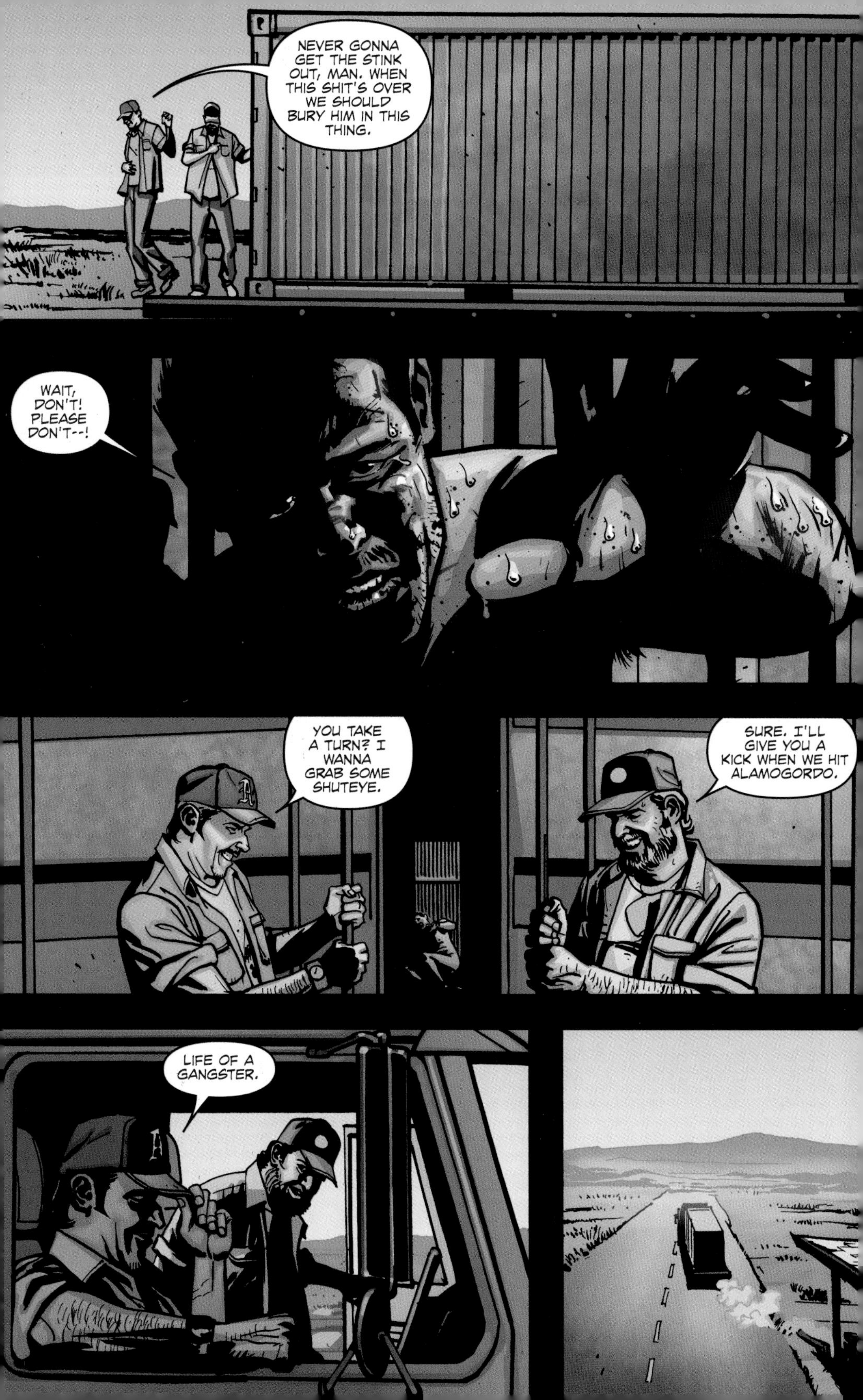
NEVER GONNA GET THE STINK OUT, MAN. WHEN THIS SHIT'S OVER WE SHOULD BURY HIM IN THIS THING.
WAIT, DON'T! PLEASE DON'T--!
YOU TAKE A TURN? I WANNA GRAB SOME SHUTEYE.
SURE. I'LL GIVE YOU A KICK WHEN WE HIT ALAMOGORDO.
LIFE OF A GANGSTER.

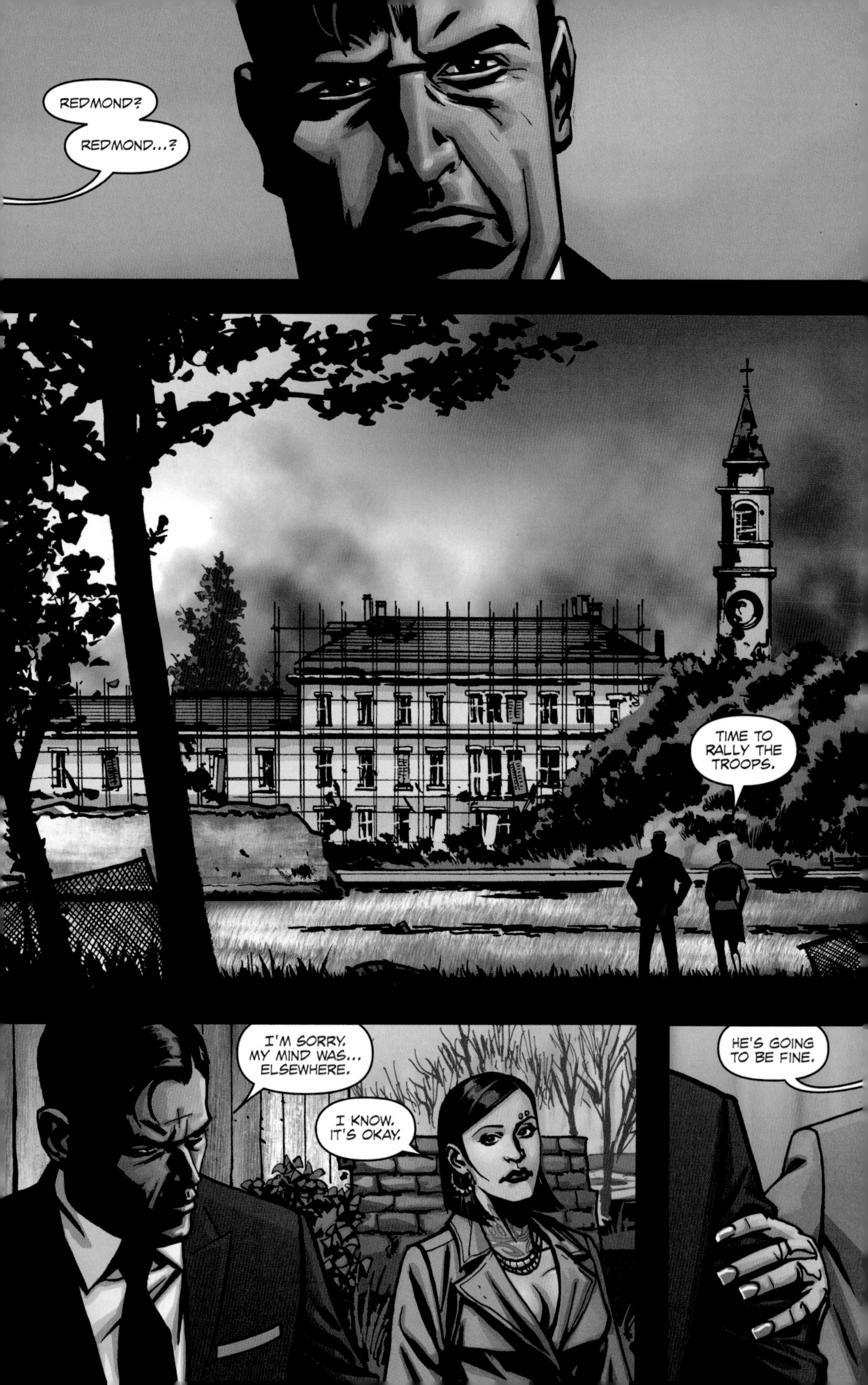
REDMOND?
REDMOND...?
TIME TO RALLY THE TROOPS.
I'M SORRY. MY MIND WAS... ELSEWHERE.
I KNOW. IT'S OKAY.
HE'S GOING TO BE FINE.

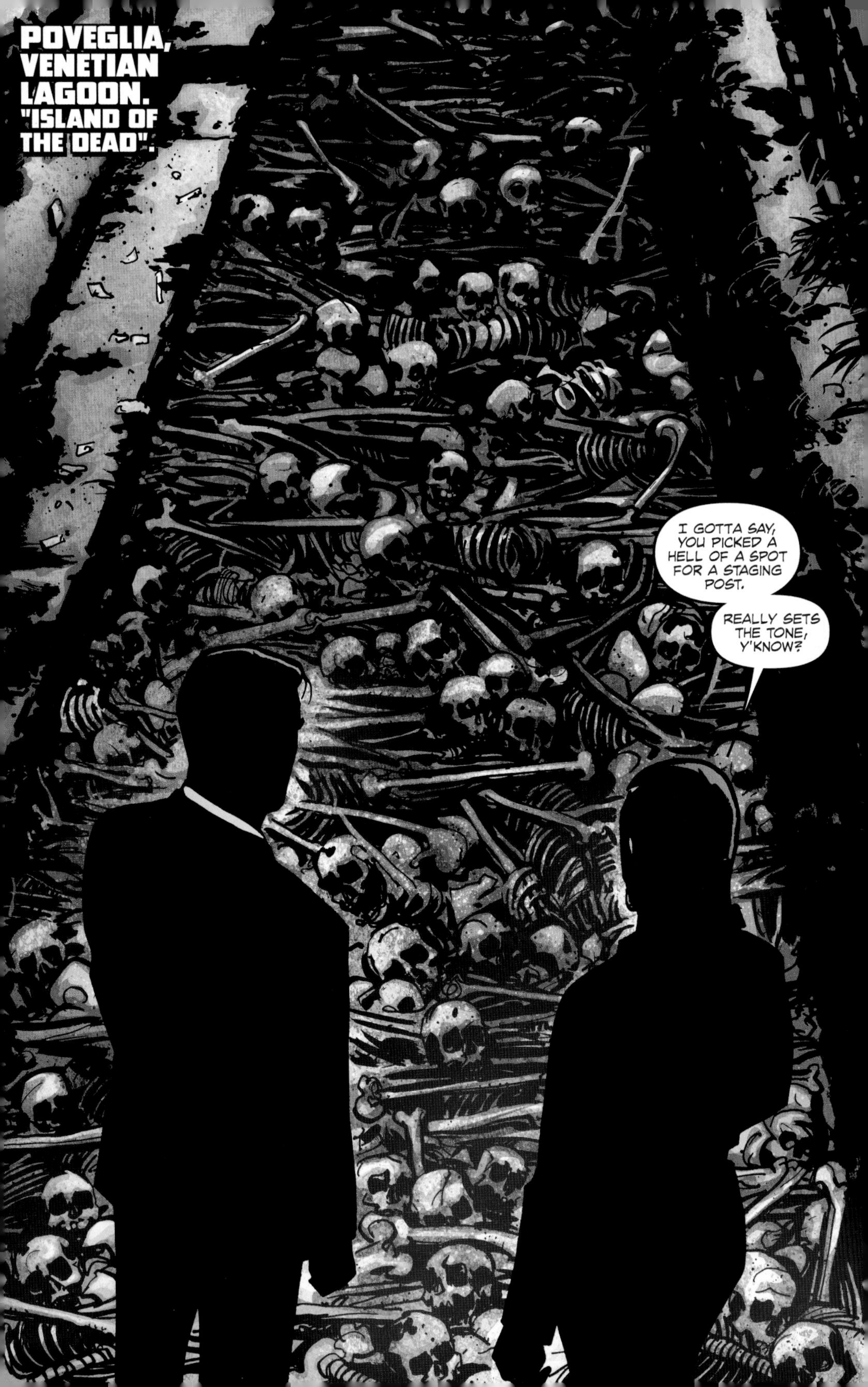
POVEGLIA, VENETIAN LAGOON. "ISLAND OF THE DEAD".
I GOTTA SAY, YOU PICKED A HELL OF A SPOT FOR A STAGING POST.
REALLY SETS THE TONE, Y'KNOW?

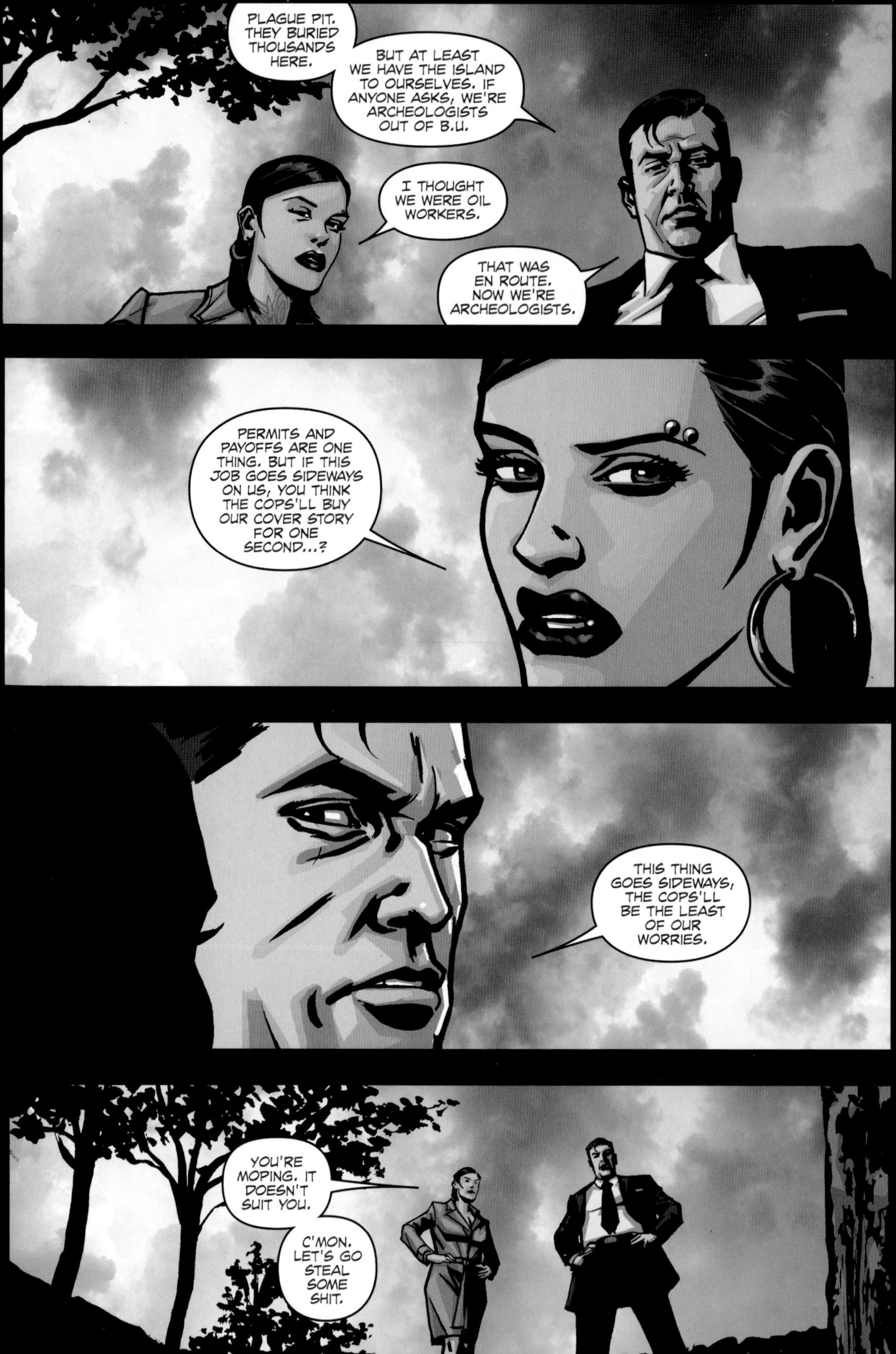
PLAGUE PIT. THEY BURIED THOUSANDS HERE.
BUT AT LEAST WE HAVE THE ISLAND TO OURSELVES. IF ANYONE ASKS, WE'RE ARCHEOLOGISTS OUT OF B.U.
I THOUGHT WE WERE OIL WORKERS.
THAT WAS EN ROUTE. NOW WE'RE ARCHEOLOGISTS.
PERMITS AND PAYOFFS ARE ONE THING. BUT IF THIS JOB GOES SIDEWAYS ON US, YOU THINK THE COPS'LL BUY OUR COVER STORY FOR ONE SECOND...?
THIS THING GOES SIDEWAYS, THE COPS'LL BE THE LEAST OF OUR WORRIES.
YOU'RE MOPING. IT DOESN'T SUIT YOU.
C'MON. LET'S GO STEAL SOME SHIT.

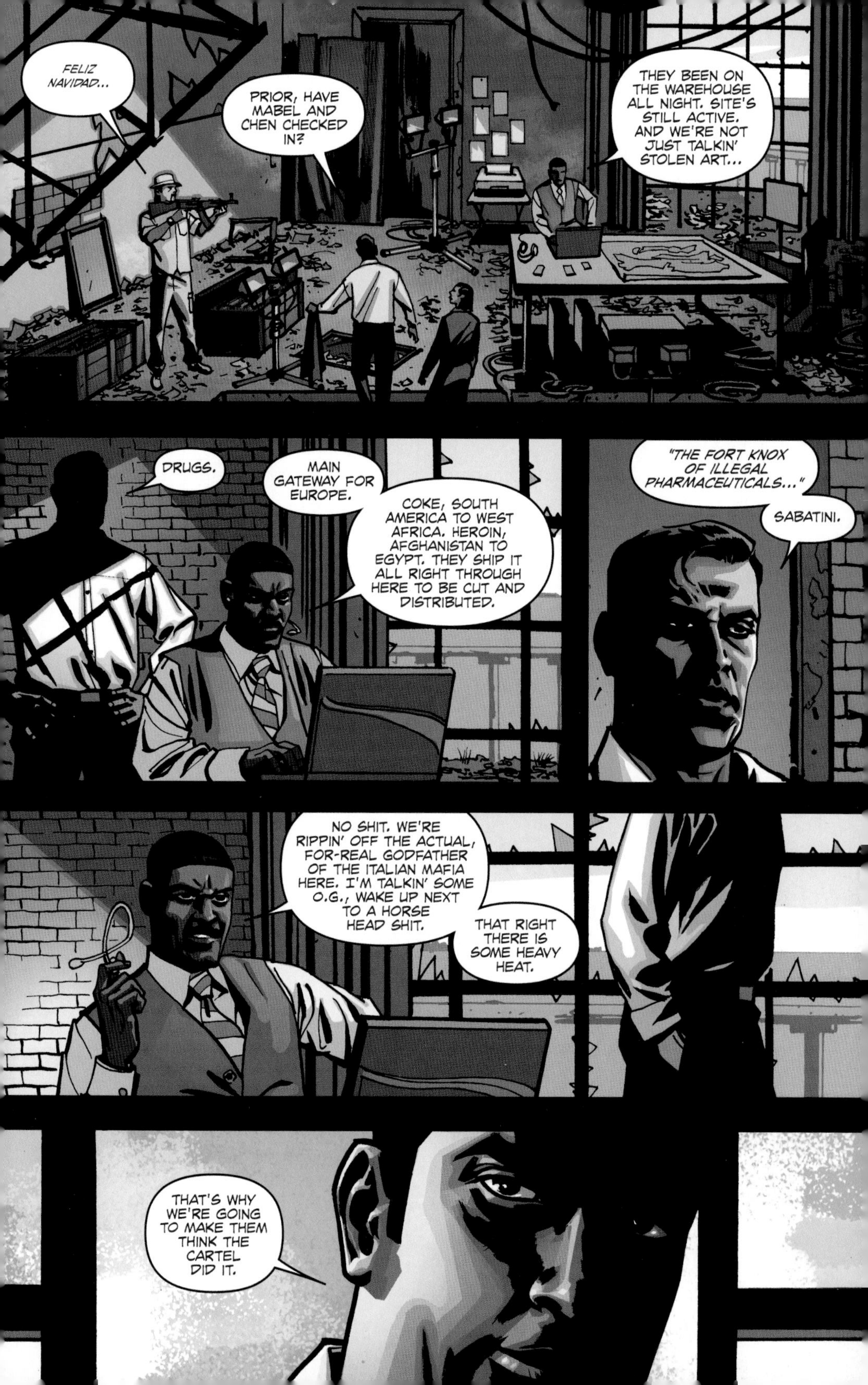
FELIZ NAVIDAD...
PRIOR, HAVE MABEL AND CHEN CHECKED IN?
THEY BEEN ON THE WAREHOUSE ALL NIGHT. SITE'S STILL ACTIVE. AND WE'RE NOT JUST TALKIN' STOLEN ART...
DRUGS.
MAIN GATEWAY FOR EUROPE.
COKE, SOUTH AMERICA TO WEST AFRICA. HEROIN, AFGHANISTAN TO EGYPT. THEY SHIP IT ALL RIGHT THROUGH HERE TO BE CUT AND DISTRIBUTED.
"THE FORT KNOX OF ILLEGAL PHARMACEUTICALS..."
SABATINI.
NO SHIT. WE'RE RIPPIN' OFF THE ACTUAL, FOR-REAL GODFATHER OF THE ITALIAN MAFIA HERE. I'M TALKIN' SOME O.G., WAKE UP NEXT TO A HORSE HEAD SHIT.
THAT RIGHT THERE IS SOME HEAVY HEAT.
THAT'S WHY WE'RE GOING TO MAKE THEM THINK THE CARTEL DID IT.

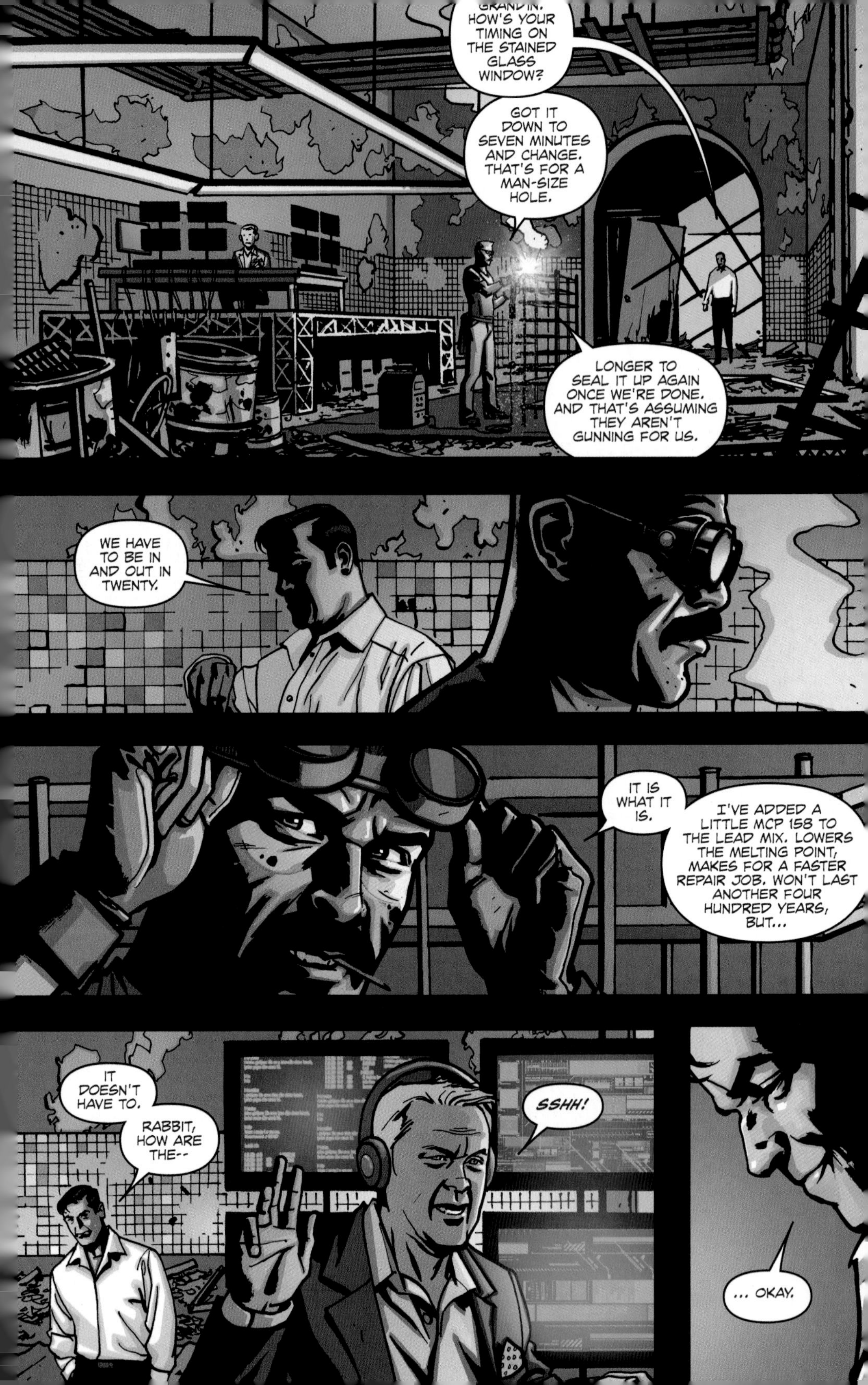

HOW'S YOUR TIMING ON THE STAINED GLASS WINDOW?
GOT IT DOWN TO SEVEN MINUTES AND CHANGE. THAT'S FOR A MAN-SIZE HOLE.
LONGER TO SEAL IT UP AGAIN ONCE WE'RE DONE. AND THAT'S ASSUMING THEY AREN'T GUNNING FOR US.
WE HAVE TO BE IN AND OUT IN TWENTY.
IT IS WHAT IT IS.
I'VE ADDED A LITTLE MCP 158 TO THE LEAD MIX. LOWERS THE MELTING POINT, MAKES FOR A FASTER REPAIR JOB. WON'T LAST ANOTHER FOUR HUNDRED YEARS, BUT...
IT DOESN'T HAVE TO.
RABBIT, HOW ARE THE--
SSHH!
... OKAY.

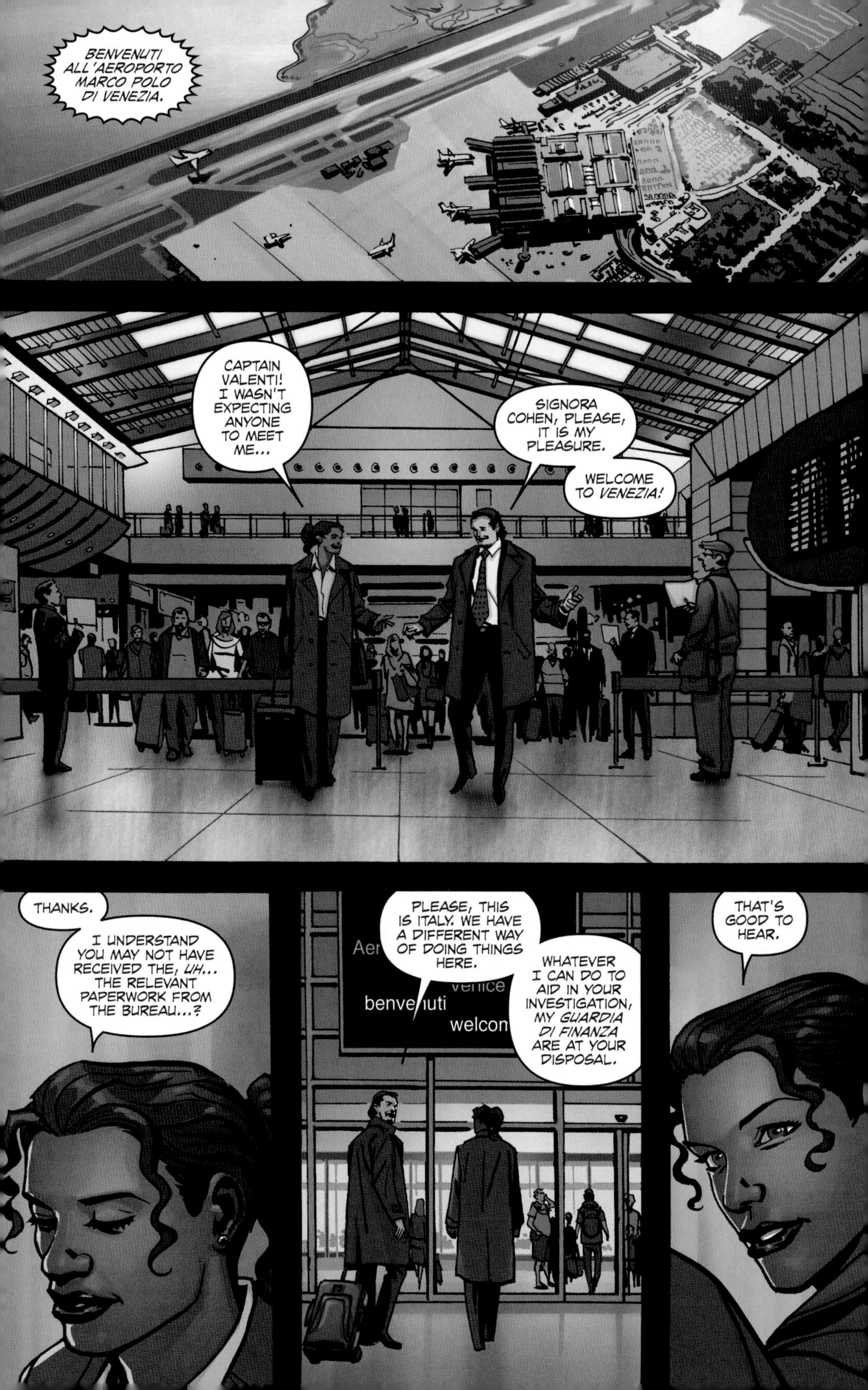

BENVENUTI ALL'AEROPORTO MARCO POLO DI VENEZIA.
CAPTAIN VALENTI! I WASN'T EXPECTING ANYONE TO MEET ME...
SIGNORA COHEN, PLEASE, IT IS MY PLEASURE.
WELCOME TO VENEZIA!
THANKS.
I UNDERSTAND YOU MAY NOT HAVE RECEIVED THE, UH... THE RELEVANT PAPERWORK FROM THE BUREAU...?
Aer
benvenuti
venice
welcom
PLEASE, THIS IS ITALY. WE HAVE A DIFFERENT WAY OF DOING THINGS HERE.
WHATEVER I CAN DO TO AID IN YOUR INVESTIGATION, MY GUARDIA DI FINANZA ARE AT YOUR DISPOSAL.
THAT'S GOOD TO HEAR.

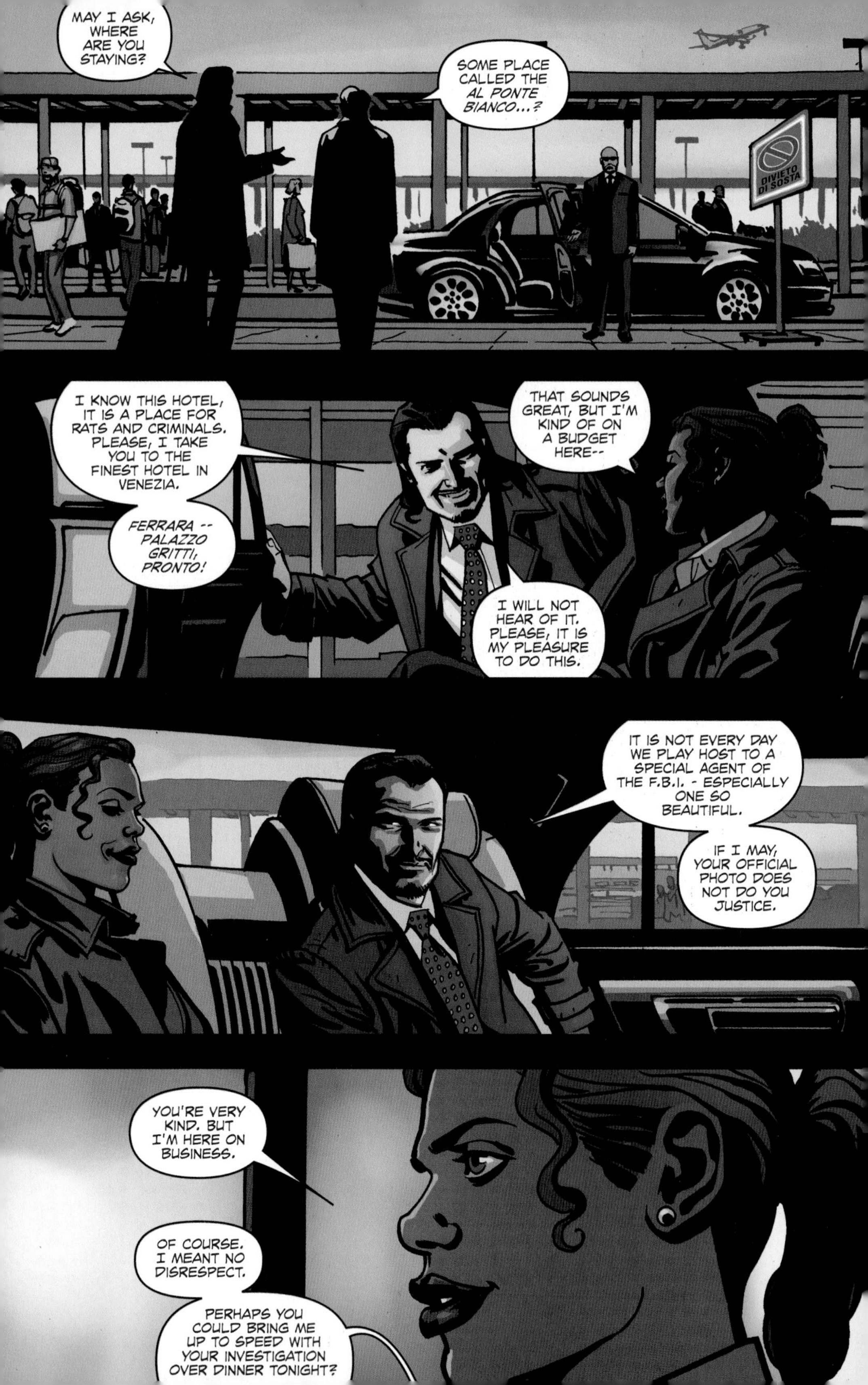
MAY I ASK, WHERE ARE YOU STAYING?
SOME PLACE CALLED THE *AL PONTE BIANCO...?*
DIVIETO DI SOSTA
I KNOW THIS HOTEL, IT IS A PLACE FOR RATS AND CRIMINALS. PLEASE, I TAKE YOU TO THE FINEST HOTEL IN VENEZIA.
FERRARA -- PALAZZO GRITTI, PRONTO!
THAT SOUNDS GREAT, BUT I'M KIND OF ON A BUDGET HERE--
I WILL NOT HEAR OF IT. PLEASE, IT IS MY PLEASURE TO DO THIS.
IT IS NOT EVERY DAY WE PLAY HOST TO A SPECIAL AGENT OF THE F.B.I. - ESPECIALLY ONE SO BEAUTIFUL.
IF I MAY, YOUR OFFICIAL PHOTO DOES NOT DO YOU JUSTICE.
YOU'RE VERY KIND. BUT I'M HERE ON BUSINESS.
OF COURSE. I MEANT NO DISRESPECT.
PERHAPS YOU COULD BRING ME UP TO SPEED WITH YOUR INVESTIGATION OVER DINNER TONIGHT?

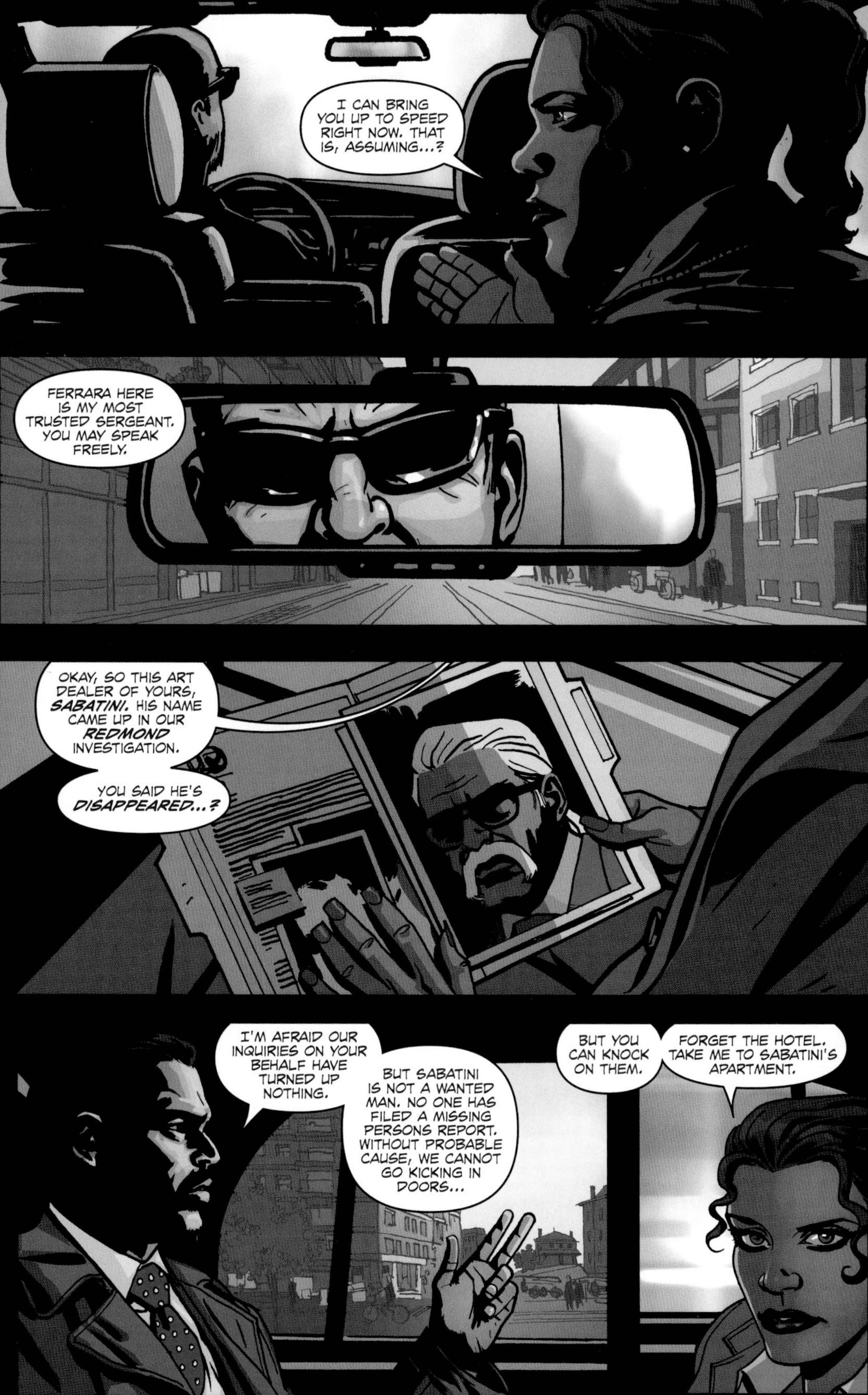
I CAN BRING YOU UP TO SPEED RIGHT NOW. THAT IS, ASSUMING...?
FERRARA HERE IS MY MOST TRUSTED SERGEANT. YOU MAY SPEAK FREELY.
OKAY, SO THIS ART DEALER OF YOURS, SABATINI. HIS NAME CAME UP IN OUR REDMOND INVESTIGATION.
YOU SAID HE'S DISAPPEARED...?
I'M AFRAID OUR INQUIRIES ON YOUR BEHALF HAVE TURNED UP NOTHING.
BUT SABATINI IS NOT A WANTED MAN. NO ONE HAS FILED A MISSING PERSONS REPORT. WITHOUT PROBABLE CAUSE, WE CANNOT GO KICKING IN DOORS...
BUT YOU CAN KNOCK ON THEM.
FORGET THE HOTEL. TAKE ME TO SABATINI'S APARTMENT.

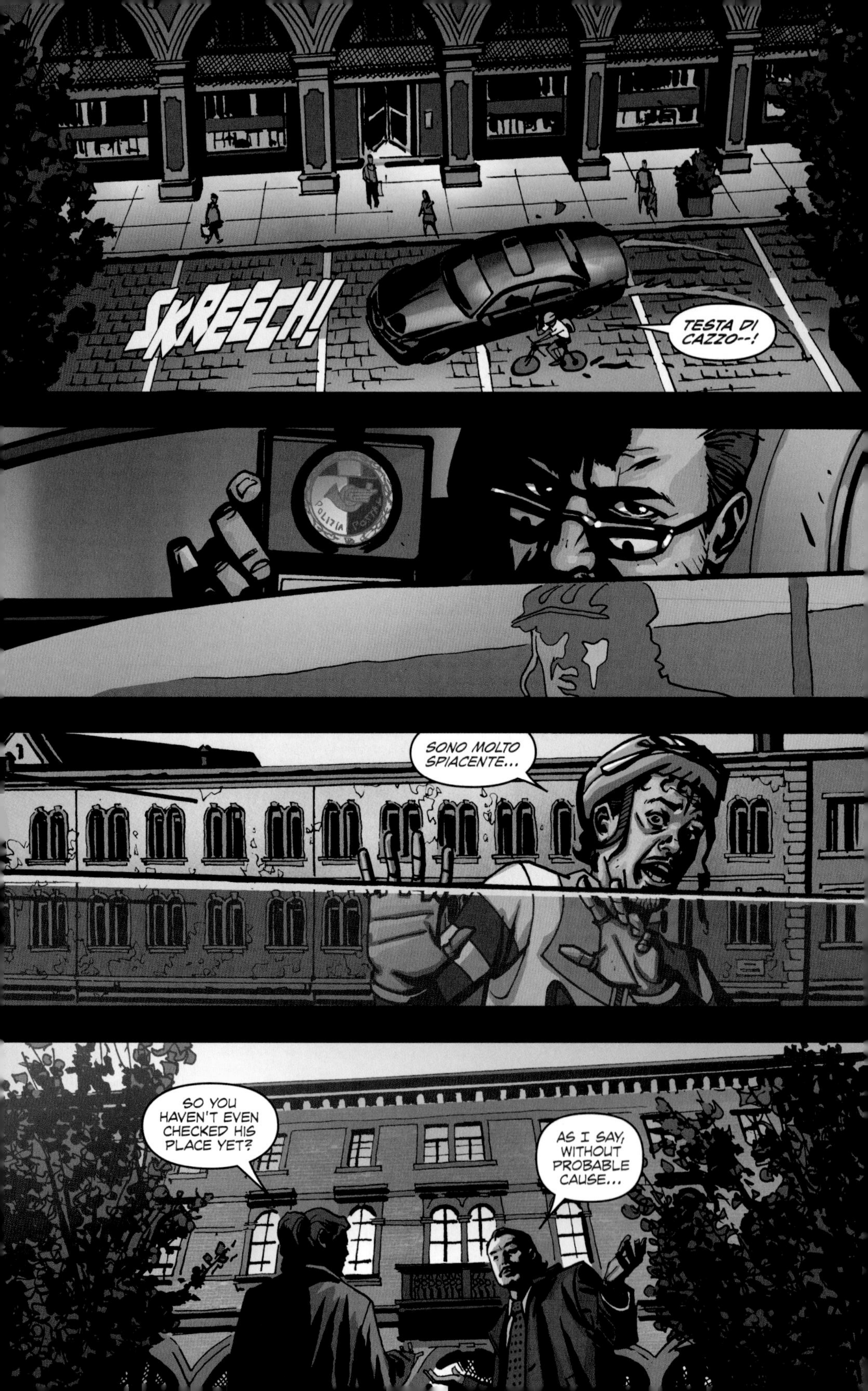
SKREECH!
TESTA DI CAZZO--!
POLIZIA
SONO MOLTO SPIACENTE...
SO YOU HAVEN'T EVEN CHECKED HIS PLACE YET?
AS I SAY, WITHOUT PROBABLE CAUSE...

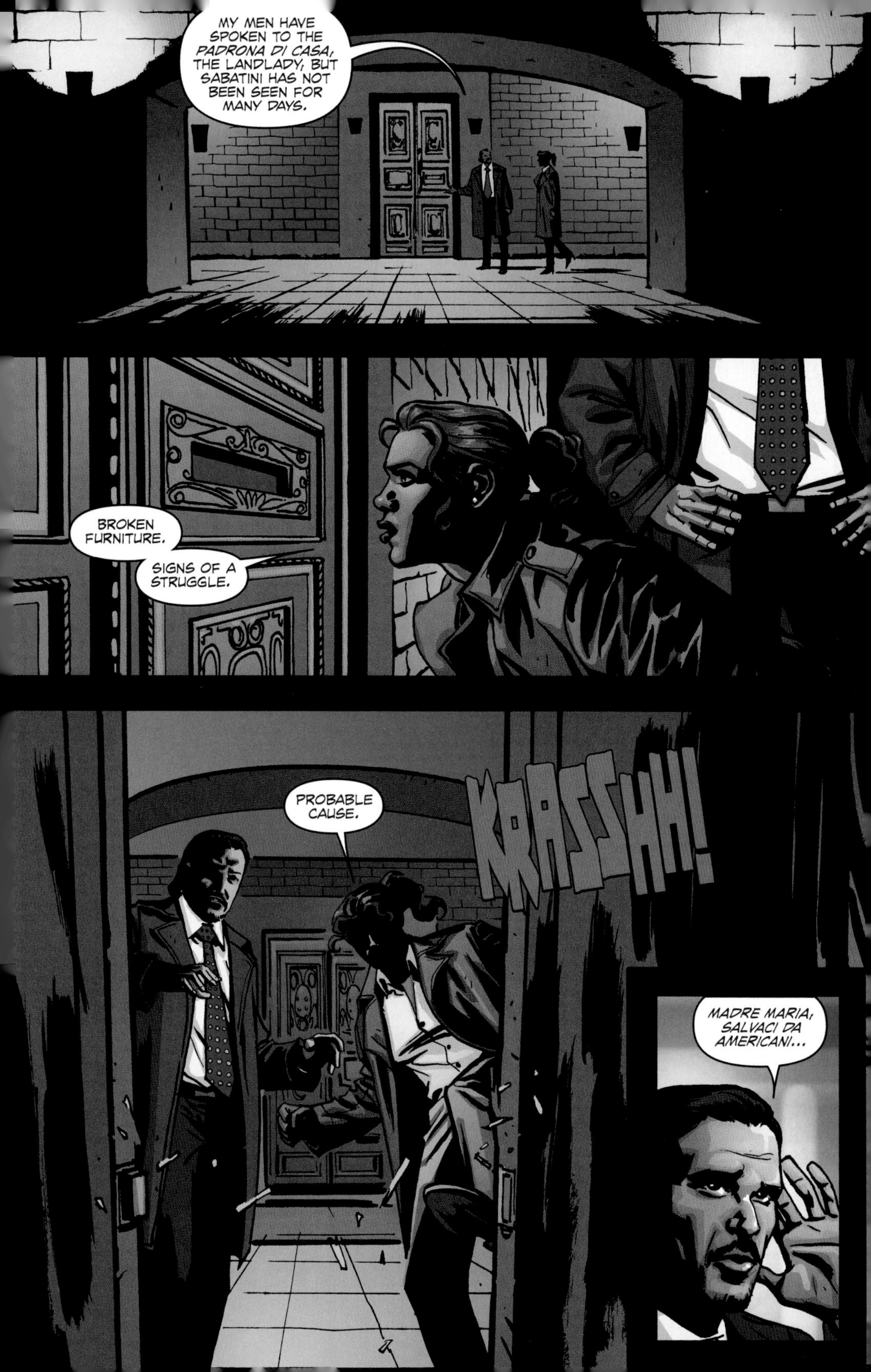
MY MEN HAVE SPOKEN TO THE *PADRONA DI CASA*, THE LANDLADY, BUT SABATINI HAS NOT BEEN SEEN FOR MANY DAYS.
BROKEN FURNITURE.
SIGNS OF A STRUGGLE.
PROBABLE CAUSE.
KRASSHH!
MADRE MARIA, SALVACI DA AMERICANI...

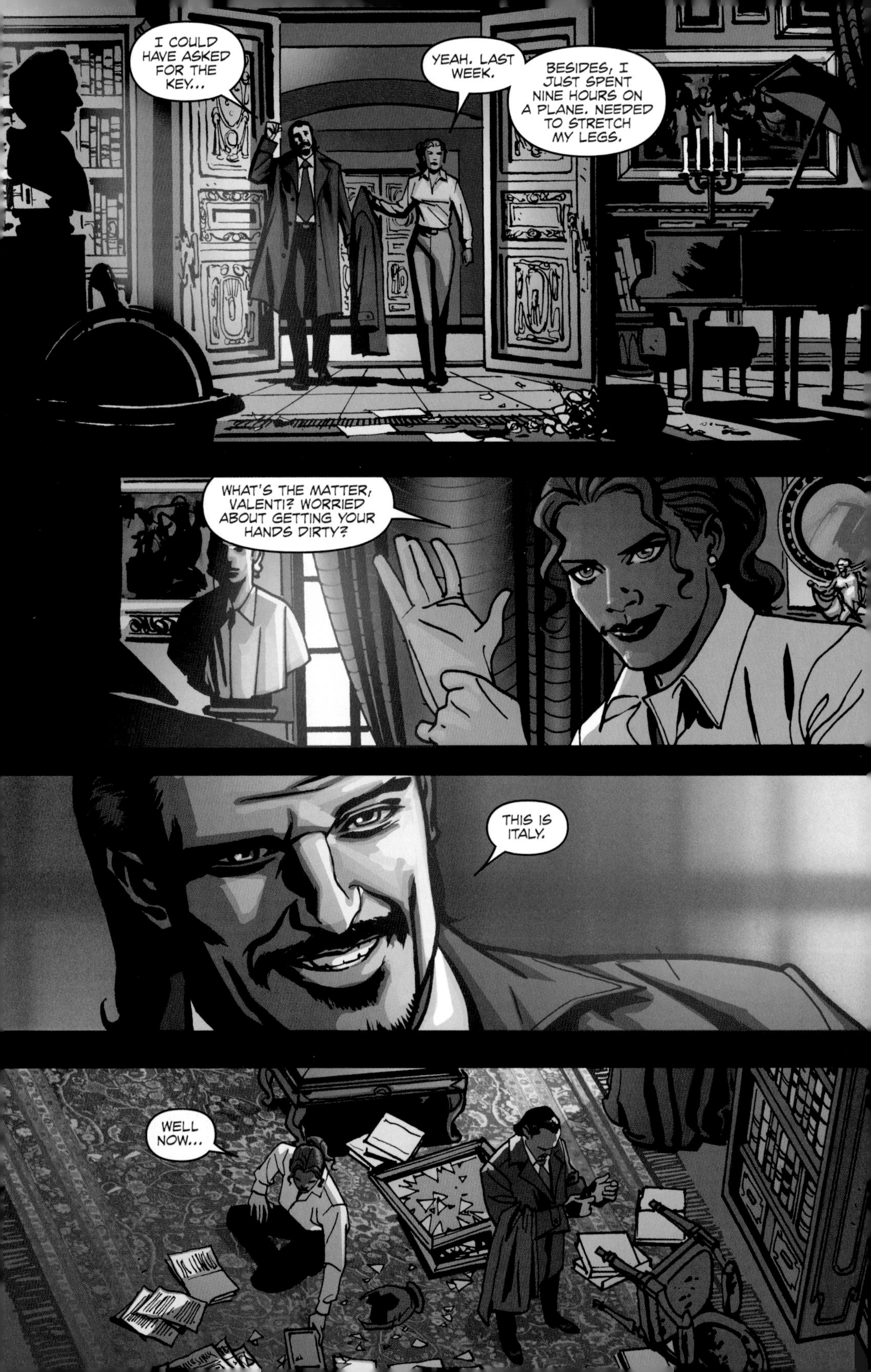
I COULD HAVE ASKED FOR THE KEY...
YEAH. LAST WEEK.
BESIDES, I JUST SPENT NINE HOURS ON A PLANE. NEEDED TO STRETCH MY LEGS.
WHAT'S THE MATTER, VALENTI? WORRIED ABOUT GETTING YOUR HANDS DIRTY?
THIS IS ITALY.
WELL NOW...

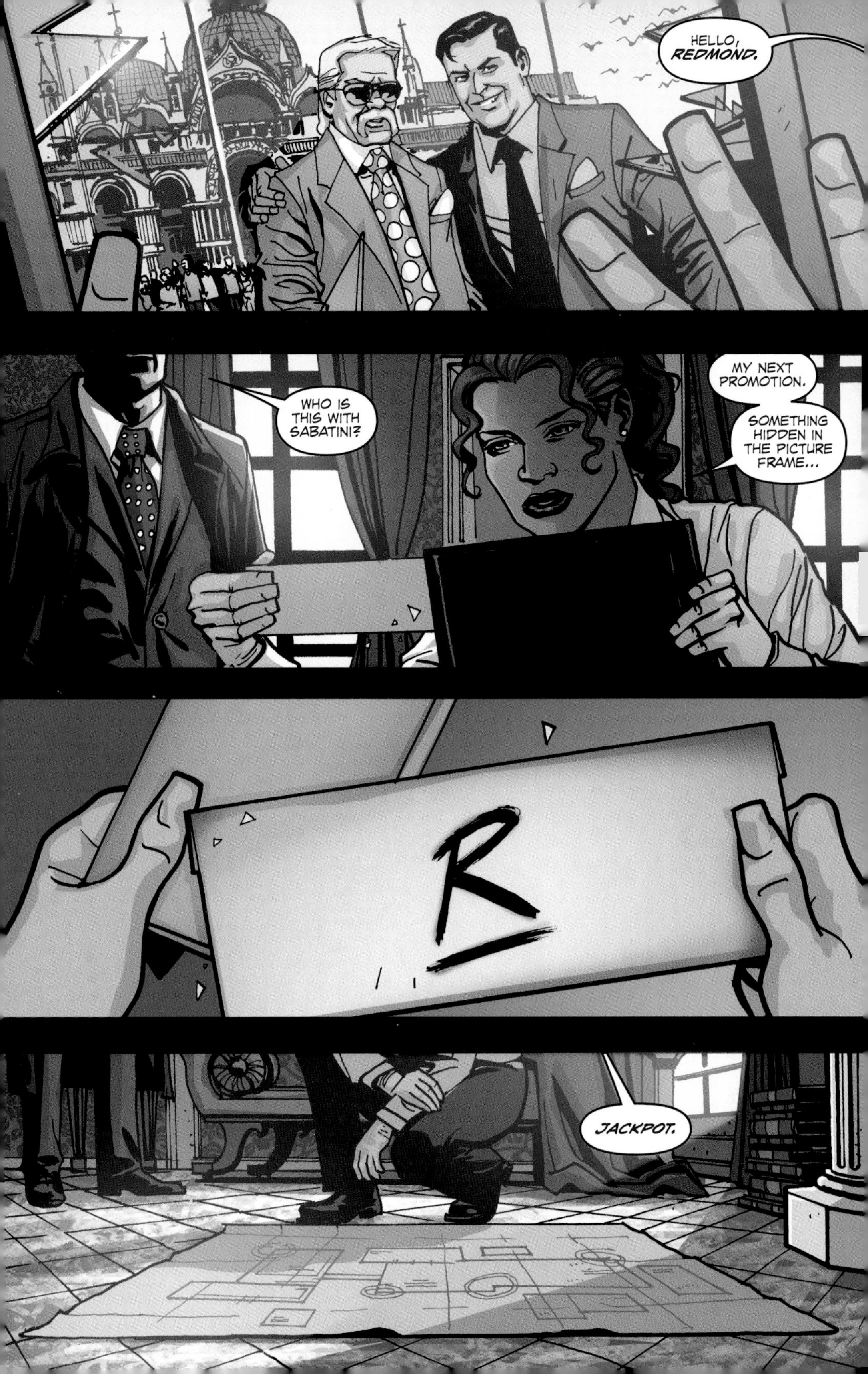
HELLO, REDMOND.
WHO IS THIS WITH SABATINI?
MY NEXT PROMOTION.
SOMETHING HIDDEN IN THE PICTURE FRAME...
R
JACKPOT.

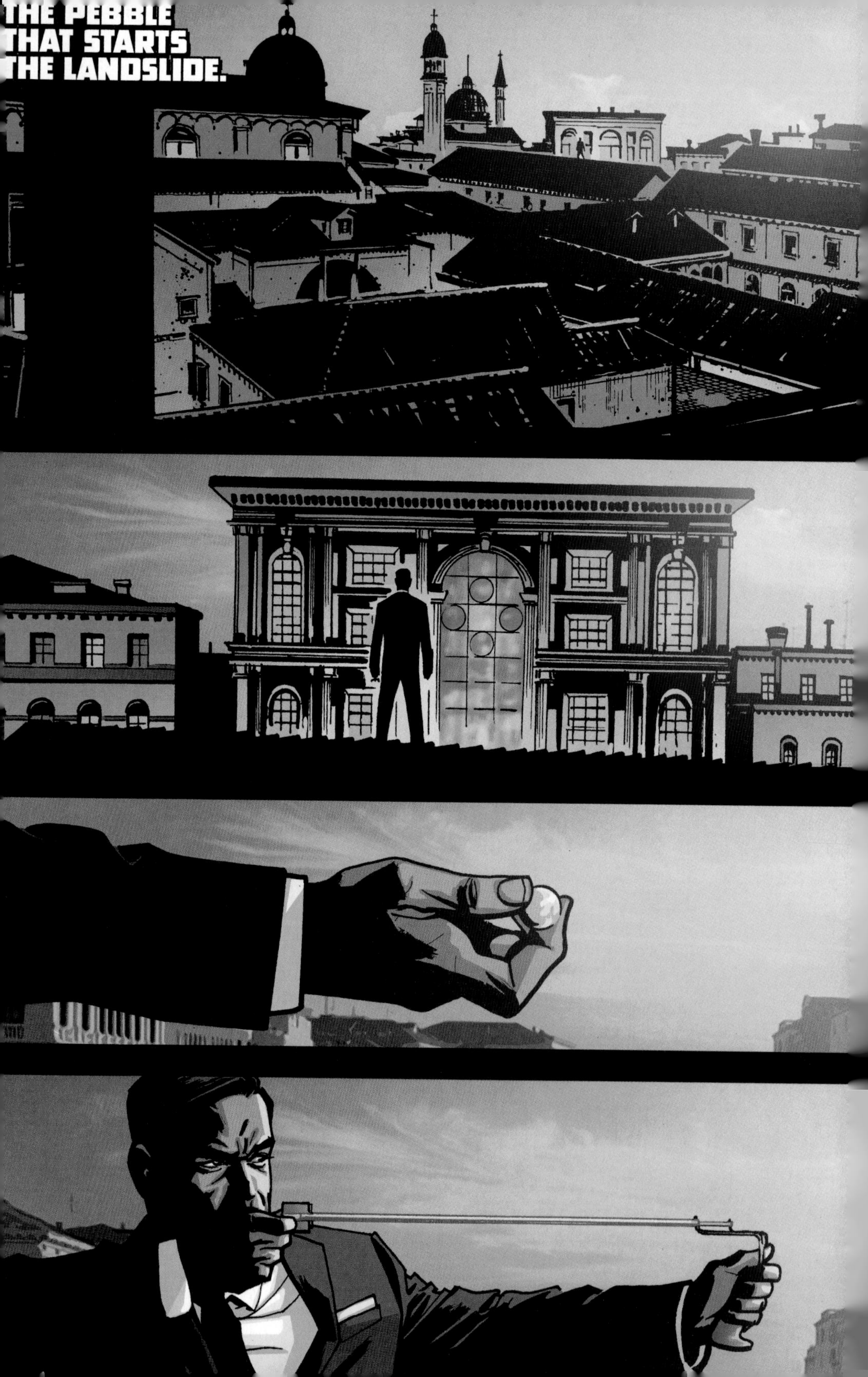
THE PEBBLE THAT STARTS THE LANDSLIDE.

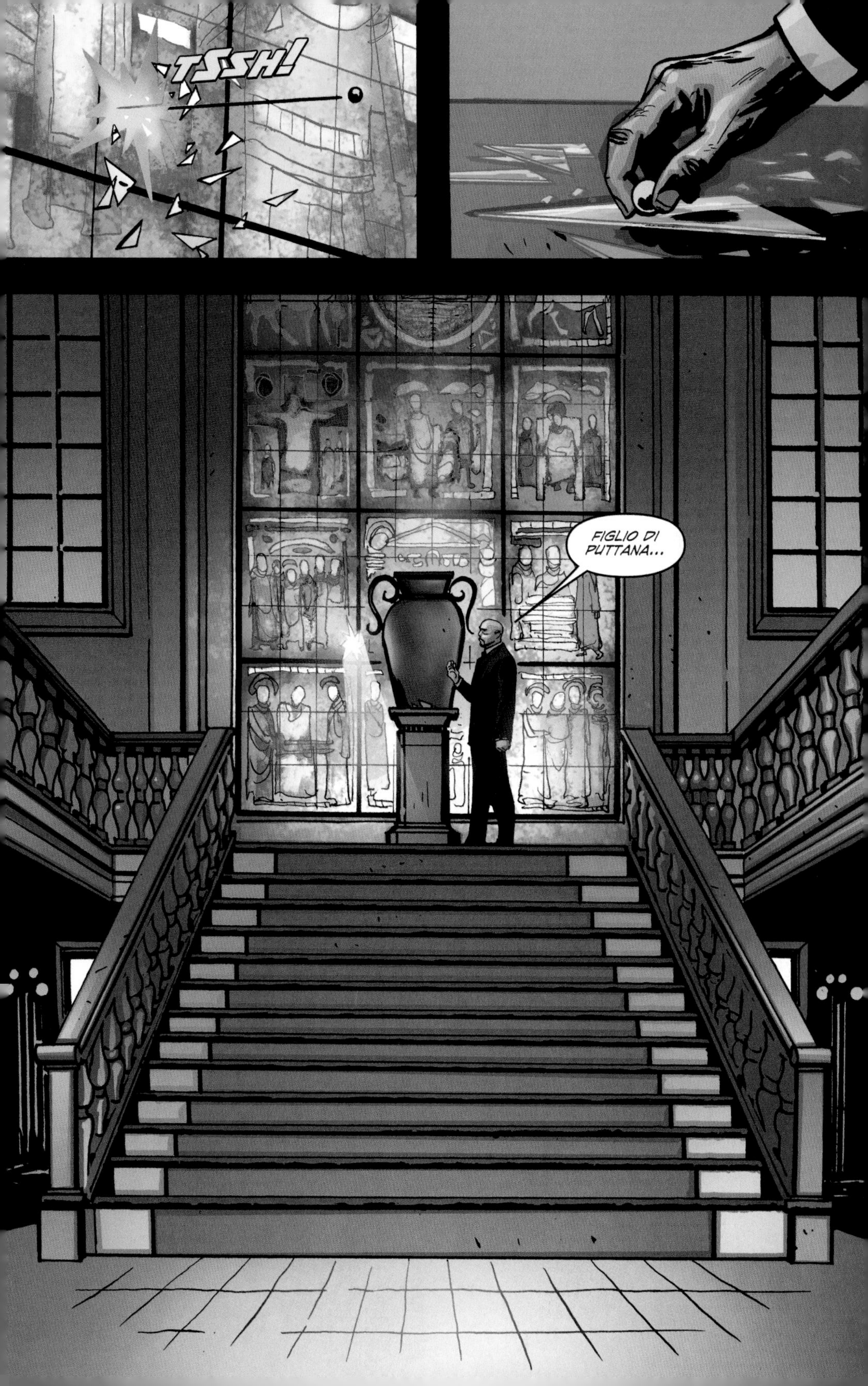
TSSH!
FIGLIO DI PUTTANA...

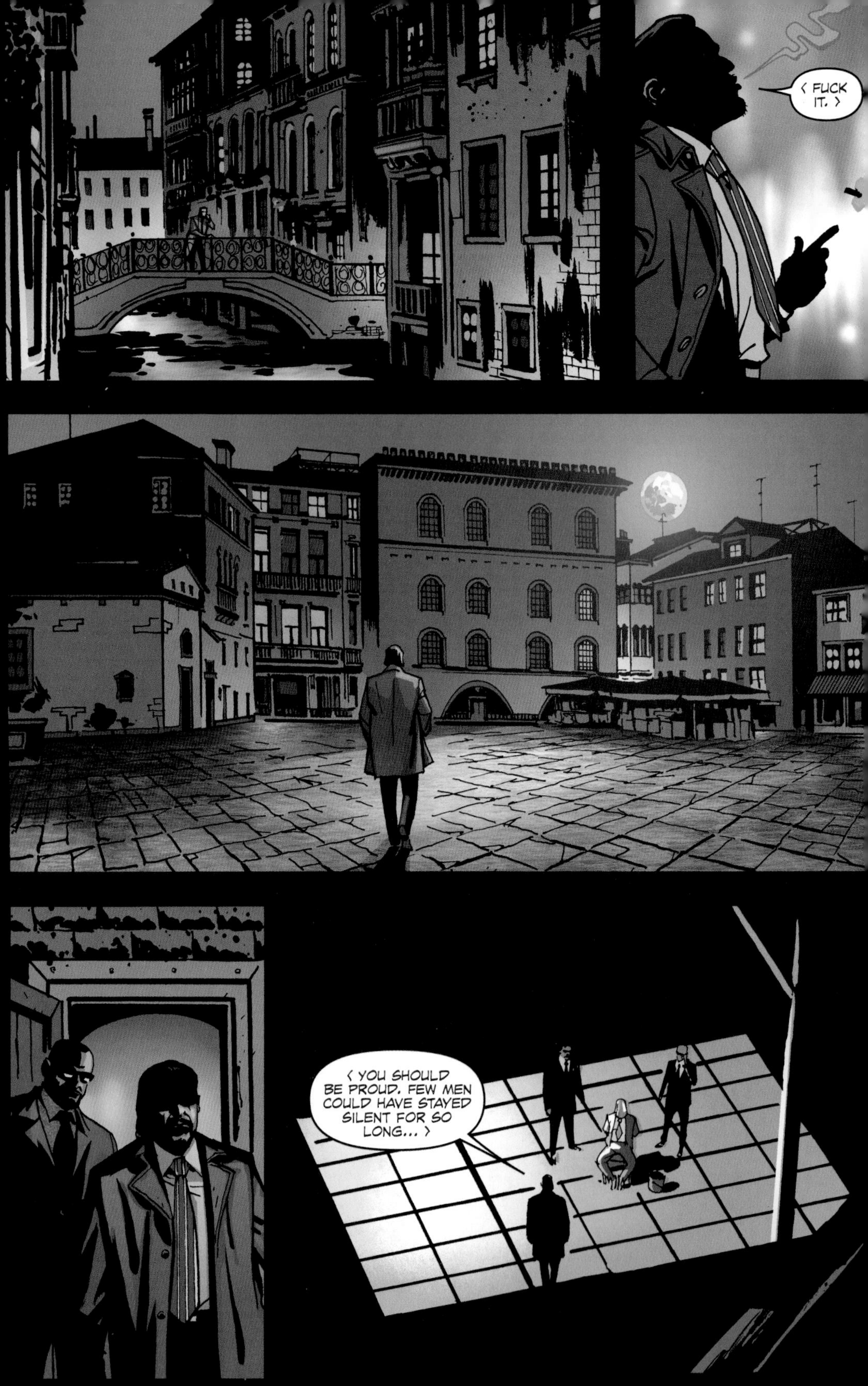
< FUCK IT. >
< YOU SHOULD BE PROUD. FEW MEN COULD HAVE STAYED SILENT FOR SO LONG... >

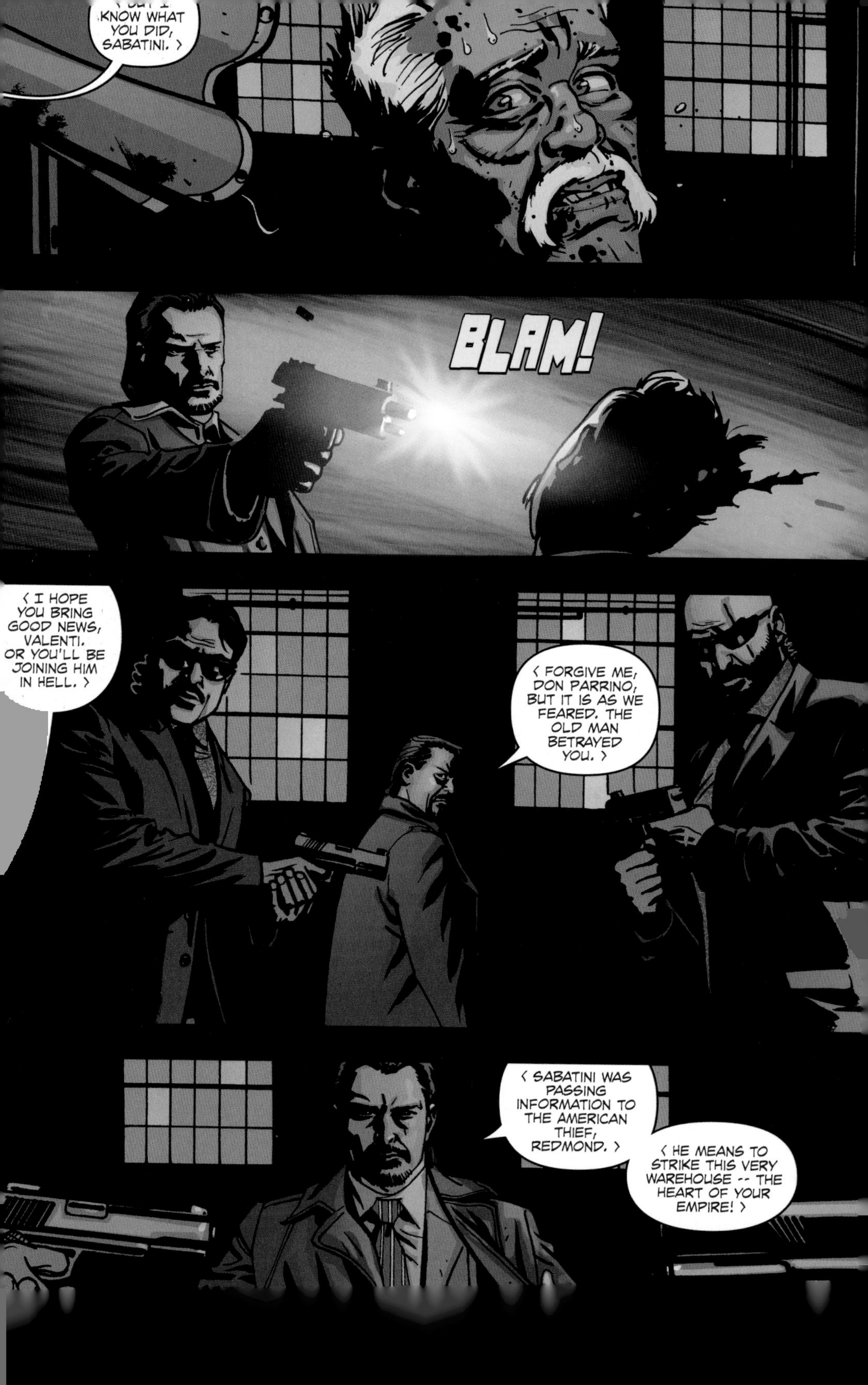
KNOW WHAT YOU DID, SABATINI. >
BLAM!
< I HOPE YOU BRING GOOD NEWS, VALENTI. OR YOU'LL BE JOINING HIM IN HELL. >
< FORGIVE ME, DON PARRINO, BUT IT IS AS WE FEARED. THE OLD MAN BETRAYED YOU. >
< SABATINI WAS PASSING INFORMATION TO THE AMERICAN THIEF, REDMOND. >
< HE MEANS TO STRIKE THIS VERY WAREHOUSE -- THE HEART OF YOUR EMPIRE! >

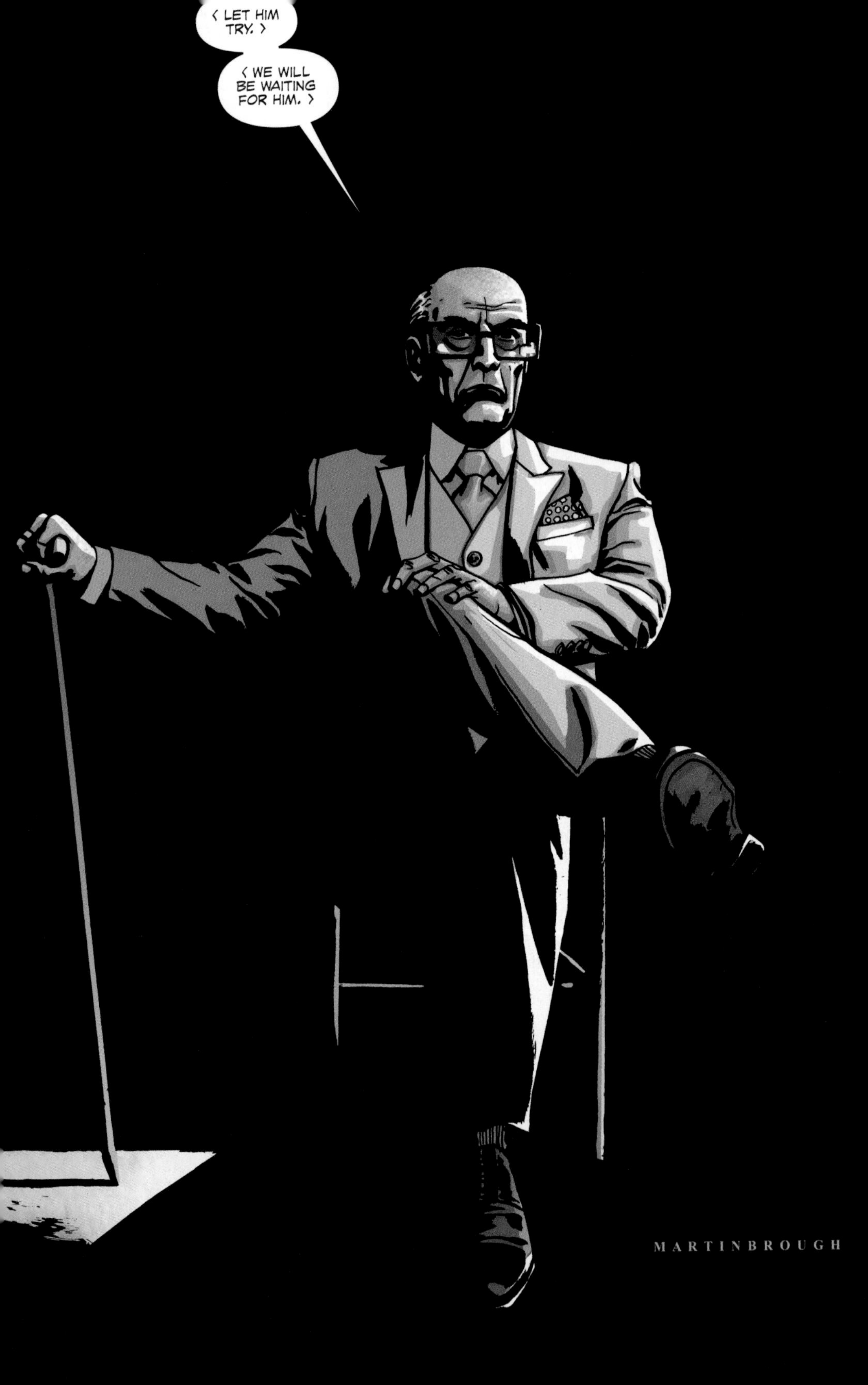
< LET HIM TRY. >
< WE WILL BE WAITING FOR HIM. >
MARTINBROUGH

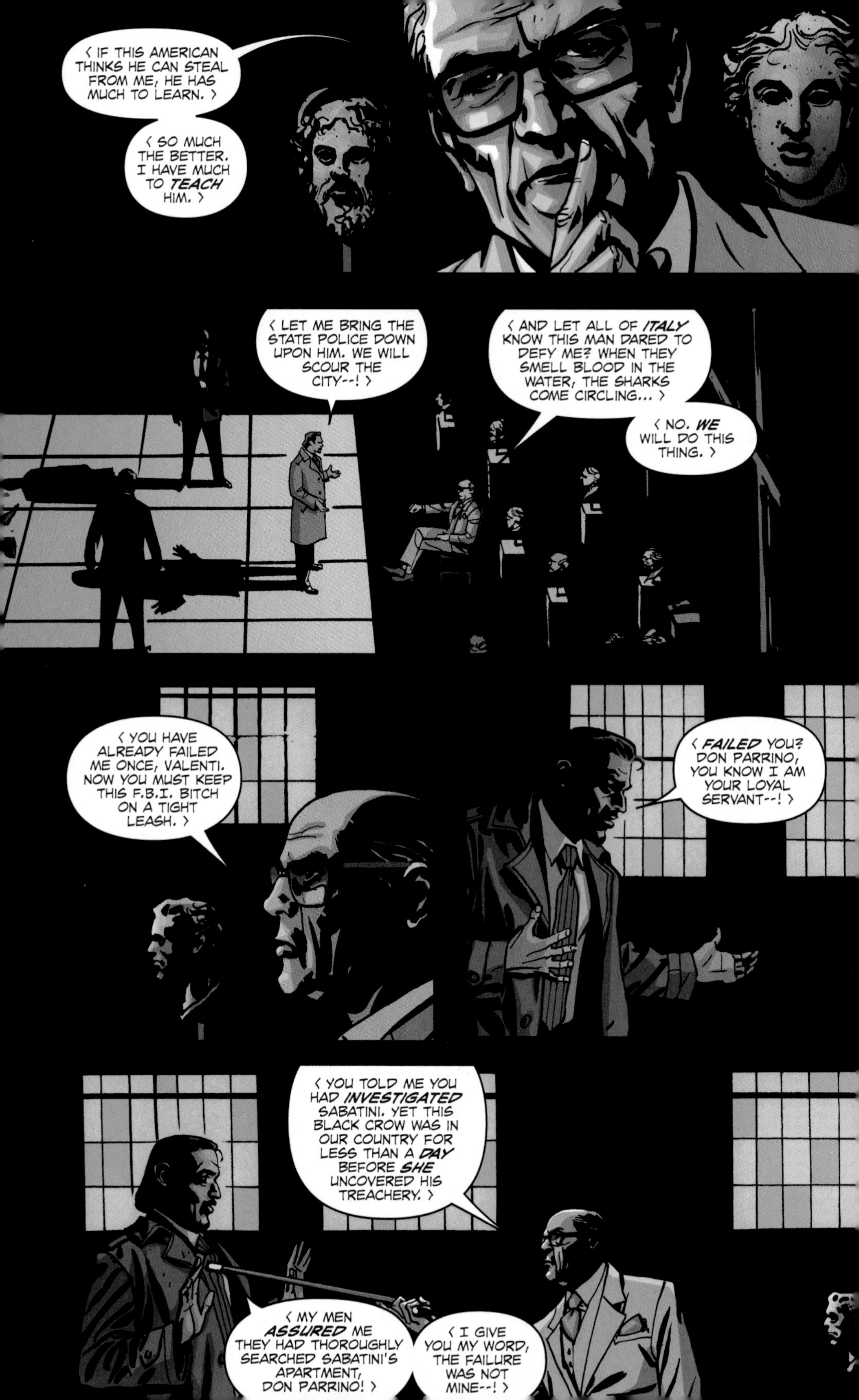
‹ IF THIS AMERICAN THINKS HE CAN STEAL FROM ME, HE HAS MUCH TO LEARN. ›
‹ SO MUCH THE BETTER. I HAVE MUCH TO *TEACH* HIM. ›
‹ LET ME BRING THE STATE POLICE DOWN UPON HIM. WE WILL SCOUR THE CITY--! ›
‹ AND LET ALL OF *ITALY* KNOW THIS MAN DARED TO DEFY ME? WHEN THEY SMELL BLOOD IN THE WATER, THE SHARKS COME CIRCLING... ›
‹ NO. *WE* WILL DO THIS THING. ›
‹ YOU HAVE ALREADY FAILED ME ONCE, VALENTI. NOW YOU MUST KEEP THIS F.B.I. BITCH ON A TIGHT LEASH. ›
‹ *FAILED* YOU? DON PARRINO, YOU KNOW I AM YOUR LOYAL SERVANT--! ›
‹ YOU TOLD ME YOU HAD *INVESTIGATED* SABATINI. YET THIS BLACK CROW WAS IN OUR COUNTRY FOR LESS THAN A *DAY* BEFORE *SHE* UNCOVERED HIS TREACHERY. ›
‹ MY MEN *ASSURED* ME THEY HAD THOROUGHLY SEARCHED SABATINI'S APARTMENT, DON PARRINO! ›
‹ I GIVE YOU MY WORD, THE FAILURE WAS NOT MINE--! ›

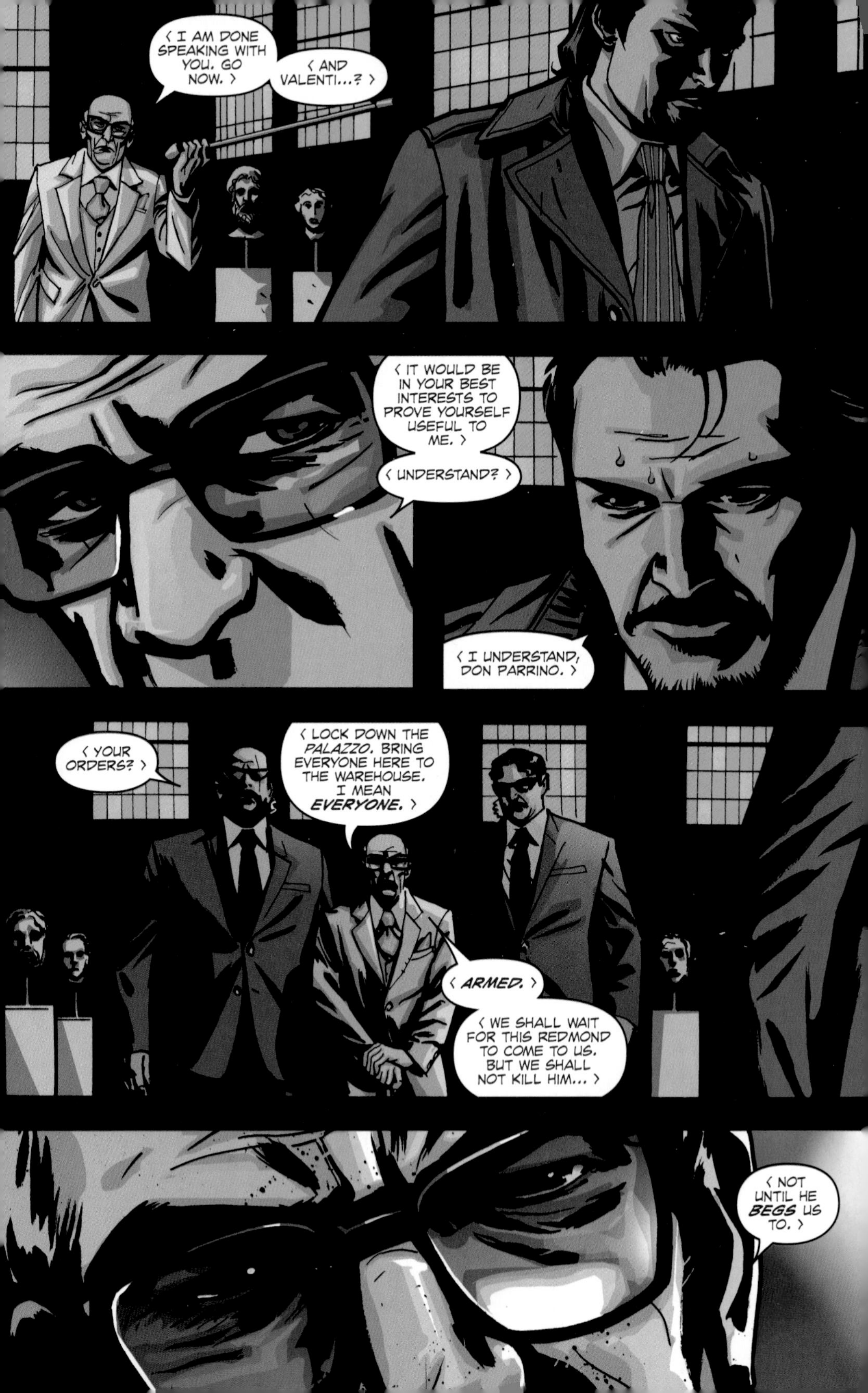

‹ I AM DONE SPEAKING WITH YOU. GO NOW. ›
‹ AND VALENTI...? ›
‹ IT WOULD BE IN YOUR BEST INTERESTS TO PROVE YOURSELF USEFUL TO ME. ›
‹ UNDERSTAND? ›
‹ I UNDERSTAND, DON PARRINO. ›
‹ YOUR ORDERS? ›
‹ LOCK DOWN THE *PALAZZO*. BRING EVERYONE HERE TO THE WAREHOUSE. I MEAN ***EVERYONE.*** ›
‹ ***ARMED.*** ›
‹ WE SHALL WAIT FOR THIS REDMOND TO COME TO US. BUT WE SHALL NOT KILL HIM... ›
‹ NOT UNTIL HE ***BEGS*** US TO. ›

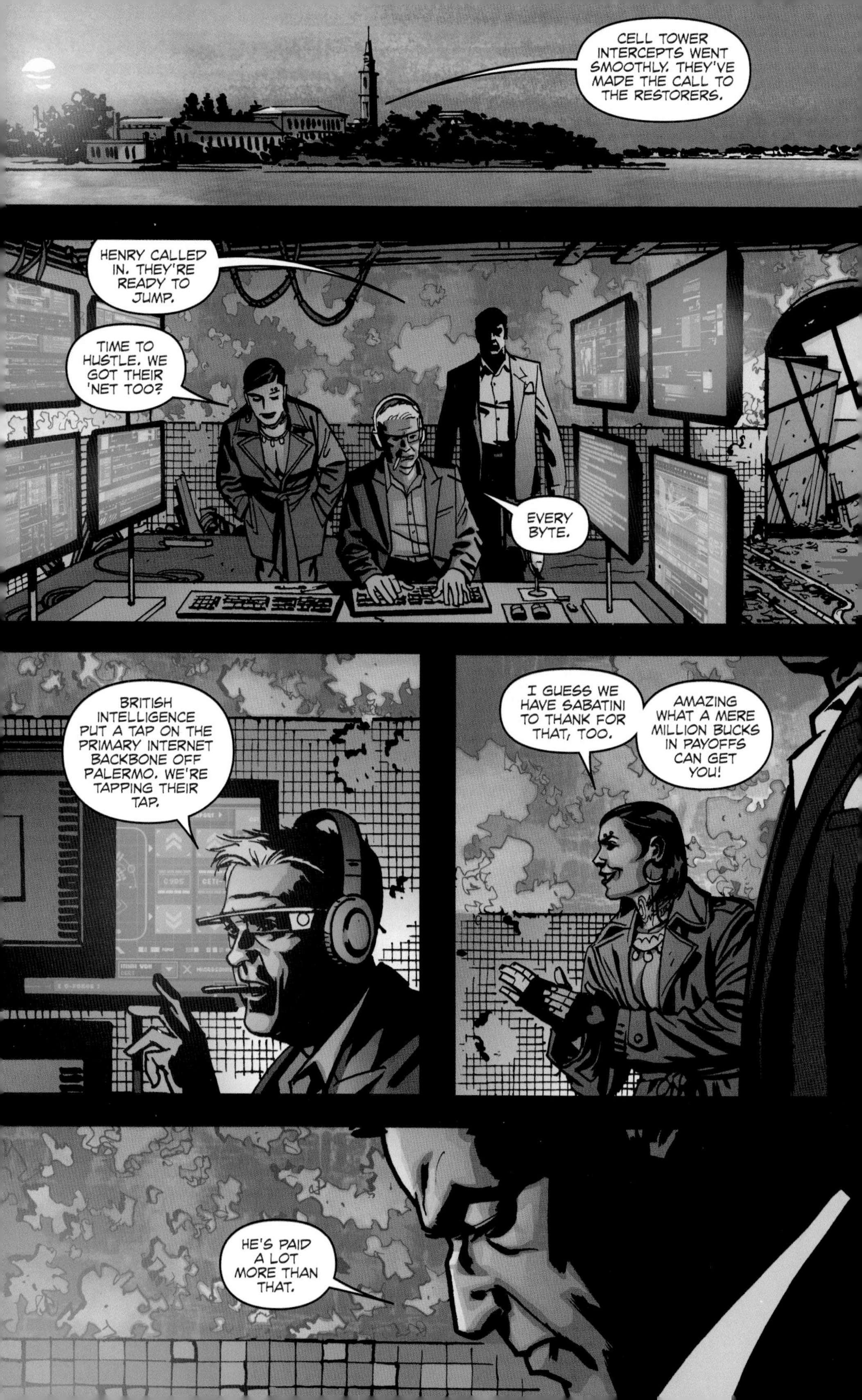
CELL TOWER INTERCEPTS WENT SMOOTHLY. THEY'VE MADE THE CALL TO THE RESTORERS.
HENRY CALLED IN. THEY'RE READY TO JUMP.
TIME TO HUSTLE. WE GOT THEIR 'NET TOO?
EVERY BYTE.
BRITISH INTELLIGENCE PUT A TAP ON THE PRIMARY INTERNET BACKBONE OFF PALERMO. WE'RE TAPPING THEIR TAP.
I GUESS WE HAVE SABATINI TO THANK FOR THAT, TOO.
AMAZING WHAT A MERE MILLION BUCKS IN PAYOFFS CAN GET YOU!
HE'S PAID A LOT MORE THAN THAT.

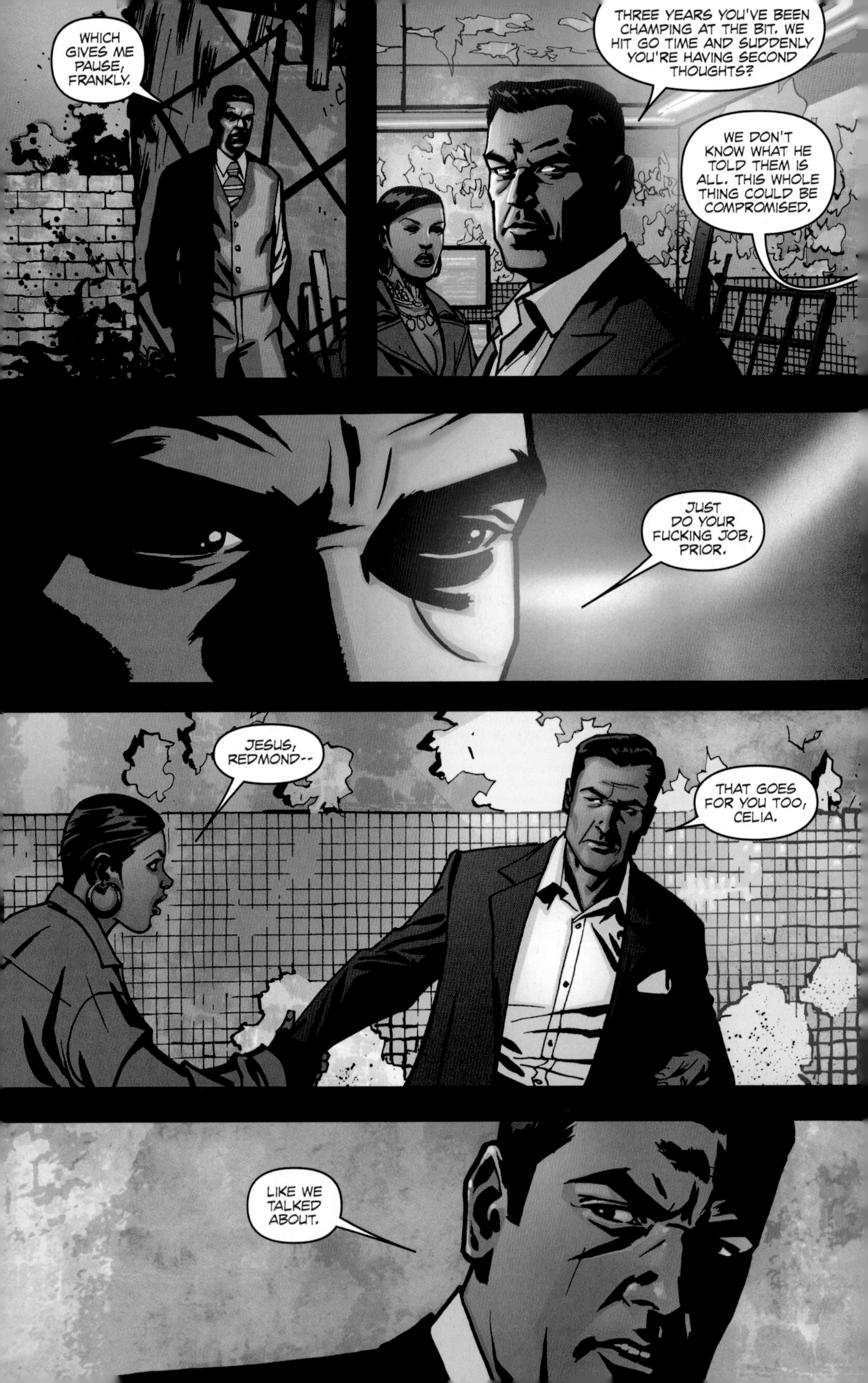
WHICH GIVES ME PAUSE, FRANKLY.
THREE YEARS YOU'VE BEEN CHAMPING AT THE BIT. WE HIT GO TIME AND SUDDENLY YOU'RE HAVING SECOND THOUGHTS?
WE DON'T KNOW WHAT HE TOLD THEM IS ALL. THIS WHOLE THING COULD BE COMPROMISED.
JUST DO YOUR FUCKING JOB, PRIOR.
JESUS, REDMOND--
THAT GOES FOR YOU TOO, CELIA.
LIKE WE TALKED ABOUT.

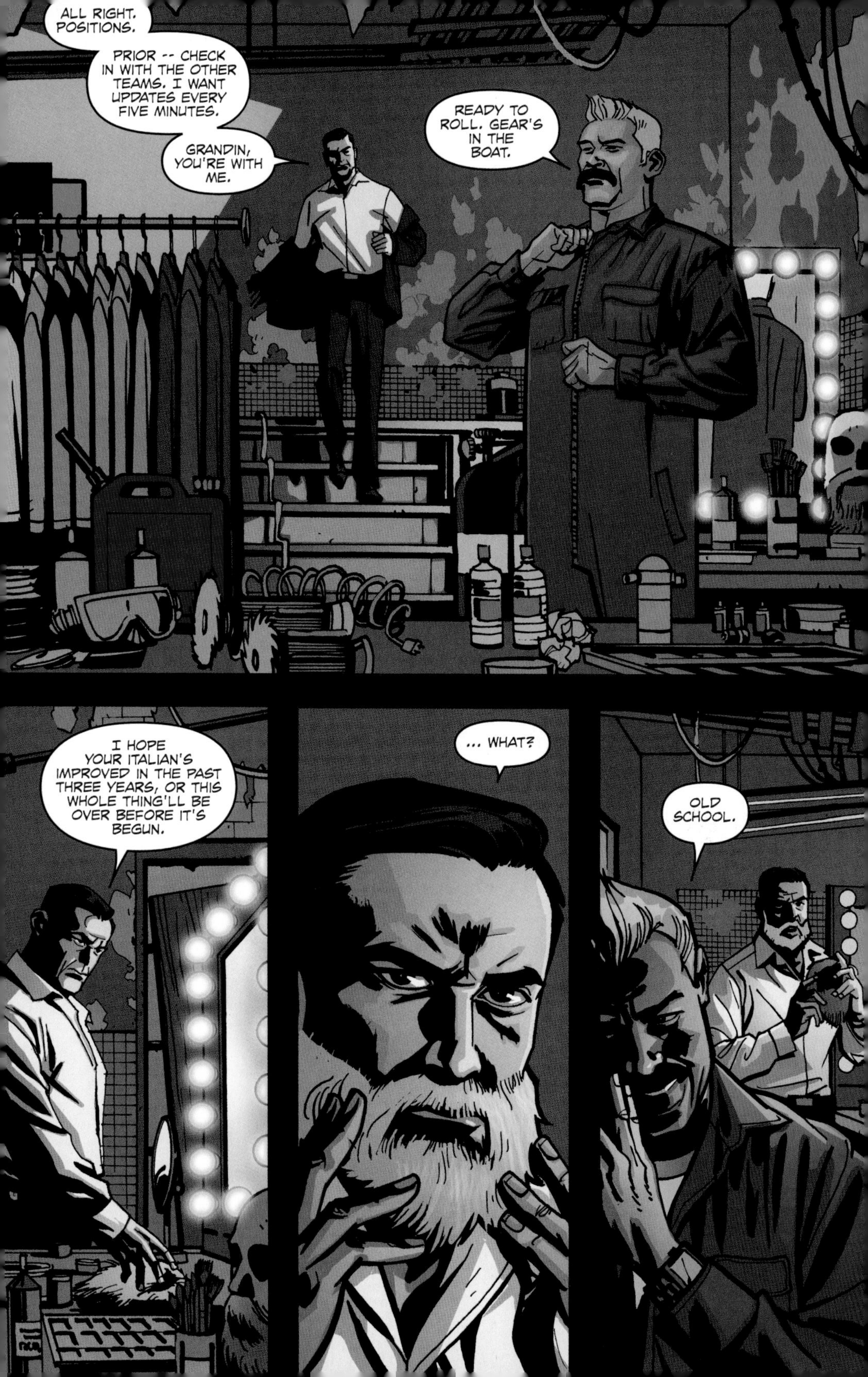
ALL RIGHT. POSITIONS.
PRIOR -- CHECK IN WITH THE OTHER TEAMS. I WANT UPDATES EVERY FIVE MINUTES.
GRANDIN, YOU'RE WITH ME.
READY TO ROLL. GEAR'S IN THE BOAT.
I HOPE YOUR ITALIAN'S IMPROVED IN THE PAST THREE YEARS, OR THIS WHOLE THING'LL BE OVER BEFORE IT'S BEGUN.
... WHAT?
OLD SCHOOL.

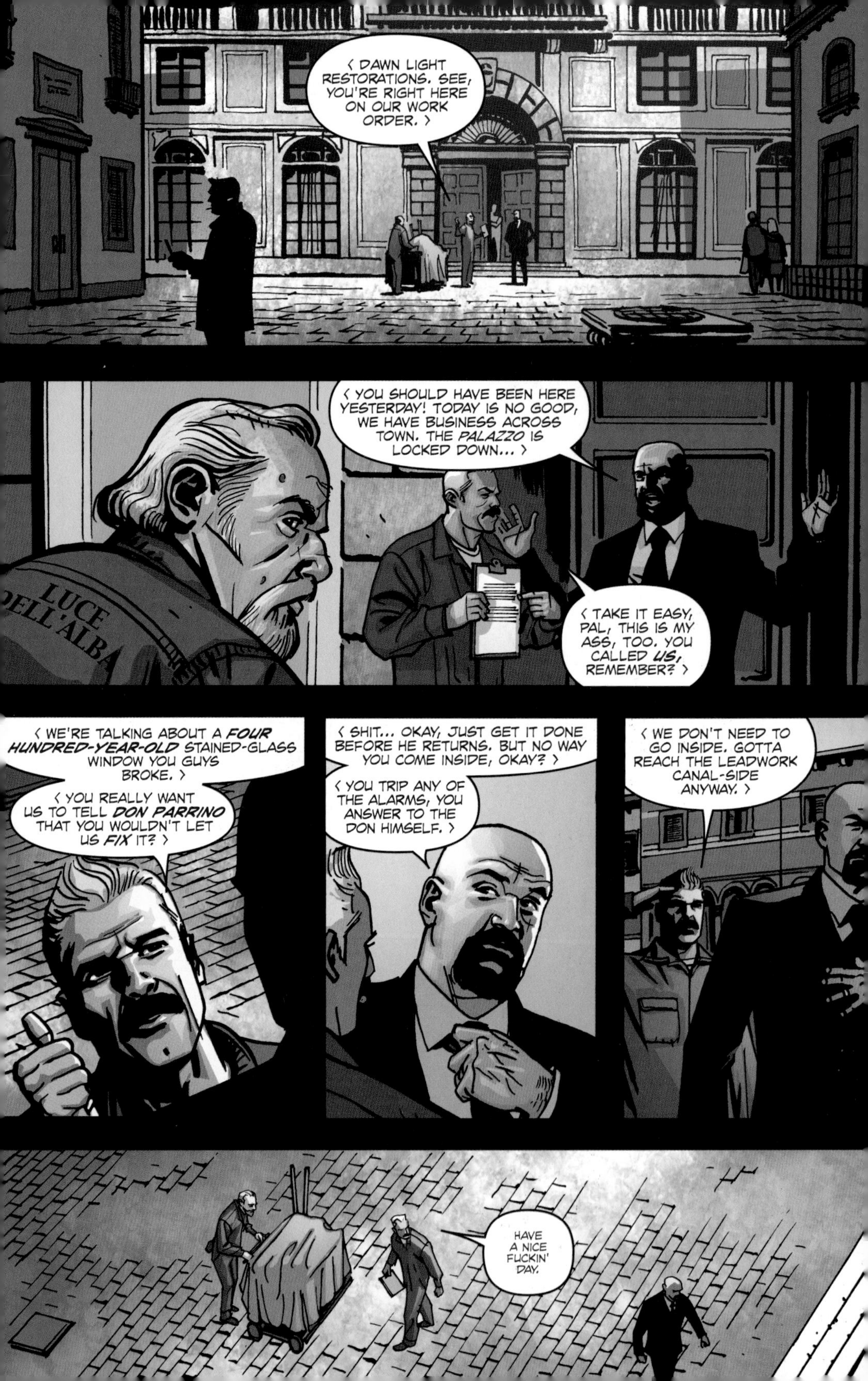

< DAWN LIGHT RESTORATIONS. SEE, YOU'RE RIGHT HERE ON OUR WORK ORDER. >
< YOU SHOULD HAVE BEEN HERE YESTERDAY! TODAY IS NO GOOD, WE HAVE BUSINESS ACROSS TOWN. THE *PALAZZO* IS LOCKED DOWN... >
LUCE DELL'ALBA
< TAKE IT EASY, PAL, THIS IS MY ASS, TOO. YOU CALLED *US*, REMEMBER? >
< WE'RE TALKING ABOUT A *FOUR HUNDRED-YEAR-OLD* STAINED-GLASS WINDOW YOU GUYS BROKE. >
< YOU REALLY WANT US TO TELL *DON PARRINO* THAT YOU WOULDN'T LET US *FIX* IT? >
< SHIT... OKAY, JUST GET IT DONE BEFORE HE RETURNS. BUT NO WAY YOU COME INSIDE, OKAY? >
< YOU TRIP ANY OF THE ALARMS, YOU ANSWER TO THE DON HIMSELF. >
< WE DON'T NEED TO GO INSIDE. GOTTA REACH THE LEADWORK CANAL-SIDE ANYWAY. >
HAVE A NICE FUCKIN' DAY.

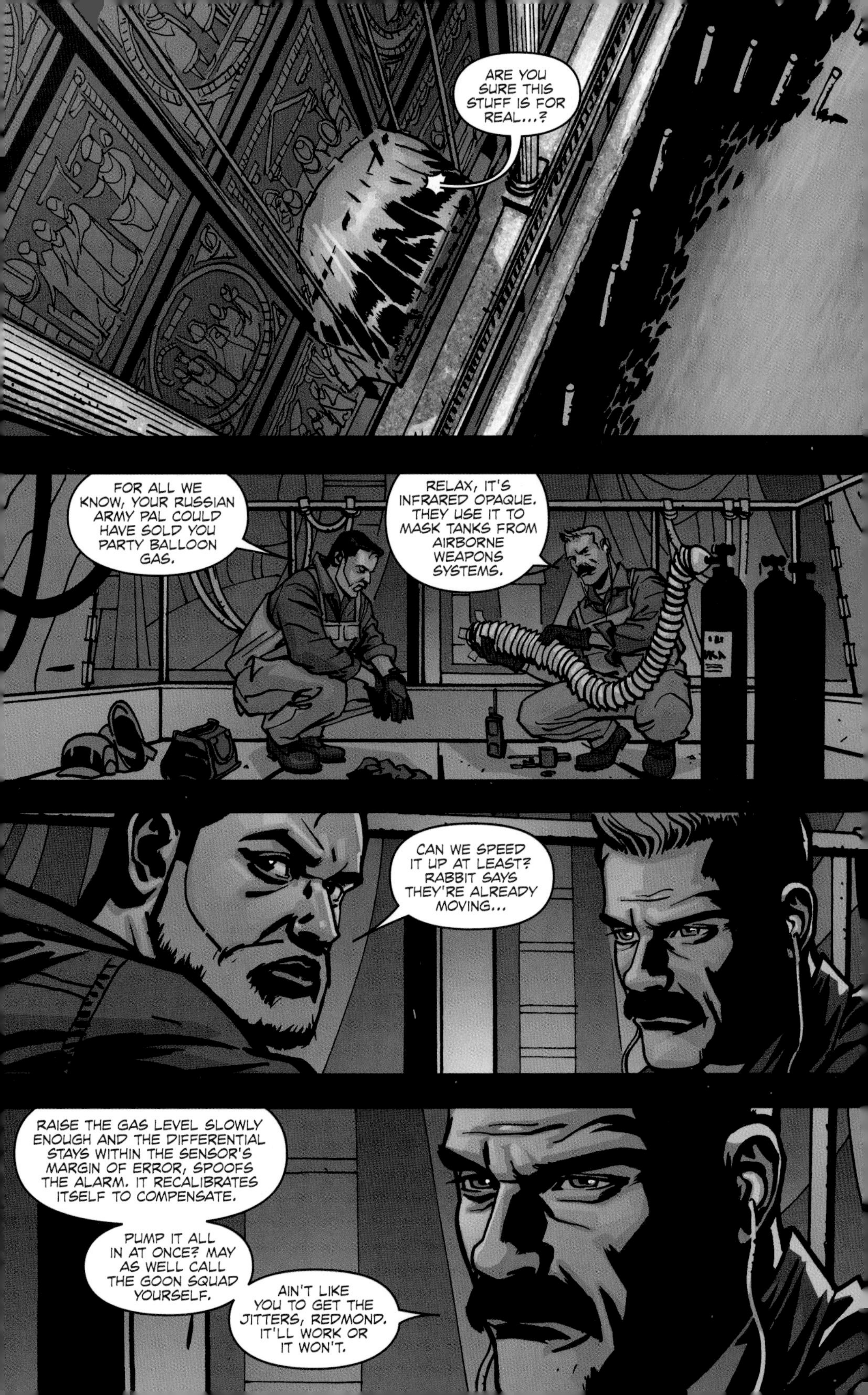
ARE YOU SURE THIS STUFF IS FOR REAL...?
FOR ALL WE KNOW, YOUR RUSSIAN ARMY PAL COULD HAVE SOLD YOU PARTY BALLOON GAS.
RELAX, IT'S INFRARED OPAQUE. THEY USE IT TO MASK TANKS FROM AIRBORNE WEAPONS SYSTEMS.
CAN WE SPEED IT UP AT LEAST? RABBIT SAYS THEY'RE ALREADY MOVING...
RAISE THE GAS LEVEL SLOWLY ENOUGH AND THE DIFFERENTIAL STAYS WITHIN THE SENSOR'S MARGIN OF ERROR, SPOOFS THE ALARM. IT RECALIBRATES ITSELF TO COMPENSATE.
PUMP IT ALL IN AT ONCE? MAY AS WELL CALL THE GOON SQUAD YOURSELF.
AIN'T LIKE YOU TO GET THE JITTERS, REDMOND. IT'LL WORK OR IT WON'T.

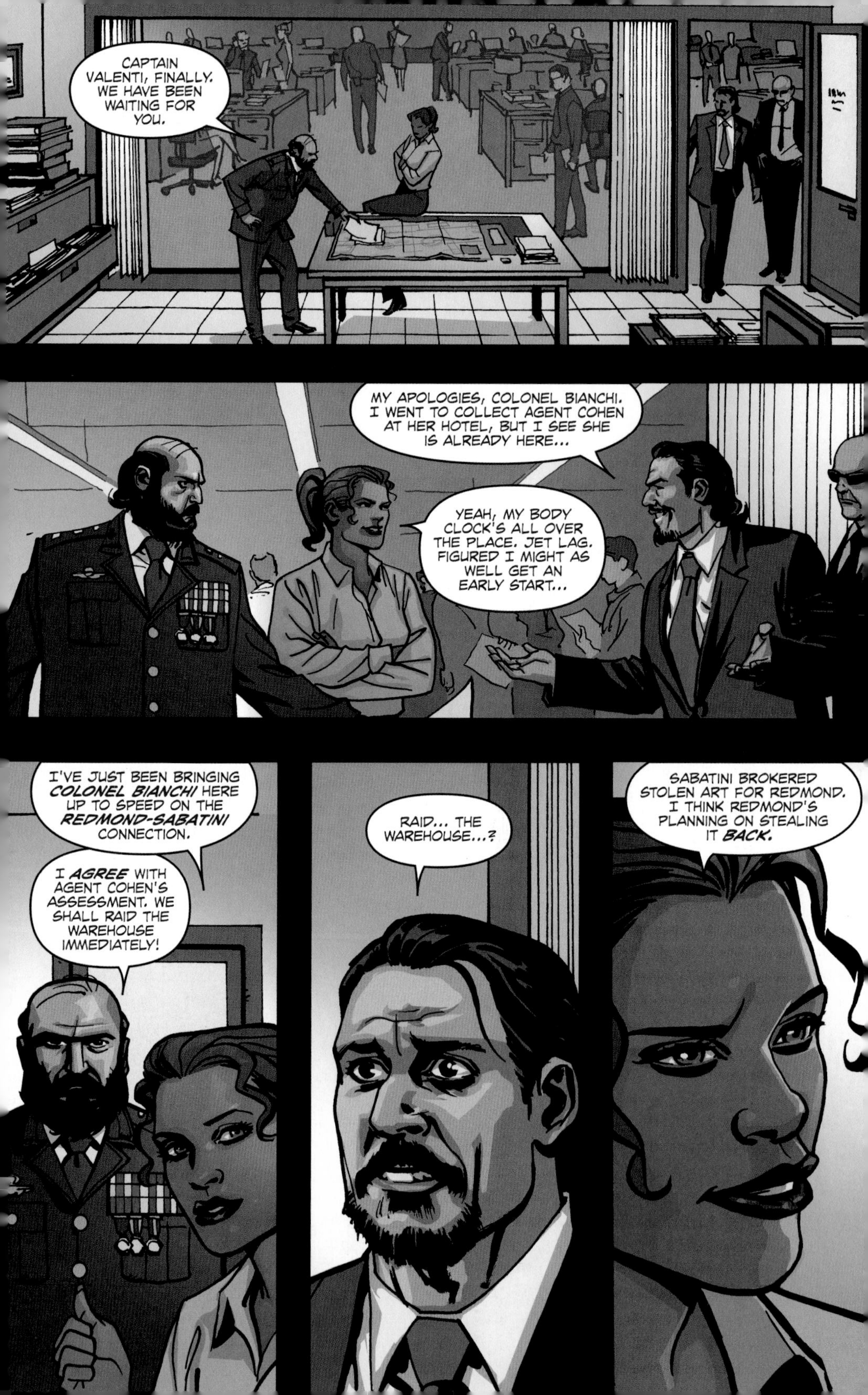
CAPTAIN VALENTI, FINALLY. WE HAVE BEEN WAITING FOR YOU.
MY APOLOGIES, COLONEL BIANCHI. I WENT TO COLLECT AGENT COHEN AT HER HOTEL, BUT I SEE SHE IS ALREADY HERE...
YEAH, MY BODY CLOCK'S ALL OVER THE PLACE. JET LAG. FIGURED I MIGHT AS WELL GET AN EARLY START...
I'VE JUST BEEN BRINGING *COLONEL BIANCHI* HERE UP TO SPEED ON THE *REDMOND-SABATINI* CONNECTION.
I *AGREE* WITH AGENT COHEN'S ASSESSMENT. WE SHALL RAID THE WAREHOUSE IMMEDIATELY!
RAID... THE WAREHOUSE...?
SABATINI BROKERED STOLEN ART FOR REDMOND. I THINK REDMOND'S PLANNING ON STEALING IT *BACK*.

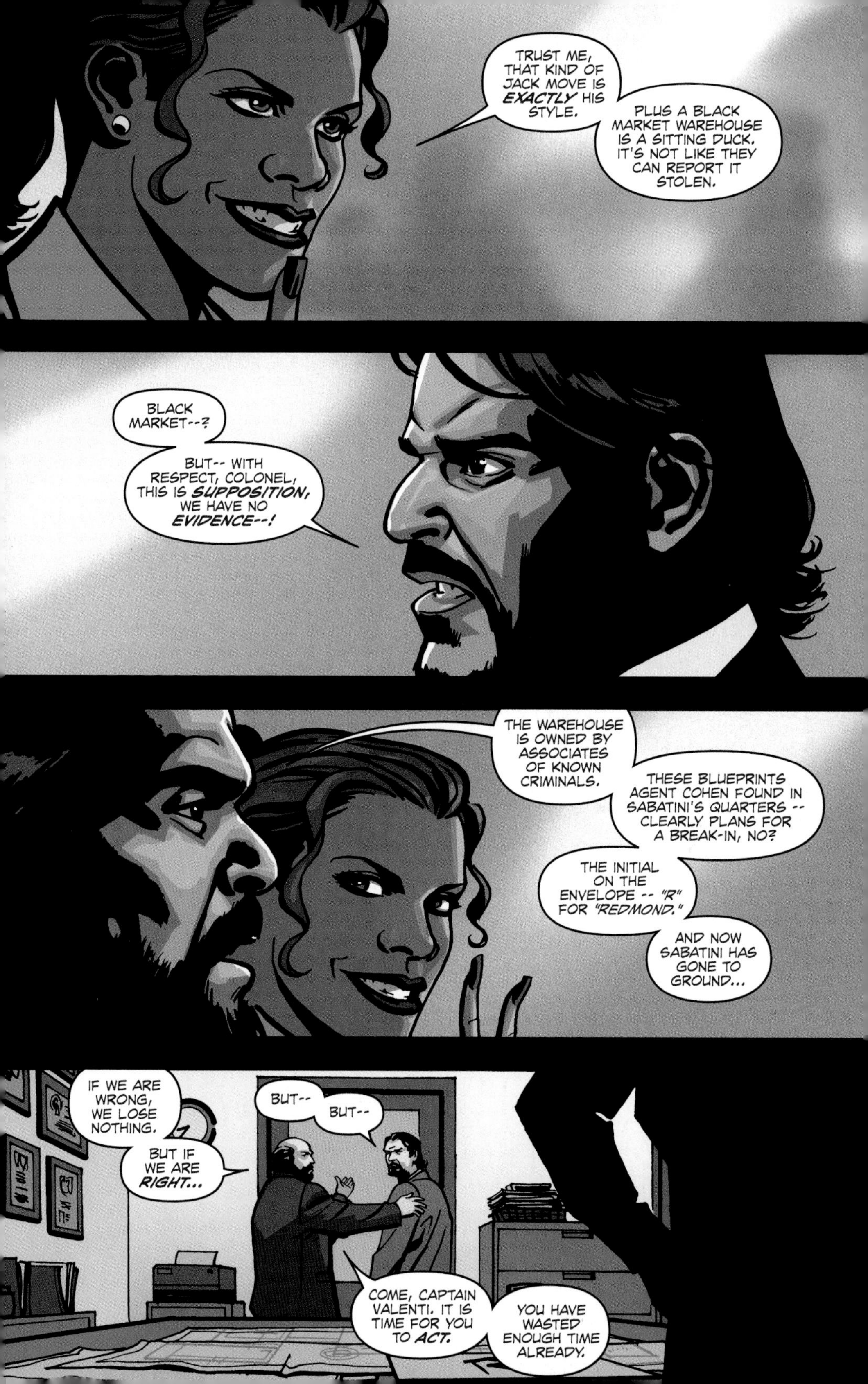
TRUST ME, THAT KIND OF JACK MOVE IS EXACTLY HIS STYLE.
PLUS A BLACK MARKET WAREHOUSE IS A SITTING DUCK. IT'S NOT LIKE THEY CAN REPORT IT STOLEN.
BLACK MARKET--?
BUT-- WITH RESPECT, COLONEL, THIS IS SUPPOSITION, WE HAVE NO EVIDENCE--!
THE WAREHOUSE IS OWNED BY ASSOCIATES OF KNOWN CRIMINALS.
THESE BLUEPRINTS AGENT COHEN FOUND IN SABATINI'S QUARTERS -- CLEARLY PLANS FOR A BREAK-IN, NO?
THE INITIAL ON THE ENVELOPE -- "R" FOR "REDMOND."
AND NOW SABATINI HAS GONE TO GROUND...
IF WE ARE WRONG, WE LOSE NOTHING.
BUT IF WE ARE RIGHT...
BUT--
BUT--
COME, CAPTAIN VALENTI. IT IS TIME FOR YOU TO ACT.
YOU HAVE WASTED ENOUGH TIME ALREADY.

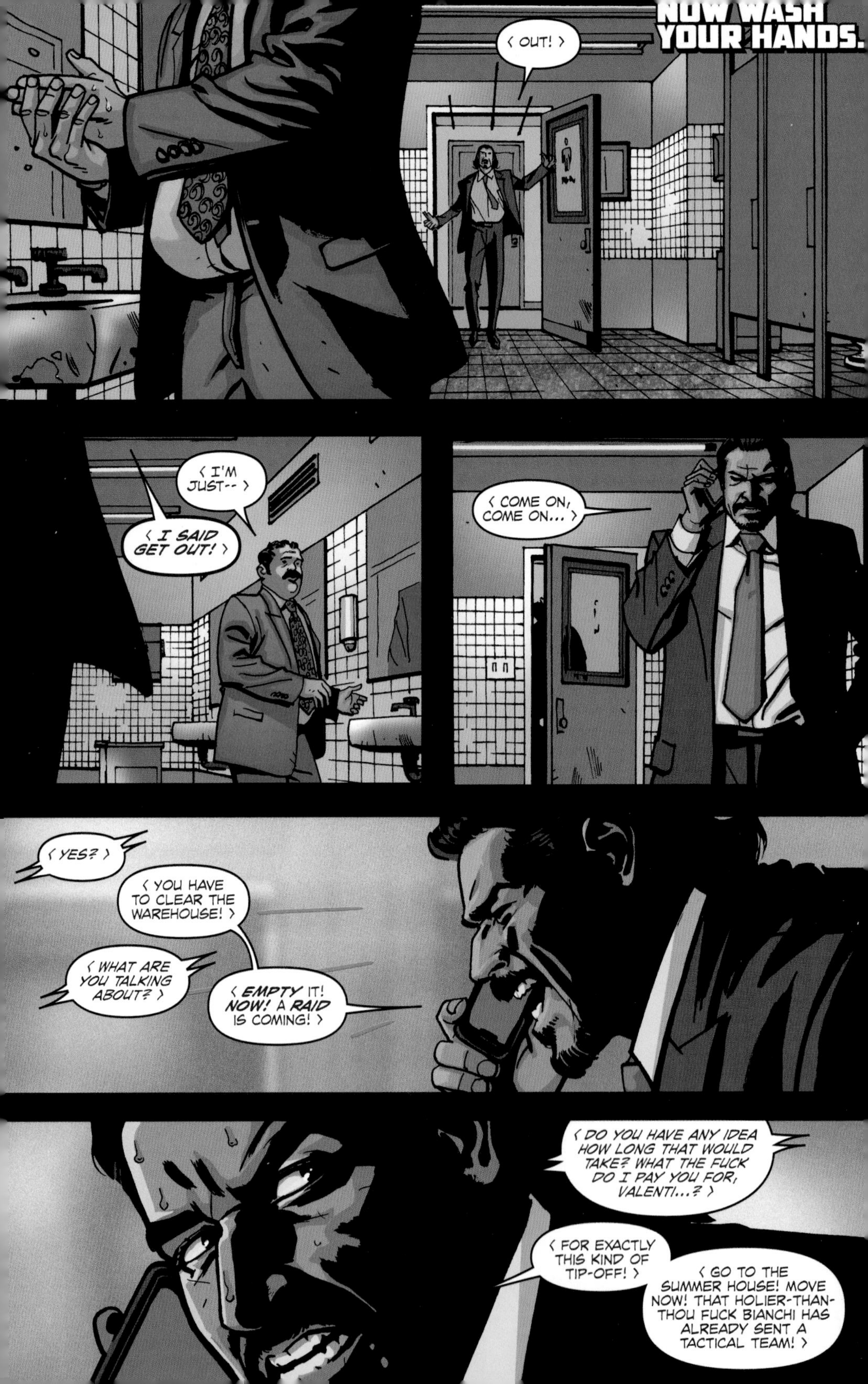
NOW WASH YOUR HANDS.
< OUT! >
< I'M JUST-- >
< I SAID GET OUT! >
< COME ON, COME ON... >
< YES? >
< YOU HAVE TO CLEAR THE WAREHOUSE! >
< WHAT ARE YOU TALKING ABOUT? >
< EMPTY IT! NOW! A RAID IS COMING! >
< DO YOU HAVE ANY IDEA HOW LONG THAT WOULD TAKE? WHAT THE FUCK DO I PAY YOU FOR, VALENTI...? >
< FOR EXACTLY THIS KIND OF TIP-OFF! >
< GO TO THE SUMMER HOUSE! MOVE NOW! THAT HOLIER-THAN-THOU FUCK BIANCHI HAS ALREADY SENT A TACTICAL TEAM! >

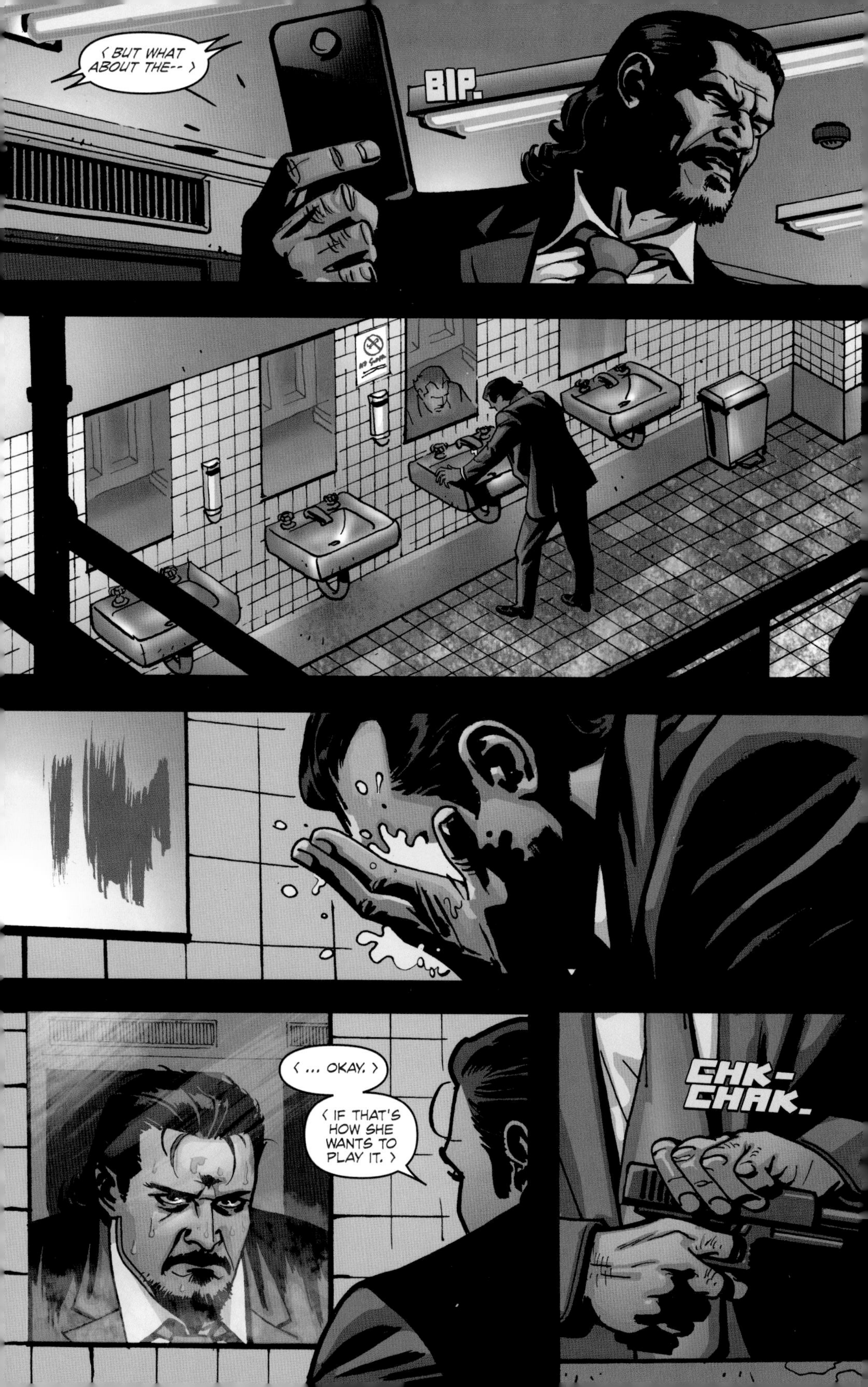

‹ BUT WHAT ABOUT THE-- ›
BIP.
‹ ... OKAY. ›
‹ IF THAT'S HOW SHE WANTS TO PLAY IT. ›
CHK-CHAK.

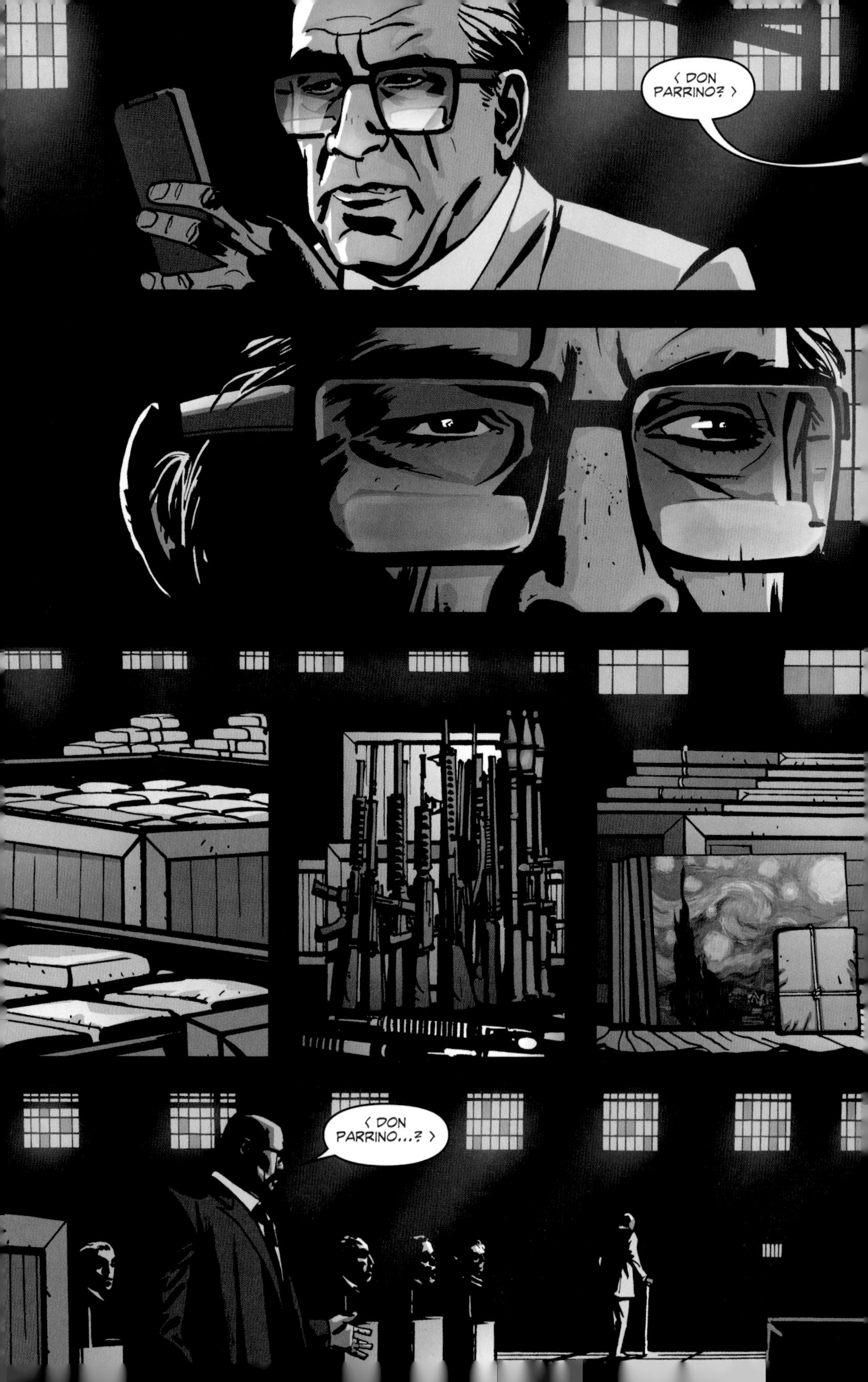
‹ DON PARRINO? ›
‹ DON PARRINO...? ›

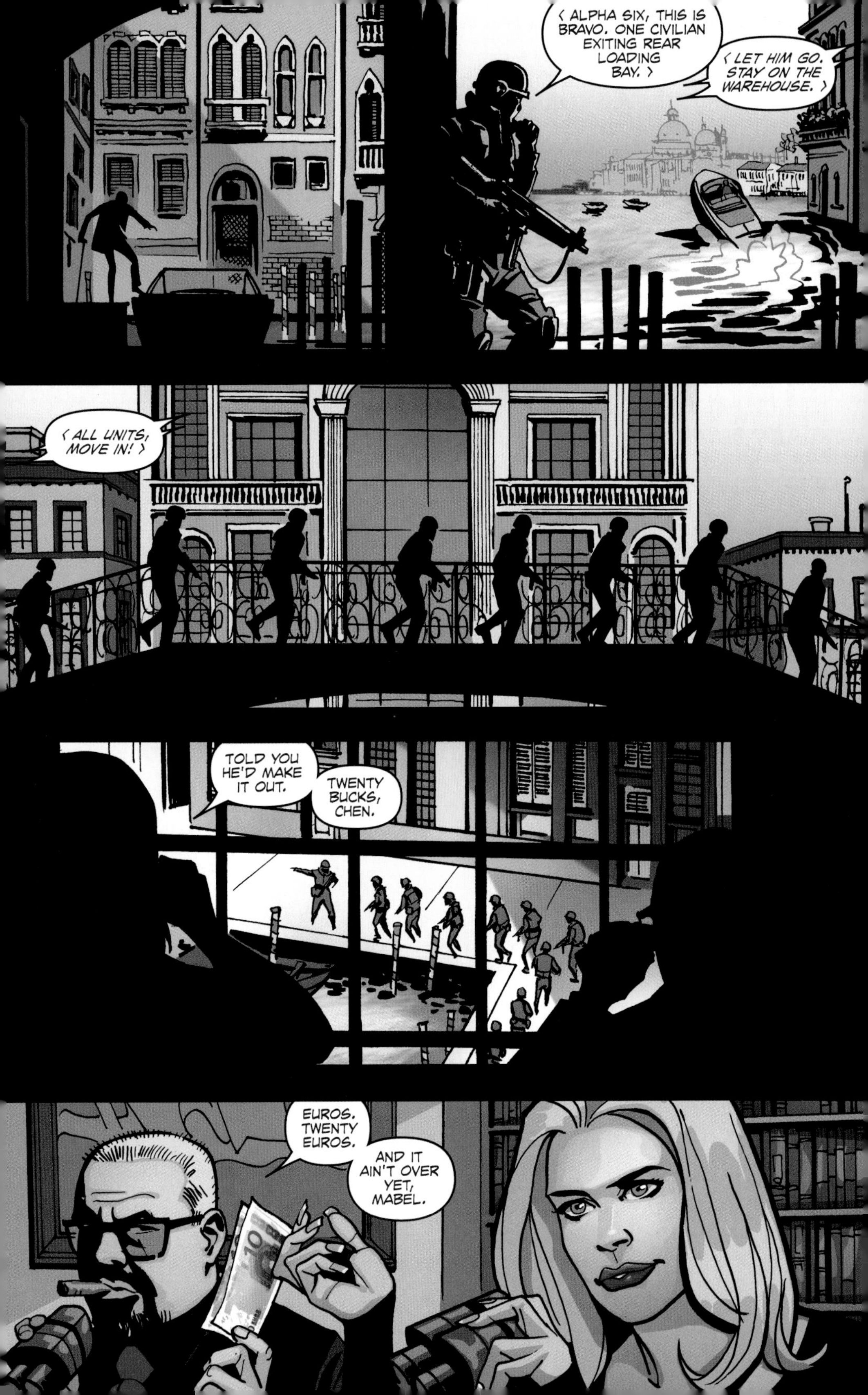
< ALPHA SIX, THIS IS BRAVO. ONE CIVILIAN EXITING REAR LOADING BAY. >
< LET HIM GO. STAY ON THE WAREHOUSE. >
< ALL UNITS, MOVE IN! >
TOLD YOU HE'D MAKE IT OUT.
TWENTY BUCKS, CHEN.
EUROS. TWENTY EUROS.
AND IT AIN'T OVER YET, MABEL.

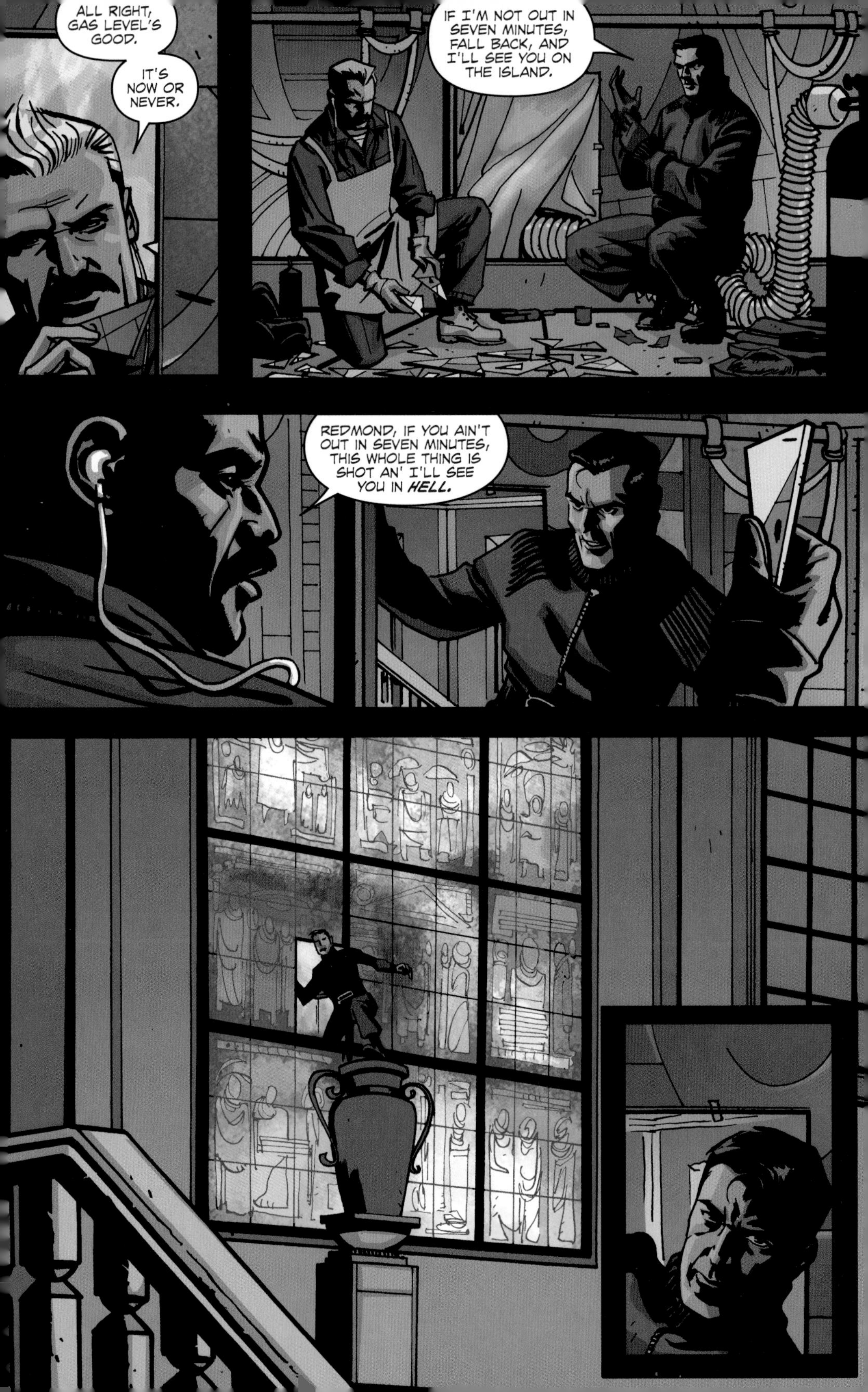
ALL RIGHT, GAS LEVEL'S GOOD.
IT'S NOW OR NEVER.
IF I'M NOT OUT IN SEVEN MINUTES, FALL BACK, AND I'LL SEE YOU ON THE ISLAND.
REDMOND, IF YOU AIN'T OUT IN SEVEN MINUTES, THIS WHOLE THING IS SHOT AN' I'LL SEE YOU IN HELL.

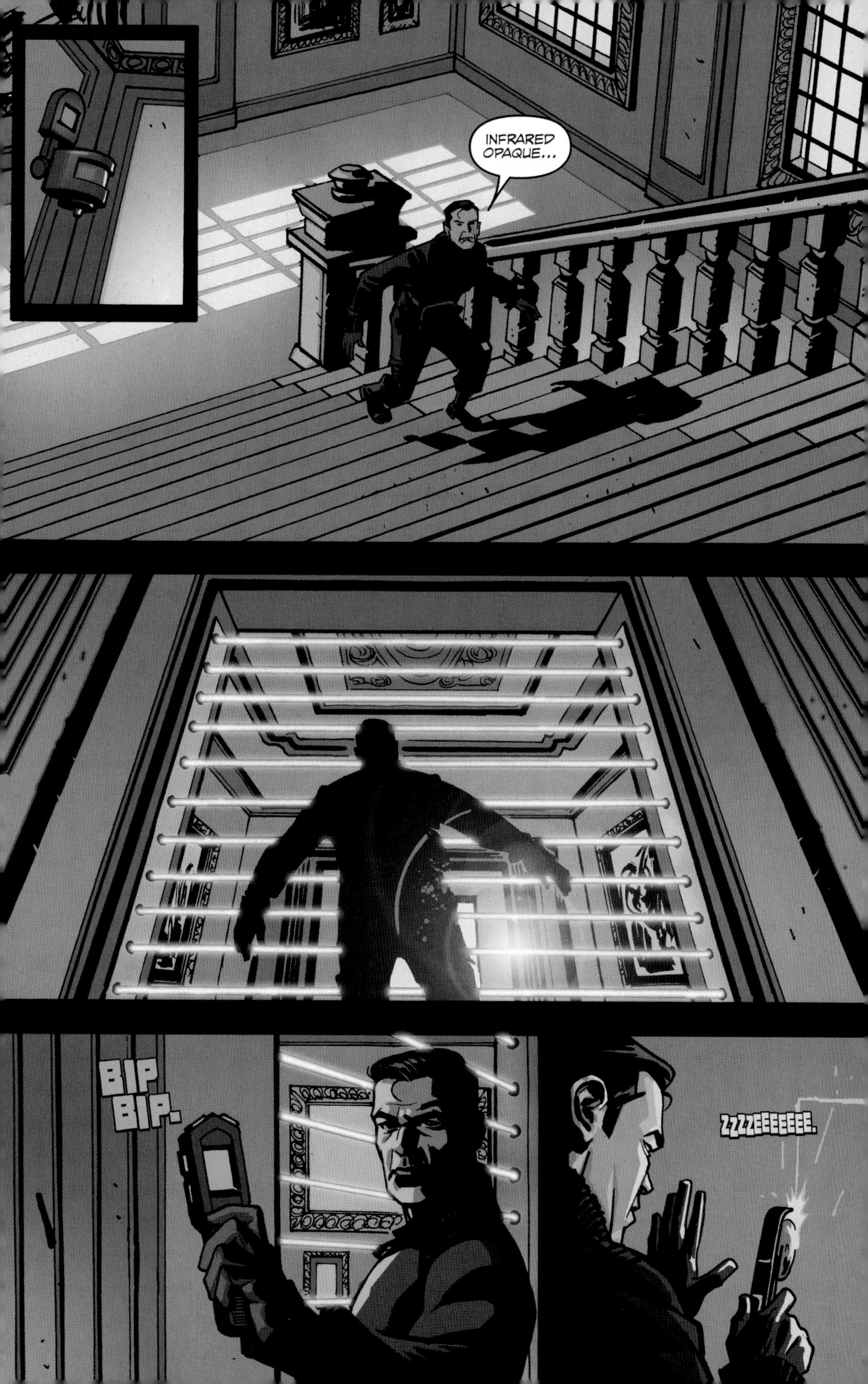
INFRARED OPAQUE...
BIP BIP.
ZZZZEEEEEEE.

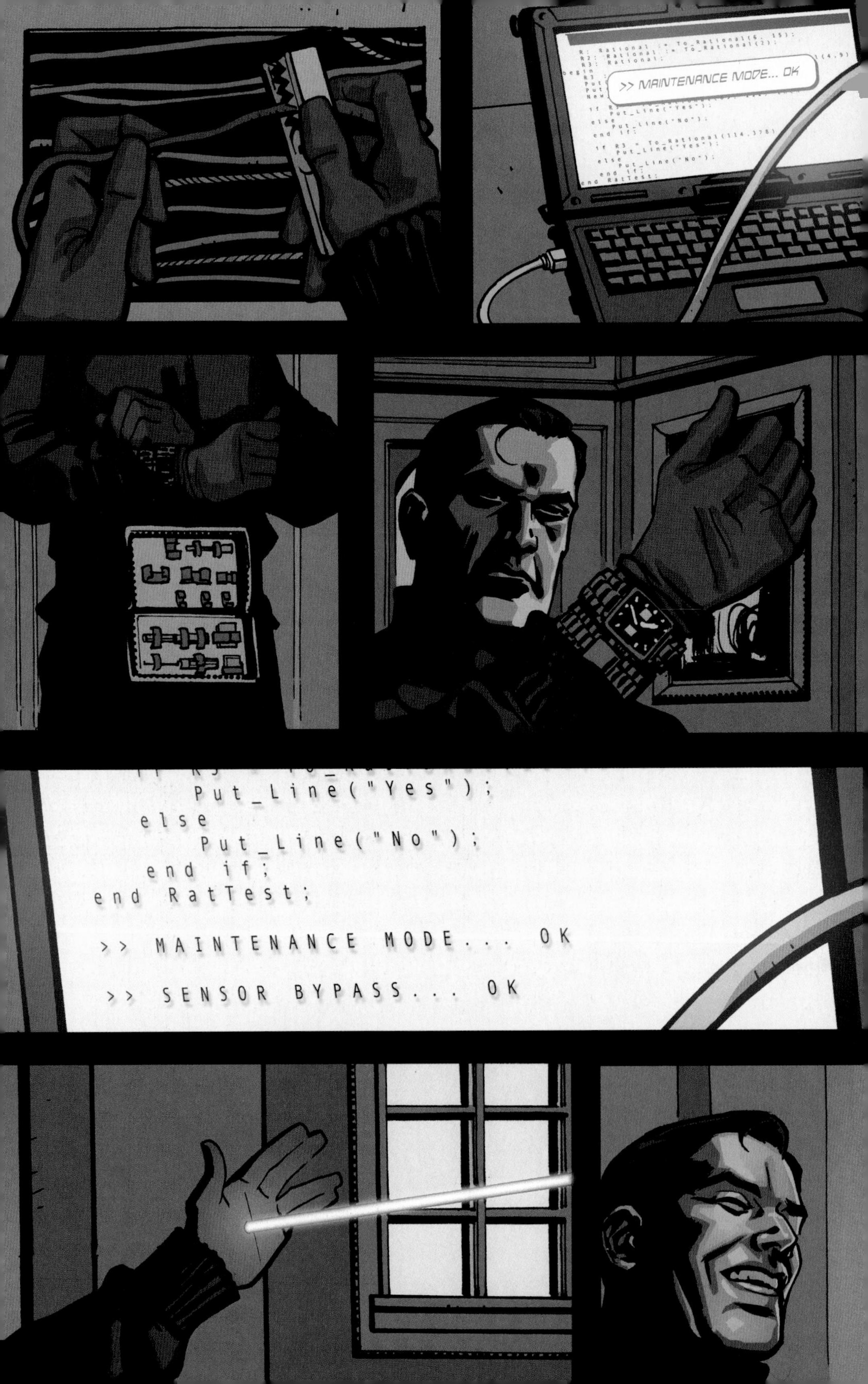
>> MAINTENANCE MODE... OK
Put_Line("Yes");
else
Put_Line("No");
end if;
end RatTest;
>> MAINTENANCE MODE... OK
>> SENSOR BYPASS... OK

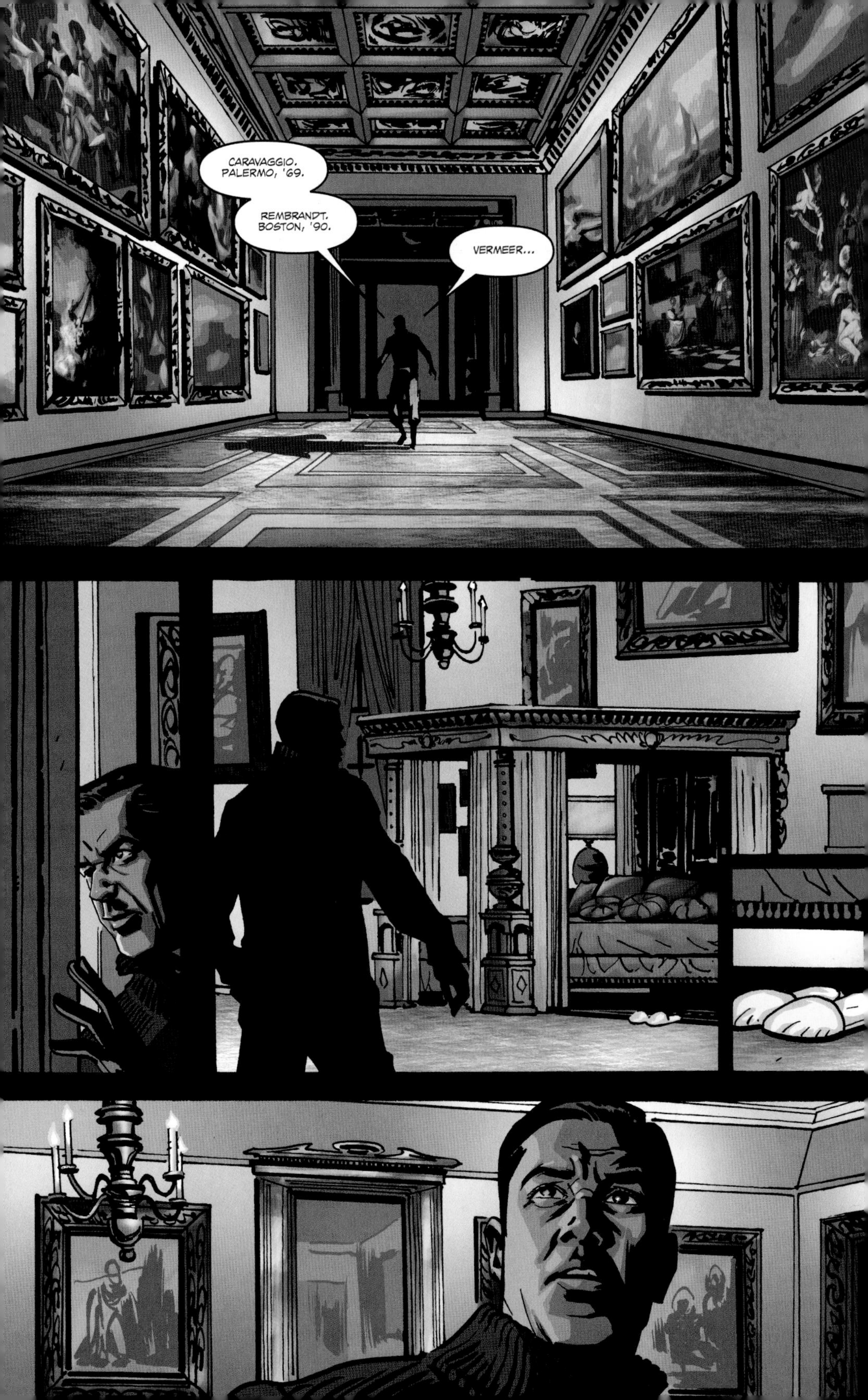
CARAVAGGIO. PALERMO, '69.
REMBRANDT. BOSTON, '90.
VERMEER...

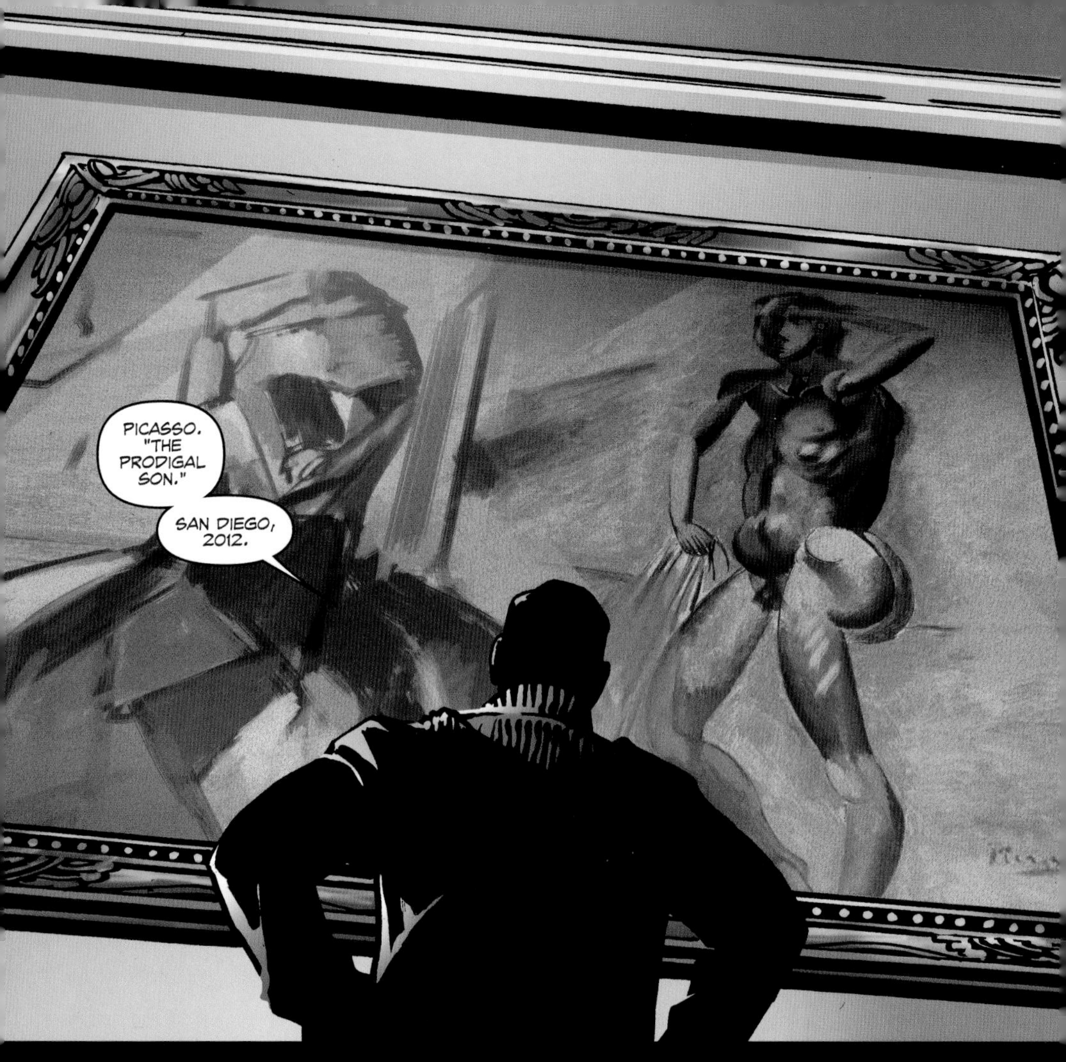
PICASSO. "THE PRODIGAL SON."
SAN DIEGO, 2012.

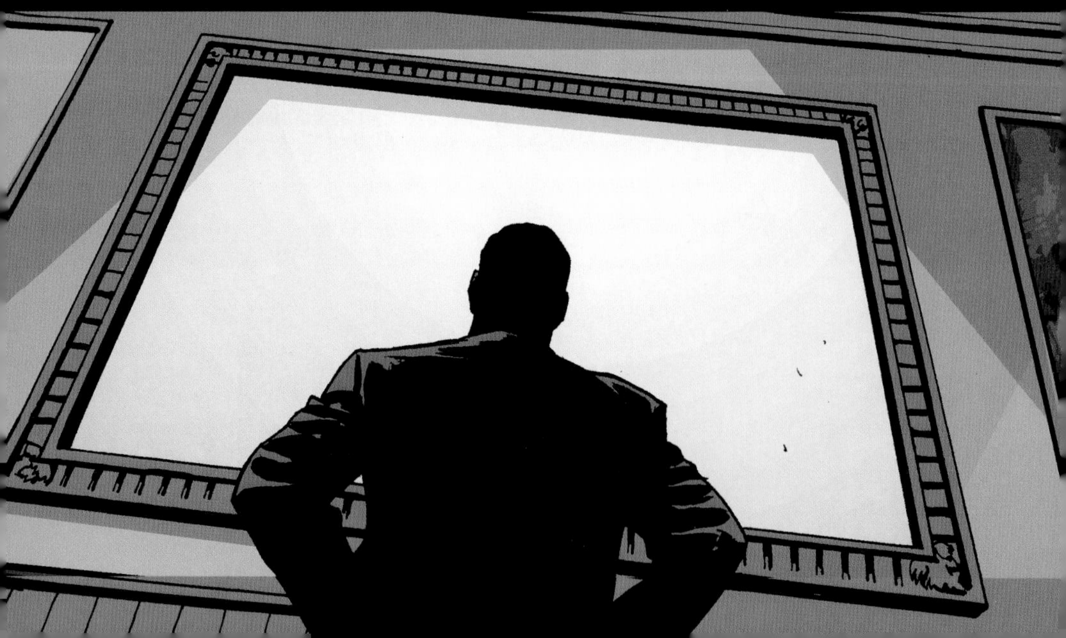

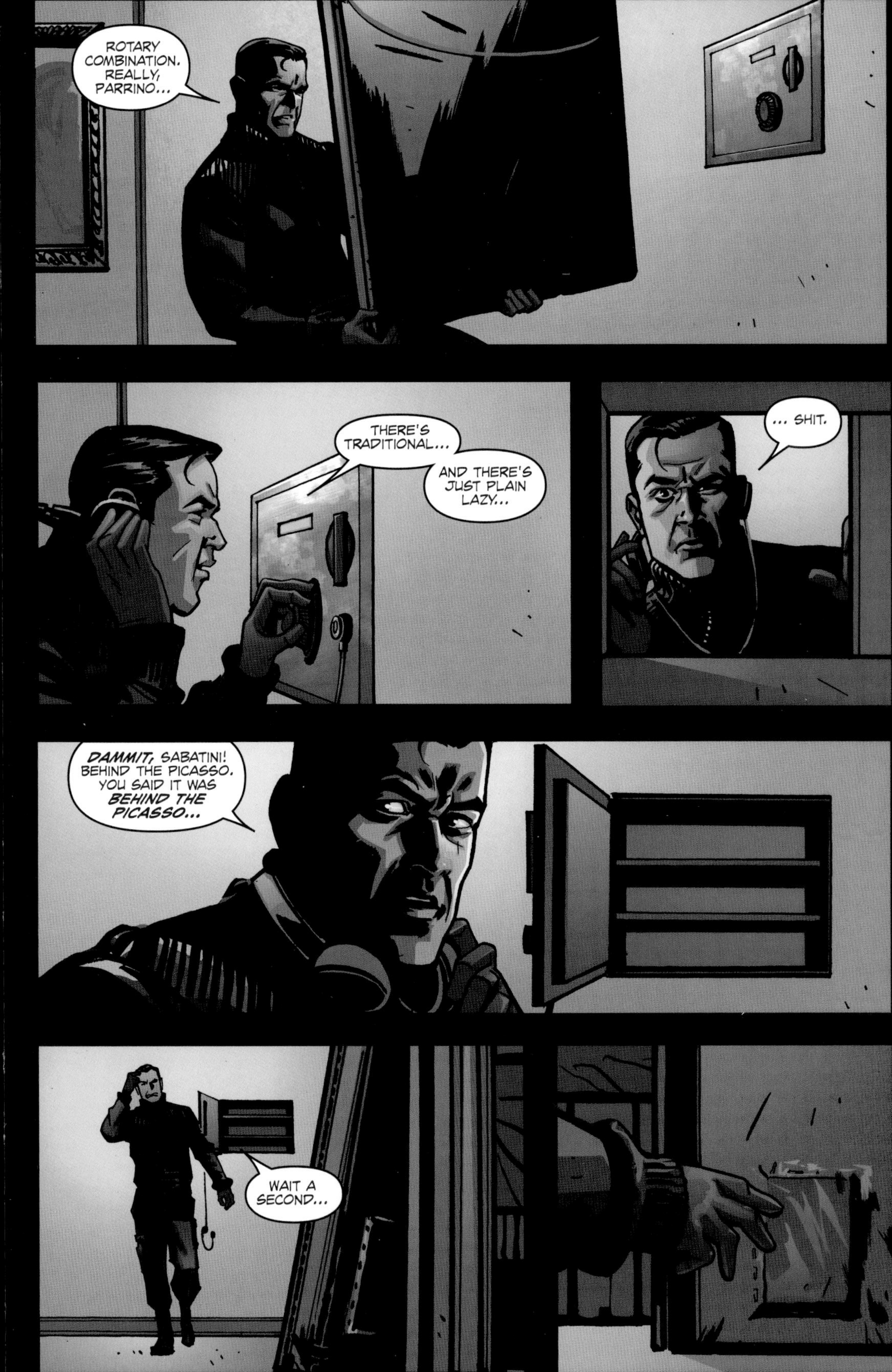
ROTARY COMBINATION. REALLY, PARRINO...
THERE'S TRADITIONAL...
AND THERE'S JUST PLAIN LAZY...
... SHIT.
DAMMIT, SABATINI! BEHIND THE PICASSO. YOU SAID IT WAS BEHIND THE PICASSO...
WAIT A SECOND...

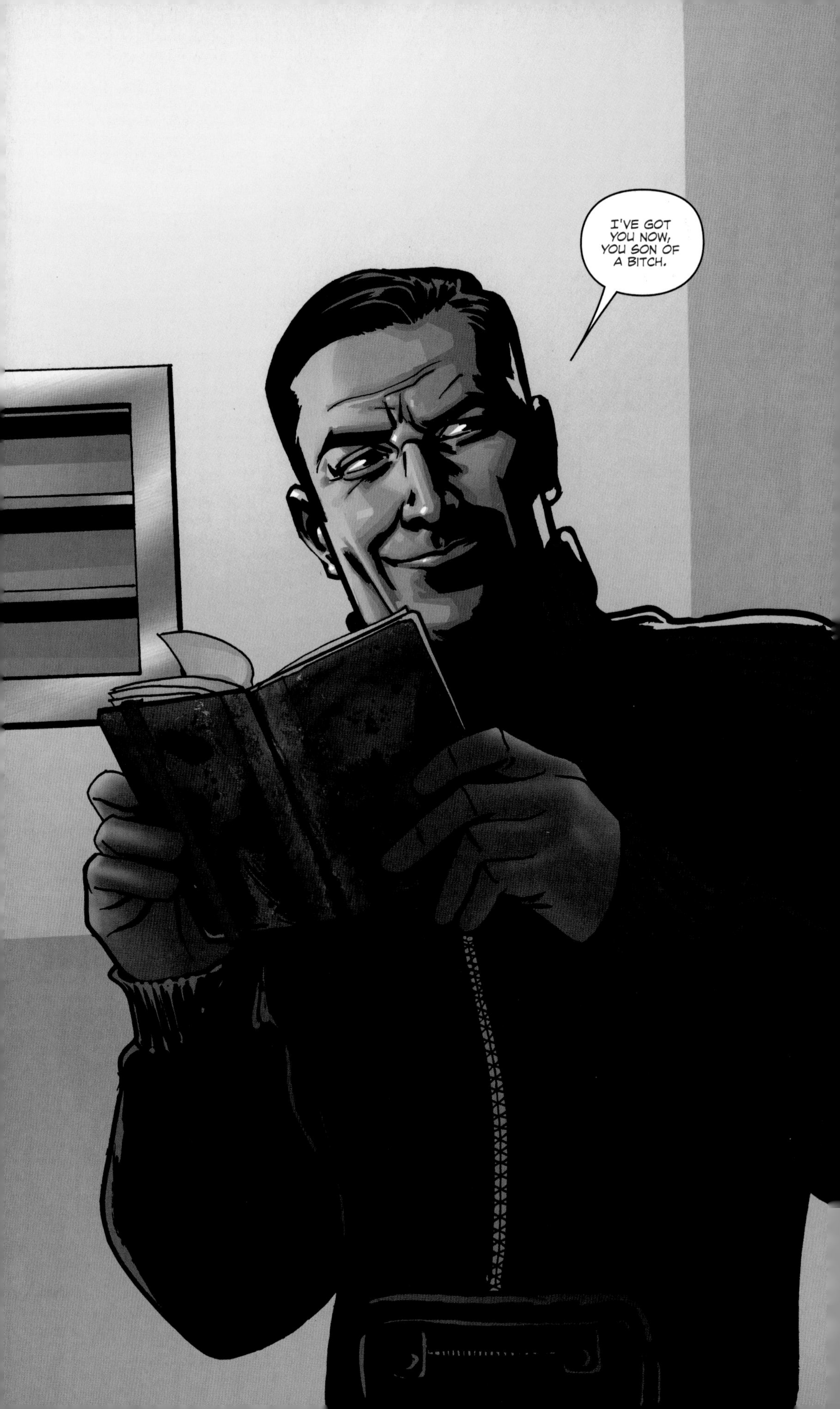
I'VE GOT YOU NOW, YOU SON OF A BITCH.

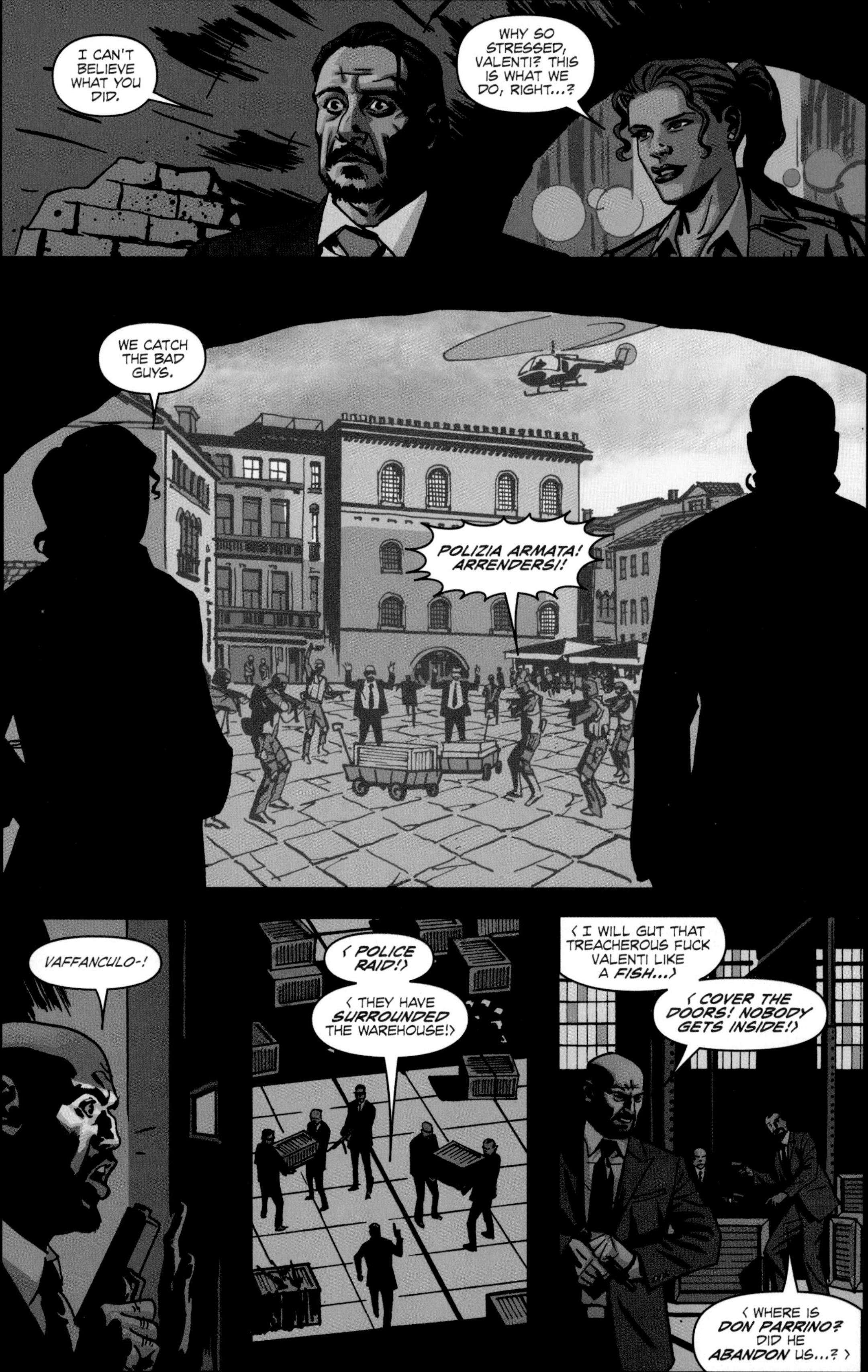
I CAN'T BELIEVE WHAT YOU DID.
WHY SO STRESSED, VALENTI? THIS IS WHAT WE DO, RIGHT...?
WE CATCH THE BAD GUYS.
POLIZIA ARMATA! ARRENDERSI!
VAFFANCULO-!
‹ POLICE RAID!›
‹ THEY HAVE SURROUNDED THE WAREHOUSE!›
‹ I WILL GUT THAT TREACHEROUS FUCK VALENTI LIKE A FISH...›
‹ COVER THE DOORS! NOBODY GETS INSIDE!›
‹ WHERE IS DON PARRINO? DID HE ABANDON US...? ›

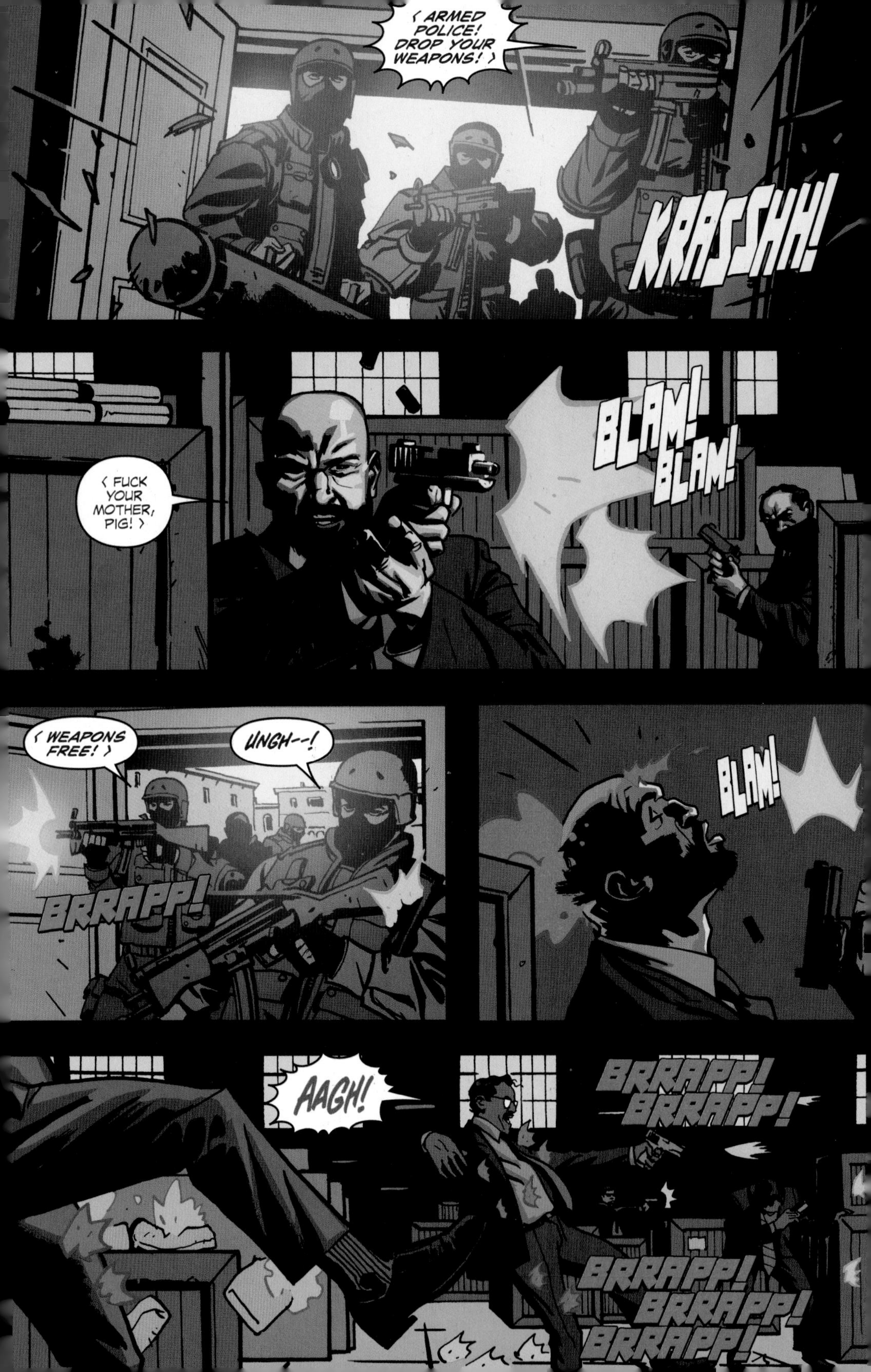
〈 ARMED POLICE! DROP YOUR WEAPONS! 〉
KRASSHH!
〈 FUCK YOUR MOTHER, PIG! 〉
BLAM! BLAM!
〈 WEAPONS FREE! 〉
UNGH--!
BRRAPP!
BLAM!
AAGH!
BRRAPP! BRRAPP!
BRRAPP! BRRAPP! BRRAPP!

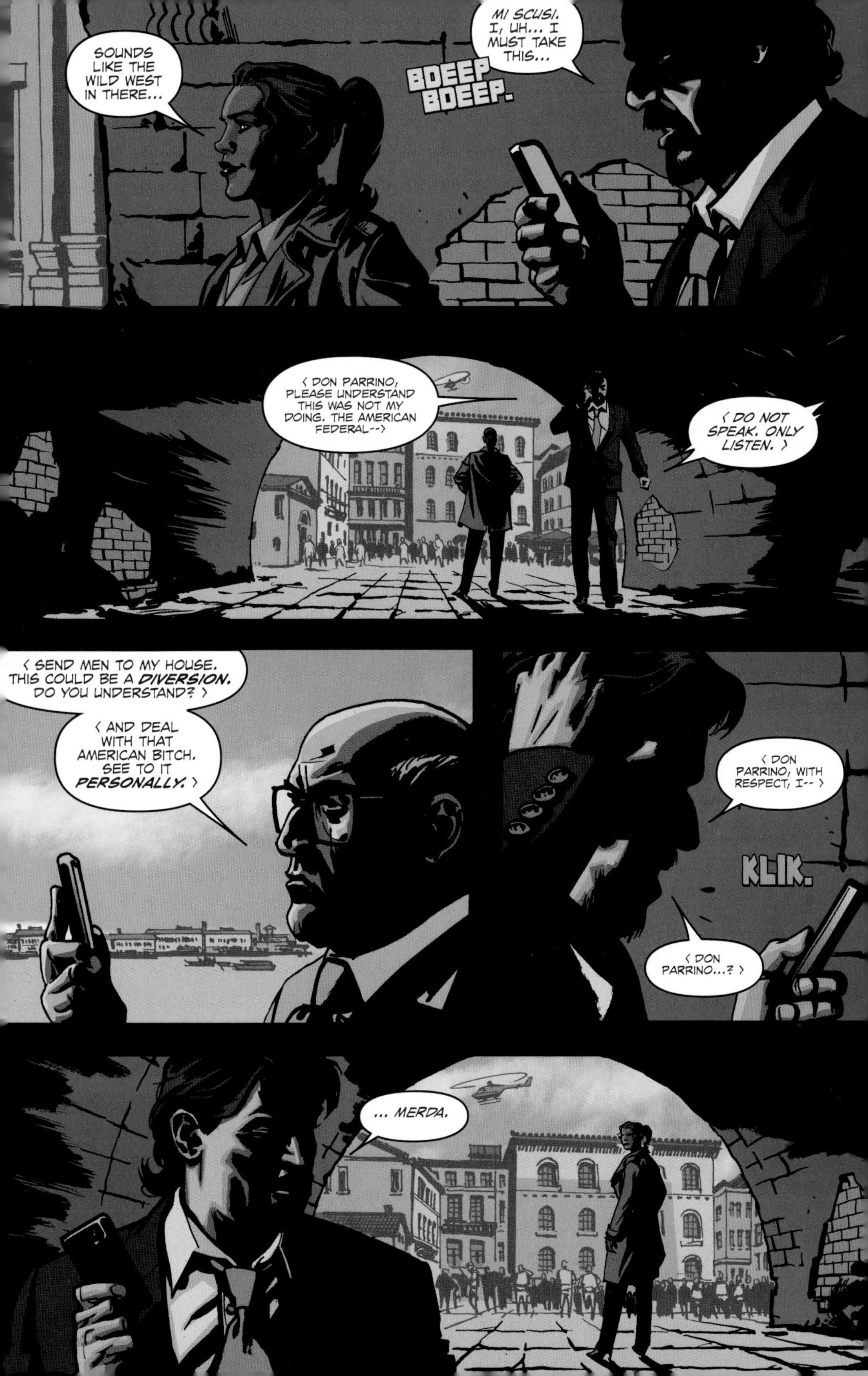
SOUNDS LIKE THE WILD WEST IN THERE...
BDEEP BDEEP.
MI SCUSI. I, UH... I MUST TAKE THIS...
‹ DON PARRINO, PLEASE UNDERSTAND THIS WAS NOT MY DOING. THE AMERICAN FEDERAL--›
‹ DO NOT SPEAK. ONLY LISTEN. ›
‹ SEND MEN TO MY HOUSE. THIS COULD BE A DIVERSION. DO YOU UNDERSTAND? ›
‹ AND DEAL WITH THAT AMERICAN BITCH. SEE TO IT PERSONALLY. ›
‹ DON PARRINO, WITH RESPECT, I-- ›
KLIK.
‹ DON PARRINO...? ›
... MERDA.

REDMOND, YOU ARE WAY OVER SCHEDULE. MOVE YOUR ASS!

EASY, GRANDIN. I'M ON MY WAY OUT.

YOU GET THE GOODS?

PARRINO'S SAFE WAS EMPTY.

SHIT! ARE WE BLOWN?

REDMOND...?

IT'S FINE, I JUST--

WAIT A SECOND...

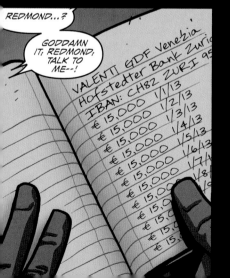

REDMOND...?

GODDAMN IT, REDMOND, TALK TO ME--!

VALENTI GDF Venezia
Hofstedter Bank Zuri
IBAN: CH82 ZURI 95
€ 15,000 1/1/13
€ 15,000 1/2/13
€ 15,000 1/3/13
€ 15,000 1/4/13
€ 15,000 1/5/13
€ 15,000 1/6/13
€ 15,000 1/7/1
€ 15,000 1/8/
€ 15,00   1/9
€ 15,0
€ 15,0
€ 15,
€ 15,

SHIT.

COHEN...

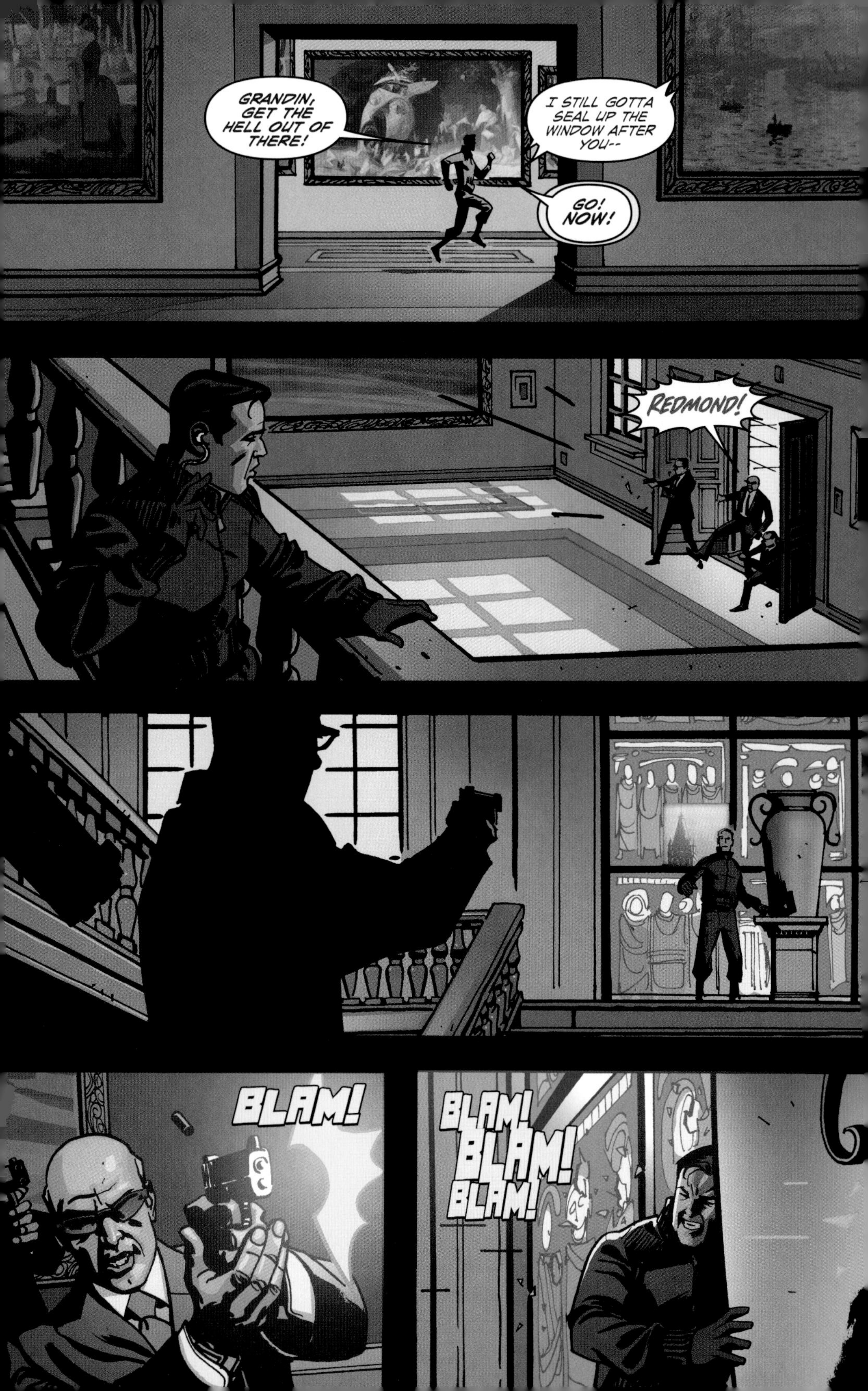
GRANDIN, GET THE HELL OUT OF THERE!
I STILL GOTTA SEAL UP THE WINDOW AFTER YOU--
GO! NOW!
REDMOND!
BLAM!
BLAM!
BLAM!
BLAM!

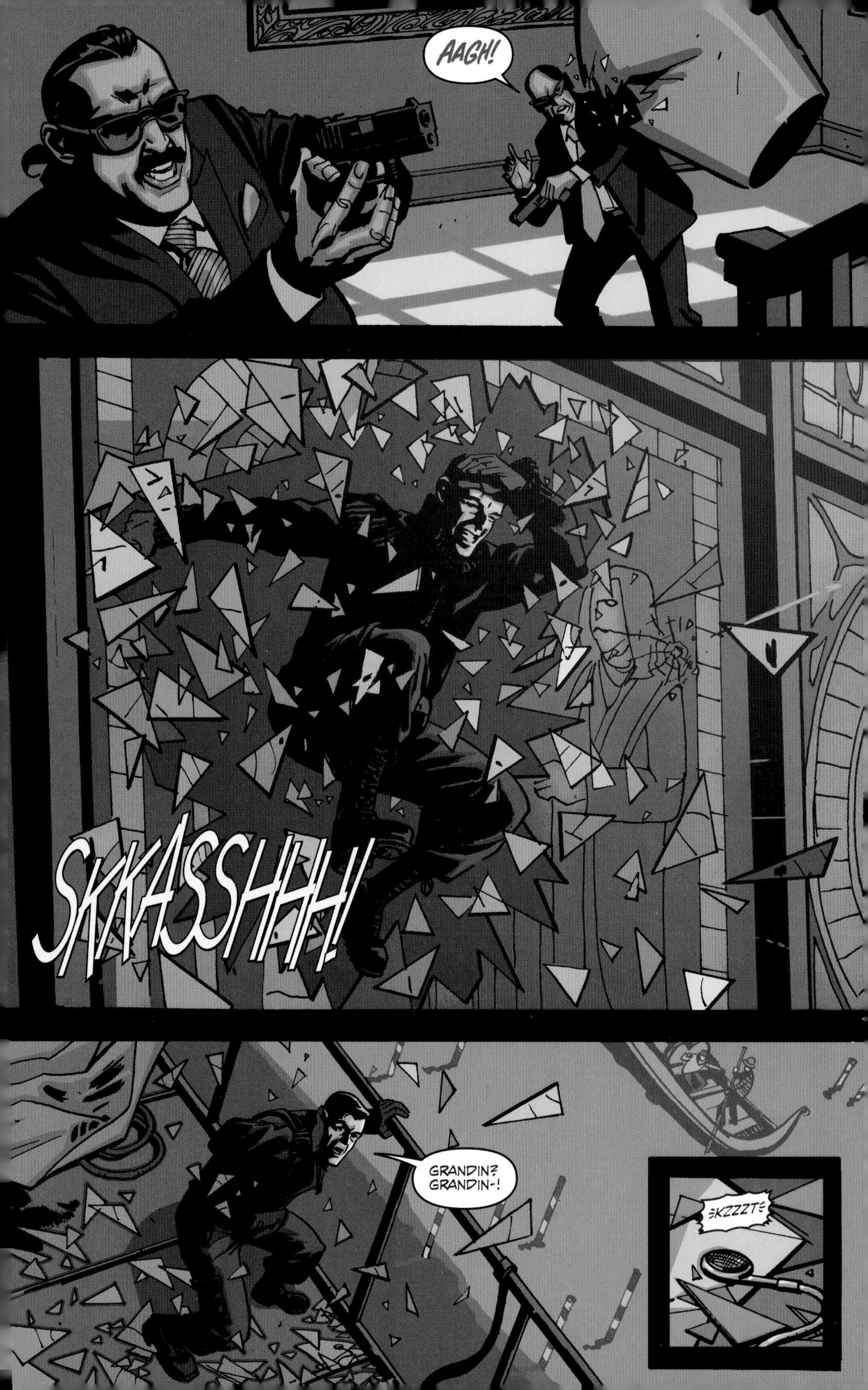
AAGH!
SKKASSHHH!
GRANDIN? GRANDIN-!
=KZZZT=

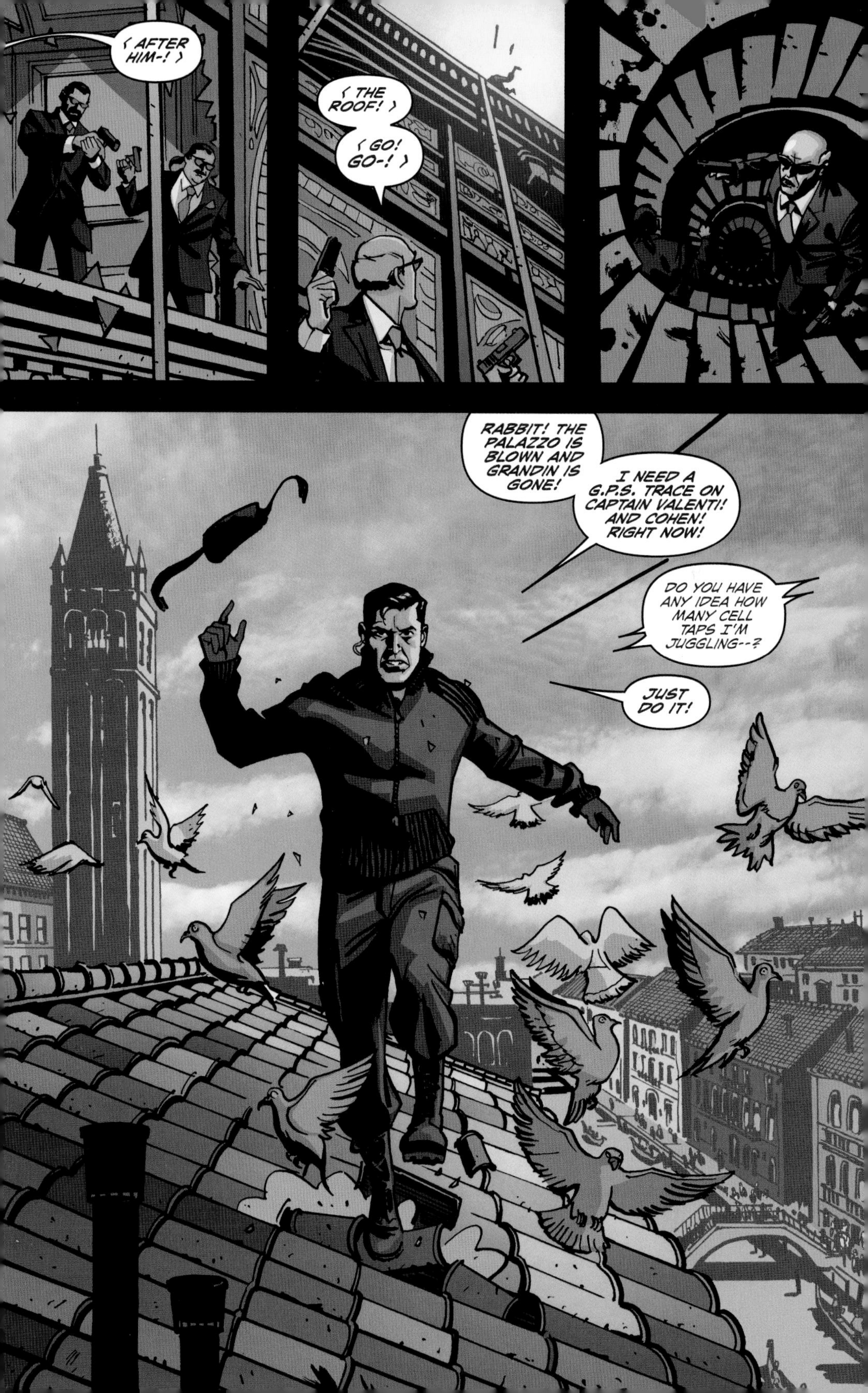
‹ AFTER HIM-! ›
‹ THE ROOF! ›
‹ GO! GO-! ›
RABBIT! THE PALAZZO IS BLOWN AND GRANDIN IS GONE!
I NEED A G.P.S. TRACE ON CAPTAIN VALENTI! AND COHEN! RIGHT NOW!
DO YOU HAVE ANY IDEA HOW MANY CELL TAPS I'M JUGGLING--?
JUST DO IT!

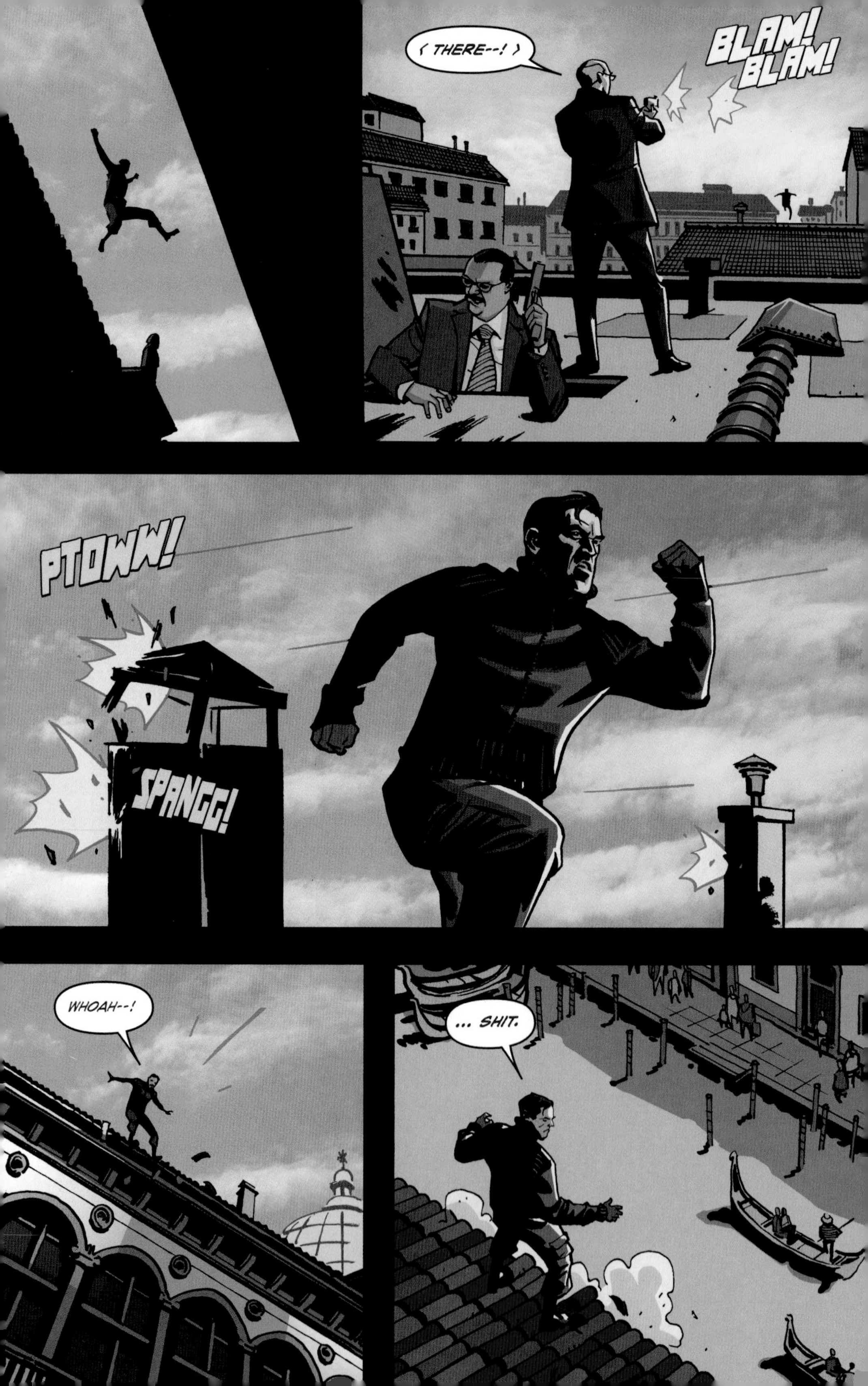
‹ THERE--! ›
BLAM! BLAM!
PTOWW!
SPANGG!
WHOAH--!
... SHIT.

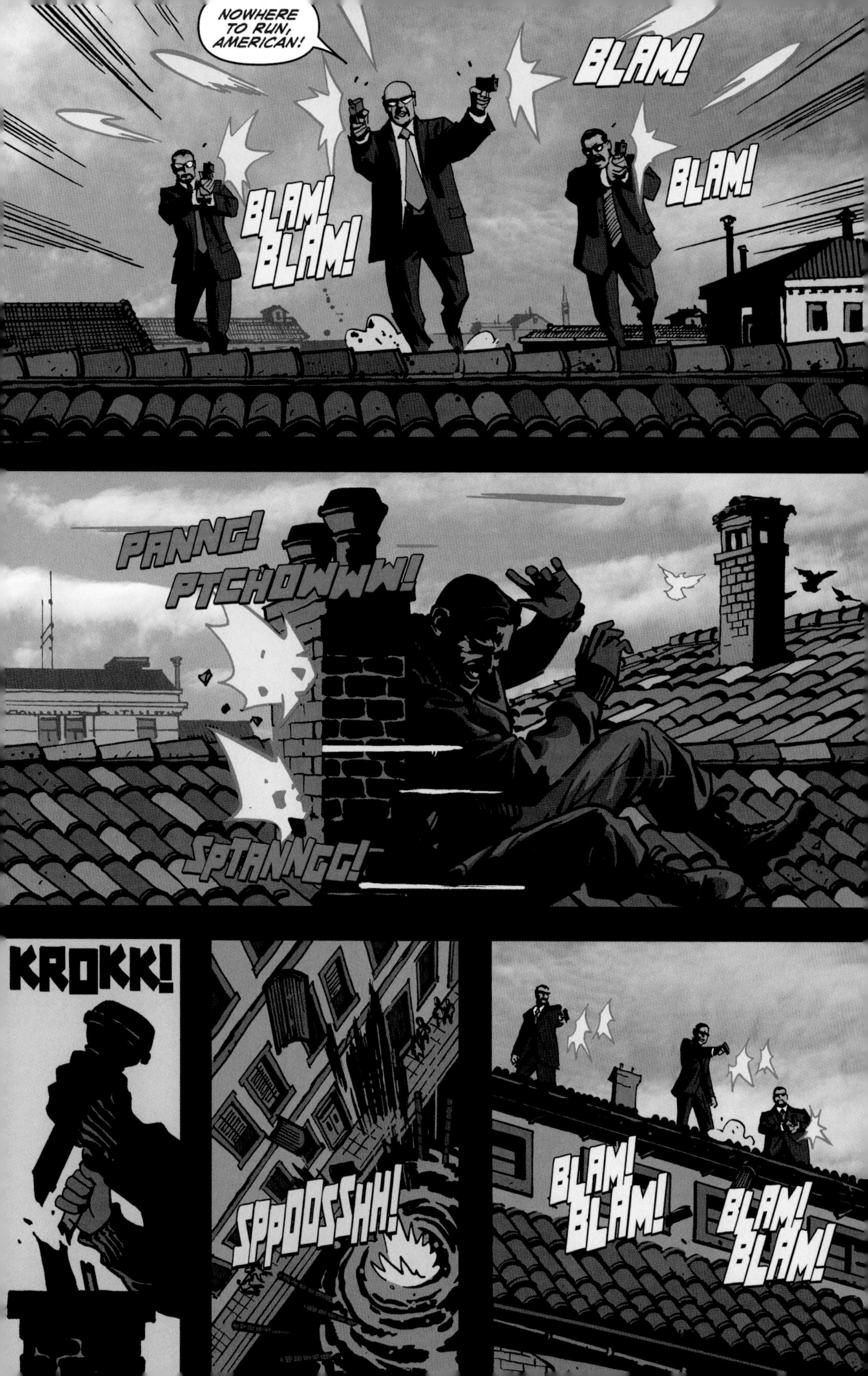
NOWHERE TO RUN, AMERICAN!
BLAM!
BLAM! BLAM!
BLAM!
PANNG!
PTCHOWWW!
SPTANNGG!
KROKK!
SPPOOSSHH!
BLAM! BLAM!
BLAM! BLAM!

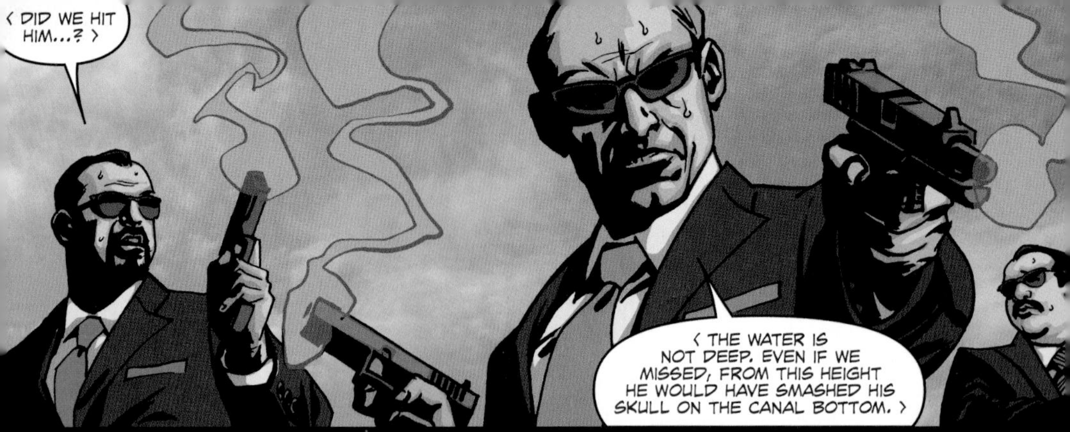
‹ DID WE HIT HIM...? ›
‹ THE WATER IS NOT DEEP. EVEN IF WE MISSED, FROM THIS HEIGHT HE WOULD HAVE SMASHED HIS SKULL ON THE CANAL BOTTOM. ›

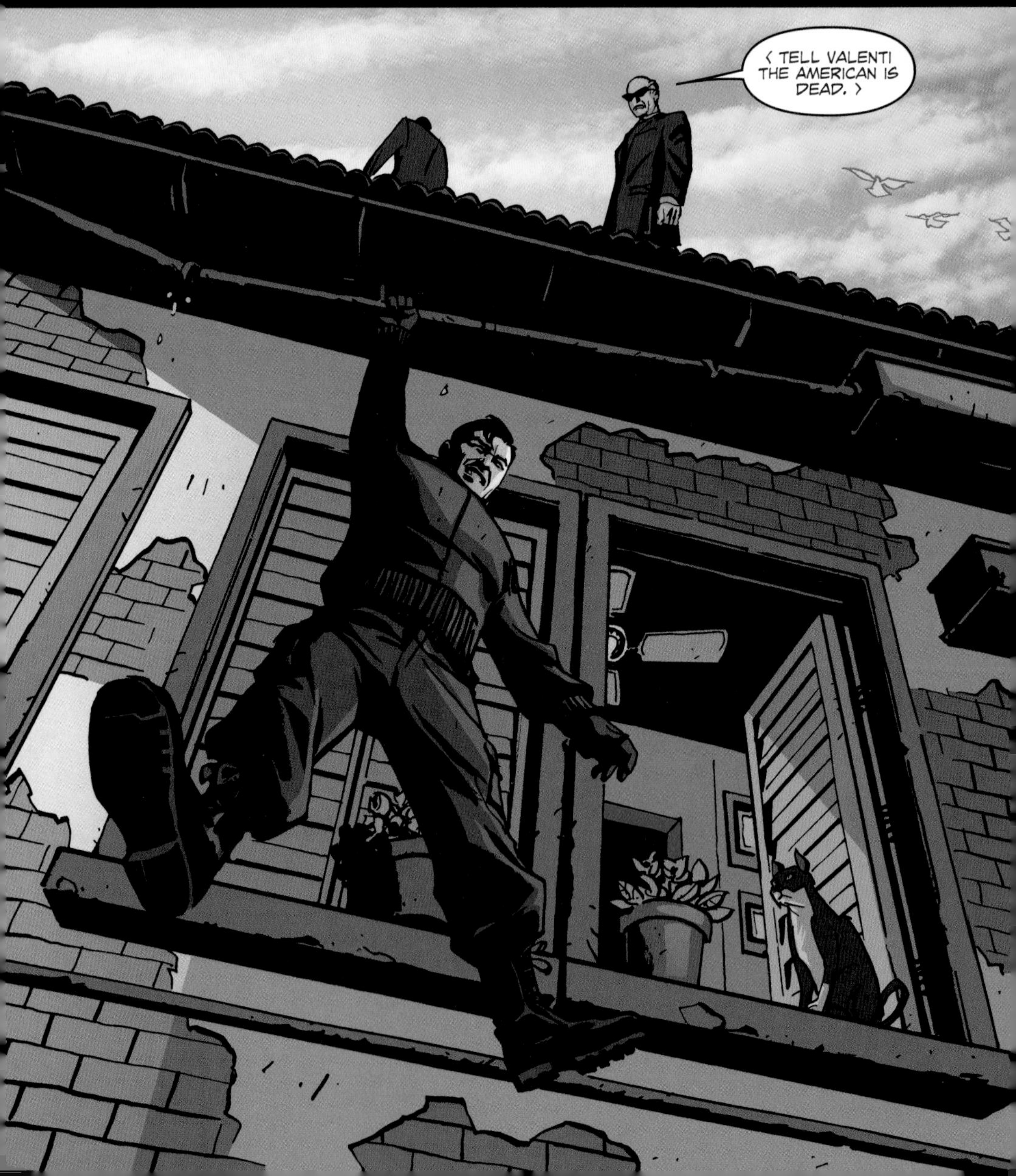
‹ TELL VALENTI THE AMERICAN IS DEAD. ›

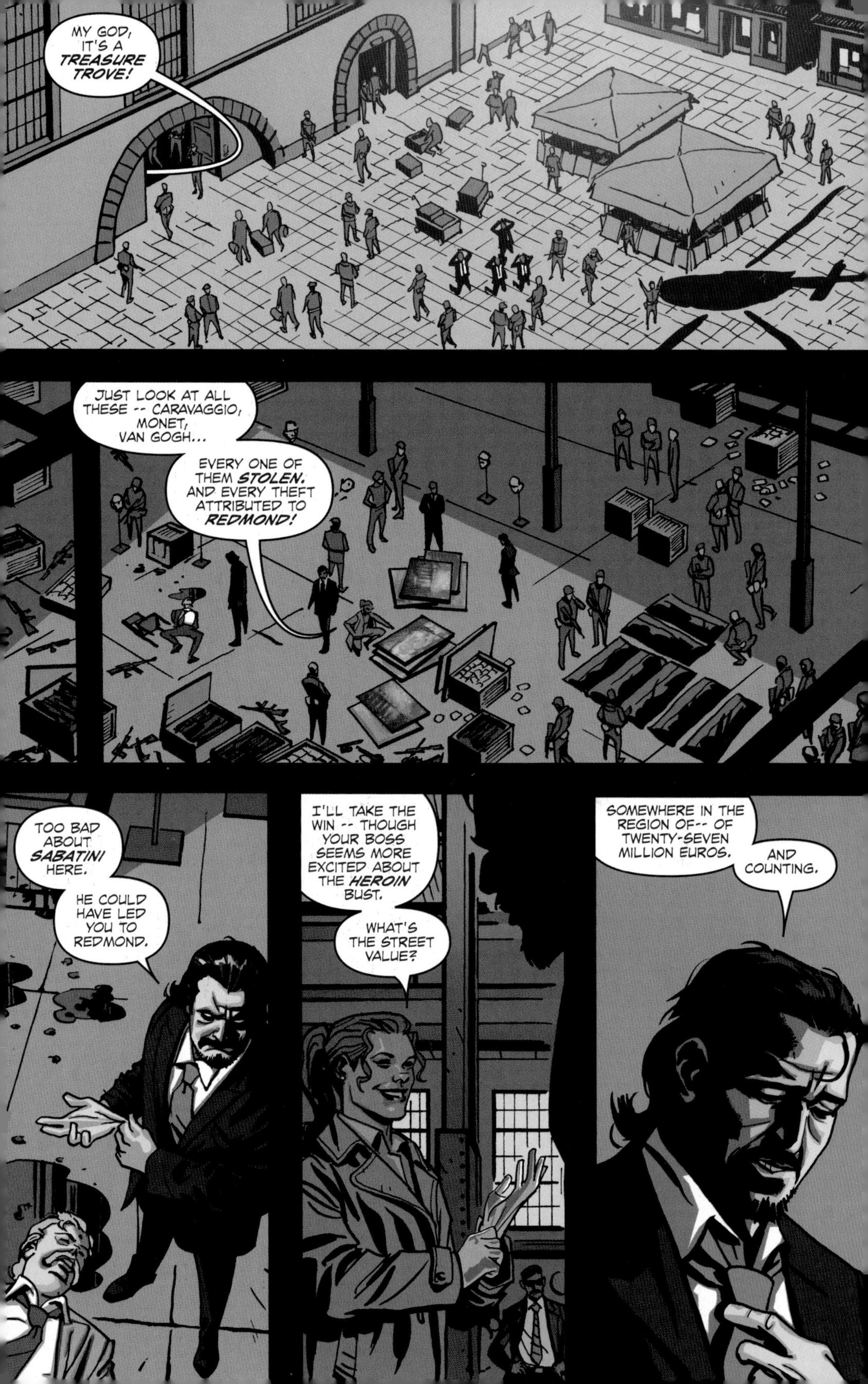
MY GOD, IT'S A TREASURE TROVE!
JUST LOOK AT ALL THESE -- CARAVAGGIO, MONET, VAN GOGH...
EVERY ONE OF THEM STOLEN. AND EVERY THEFT ATTRIBUTED TO REDMOND!
TOO BAD ABOUT SABATINI HERE.
HE COULD HAVE LED YOU TO REDMOND.
I'LL TAKE THE WIN -- THOUGH YOUR BOSS SEEMS MORE EXCITED ABOUT THE HEROIN BUST.
WHAT'S THE STREET VALUE?
SOMEWHERE IN THE REGION OF-- OF TWENTY-SEVEN MILLION EUROS.
AND COUNTING.

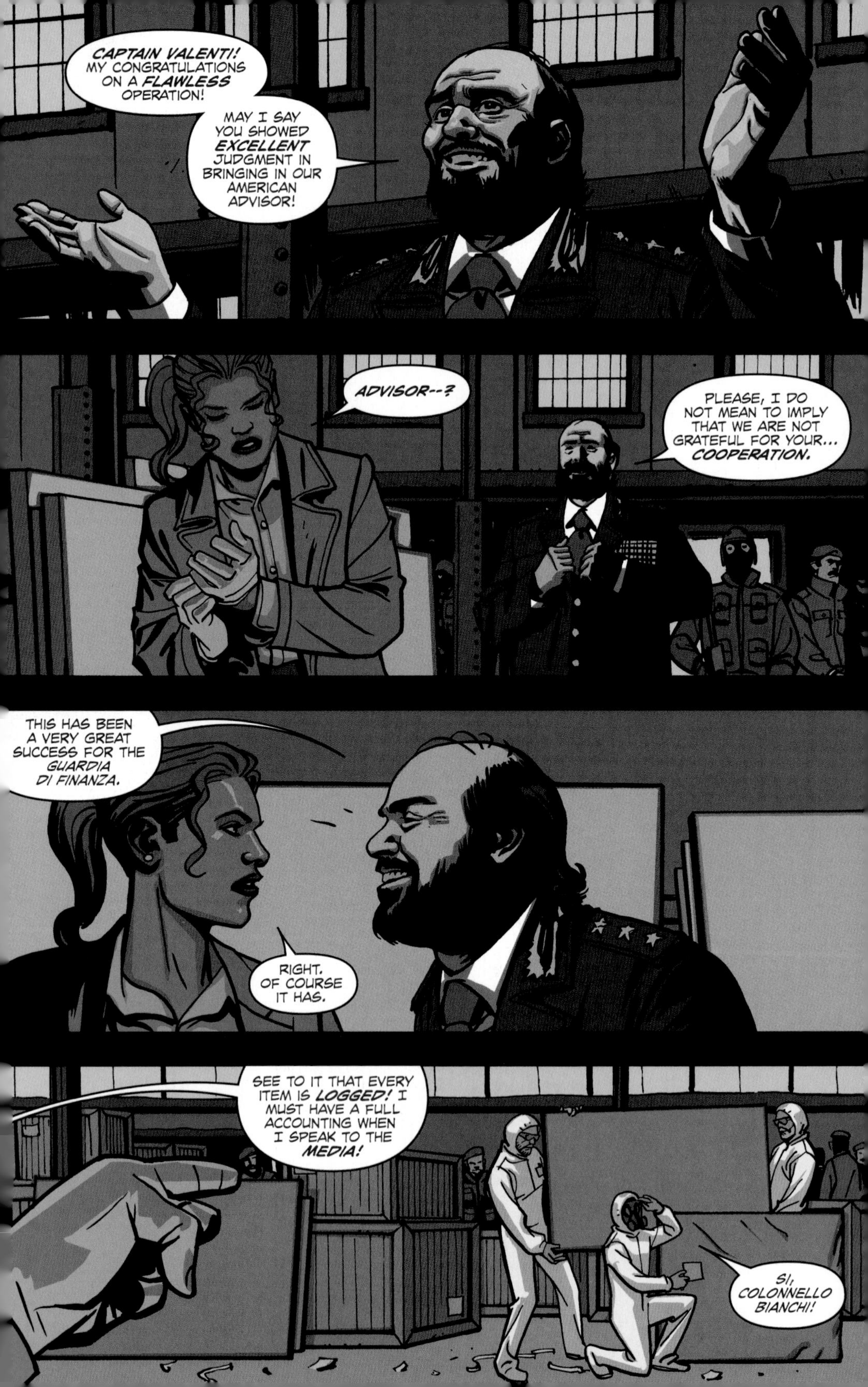
CAPTAIN VALENTI! MY CONGRATULATIONS ON A FLAWLESS OPERATION!
MAY I SAY YOU SHOWED EXCELLENT JUDGMENT IN BRINGING IN OUR AMERICAN ADVISOR!
ADVISOR--?
PLEASE, I DO NOT MEAN TO IMPLY THAT WE ARE NOT GRATEFUL FOR YOUR... COOPERATION.
THIS HAS BEEN A VERY GREAT SUCCESS FOR THE GUARDIA DI FINANZA.
RIGHT. OF COURSE IT HAS.
SEE TO IT THAT EVERY ITEM IS LOGGED! I MUST HAVE A FULL ACCOUNTING WHEN I SPEAK TO THE MEDIA!
SI, COLONNELLO BIANCHI!

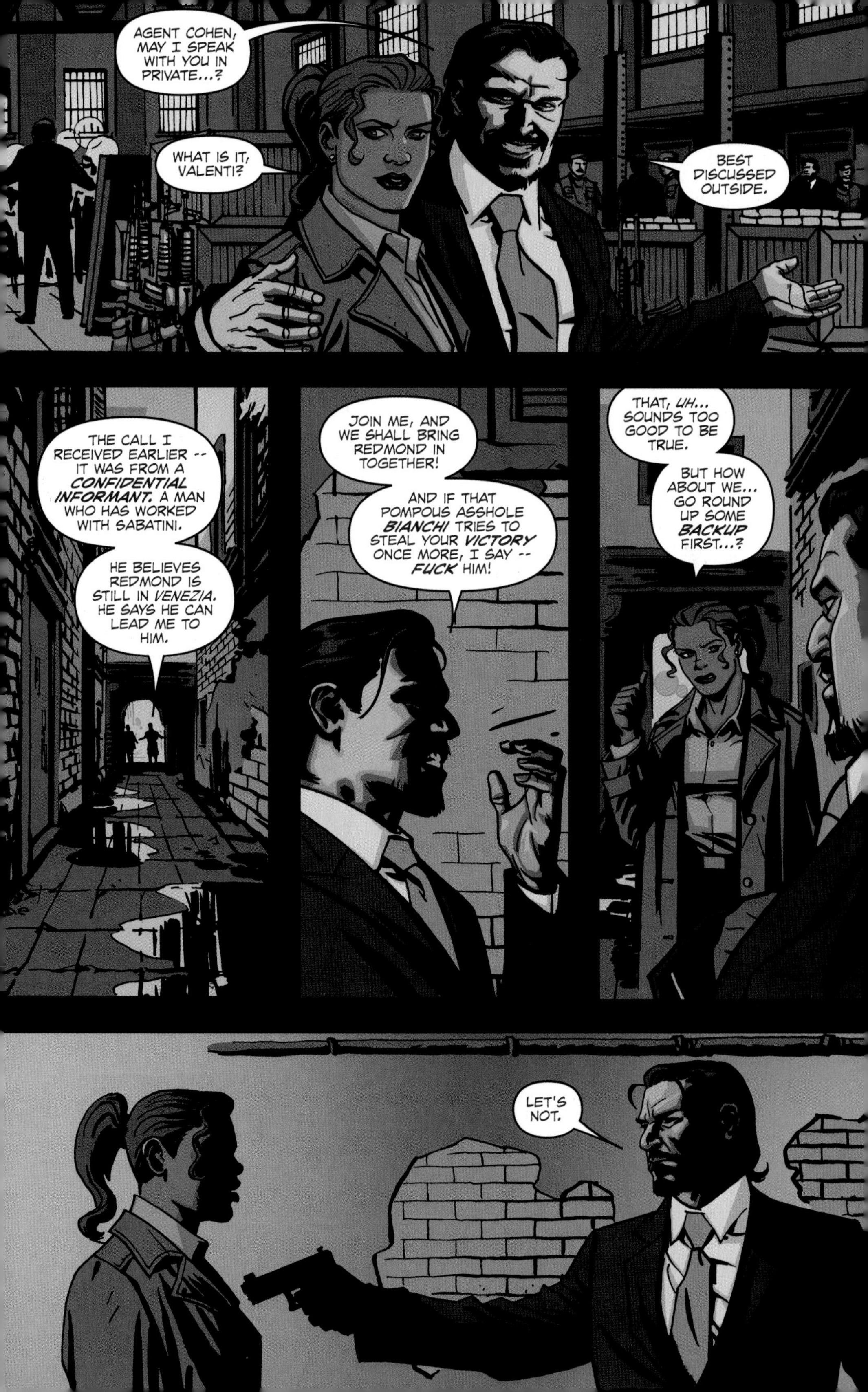
AGENT COHEN, MAY I SPEAK WITH YOU IN PRIVATE...?
WHAT IS IT, VALENTI?
BEST DISCUSSED OUTSIDE.
THE CALL I RECEIVED EARLIER -- IT WAS FROM A *CONFIDENTIAL INFORMANT.* A MAN WHO HAS WORKED WITH SABATINI.
HE BELIEVES REDMOND IS STILL IN *VENEZIA.* HE SAYS HE CAN LEAD ME TO HIM.
JOIN ME, AND WE SHALL BRING REDMOND IN TOGETHER!
AND IF THAT POMPOUS ASSHOLE *BIANCHI* TRIES TO STEAL YOUR *VICTORY* ONCE MORE, I SAY -- *FUCK* HIM!
THAT, *UH...* SOUNDS TOO GOOD TO BE TRUE.
BUT HOW ABOUT WE... GO ROUND UP SOME *BACKUP* FIRST...?
LET'S NOT.

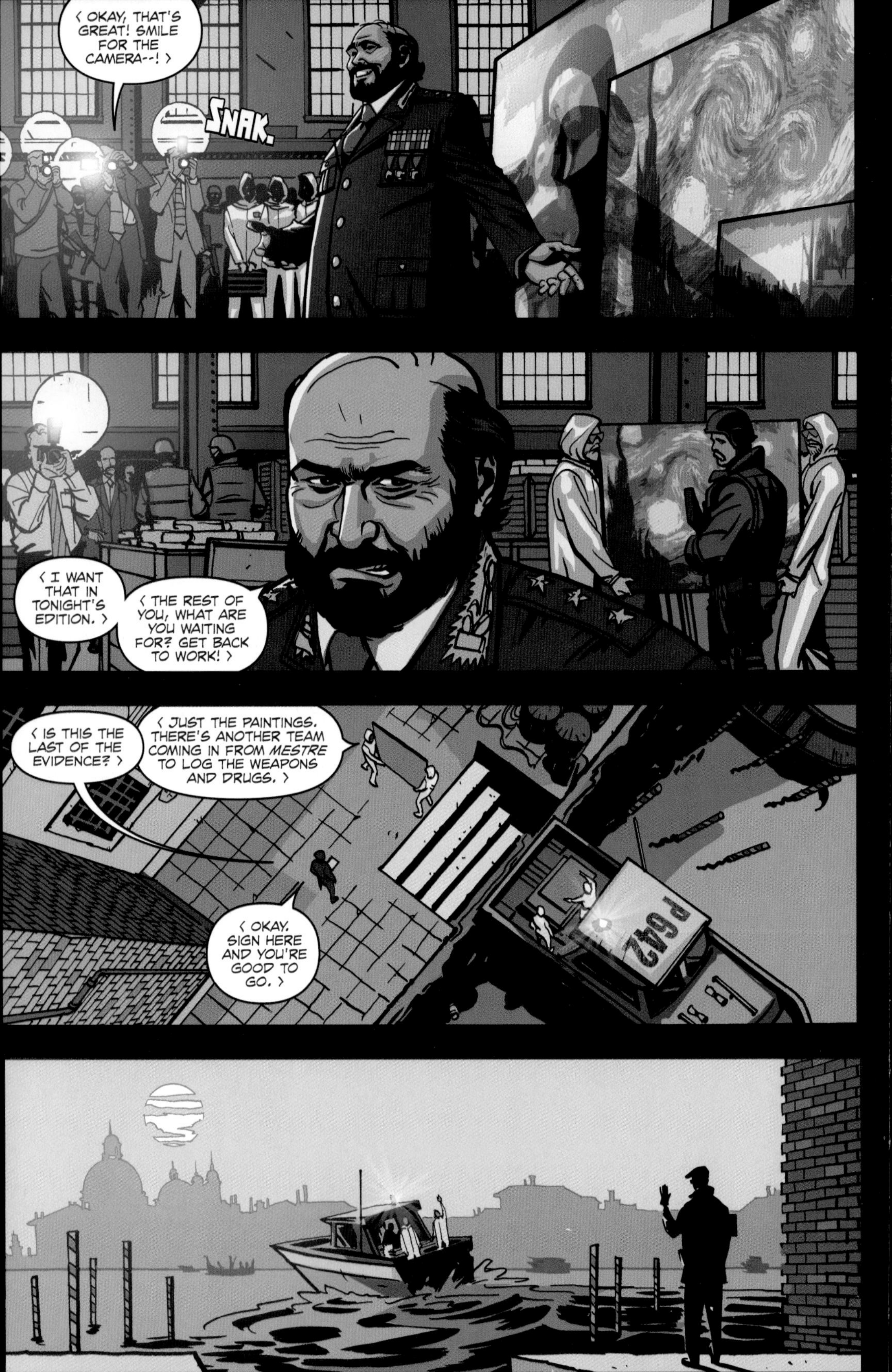

< OKAY, THAT'S GREAT! SMILE FOR THE CAMERA--! >
SNAK.
< I WANT THAT IN TONIGHT'S EDITION. >
< THE REST OF YOU, WHAT ARE YOU WAITING FOR? GET BACK TO WORK! >
< IS THIS THE LAST OF THE EVIDENCE? >
< JUST THE PAINTINGS. THERE'S ANOTHER TEAM COMING IN FROM *MESTRE* TO LOG THE WEAPONS AND DRUGS. >
< OKAY. SIGN HERE AND YOU'RE GOOD TO GO. >
P642

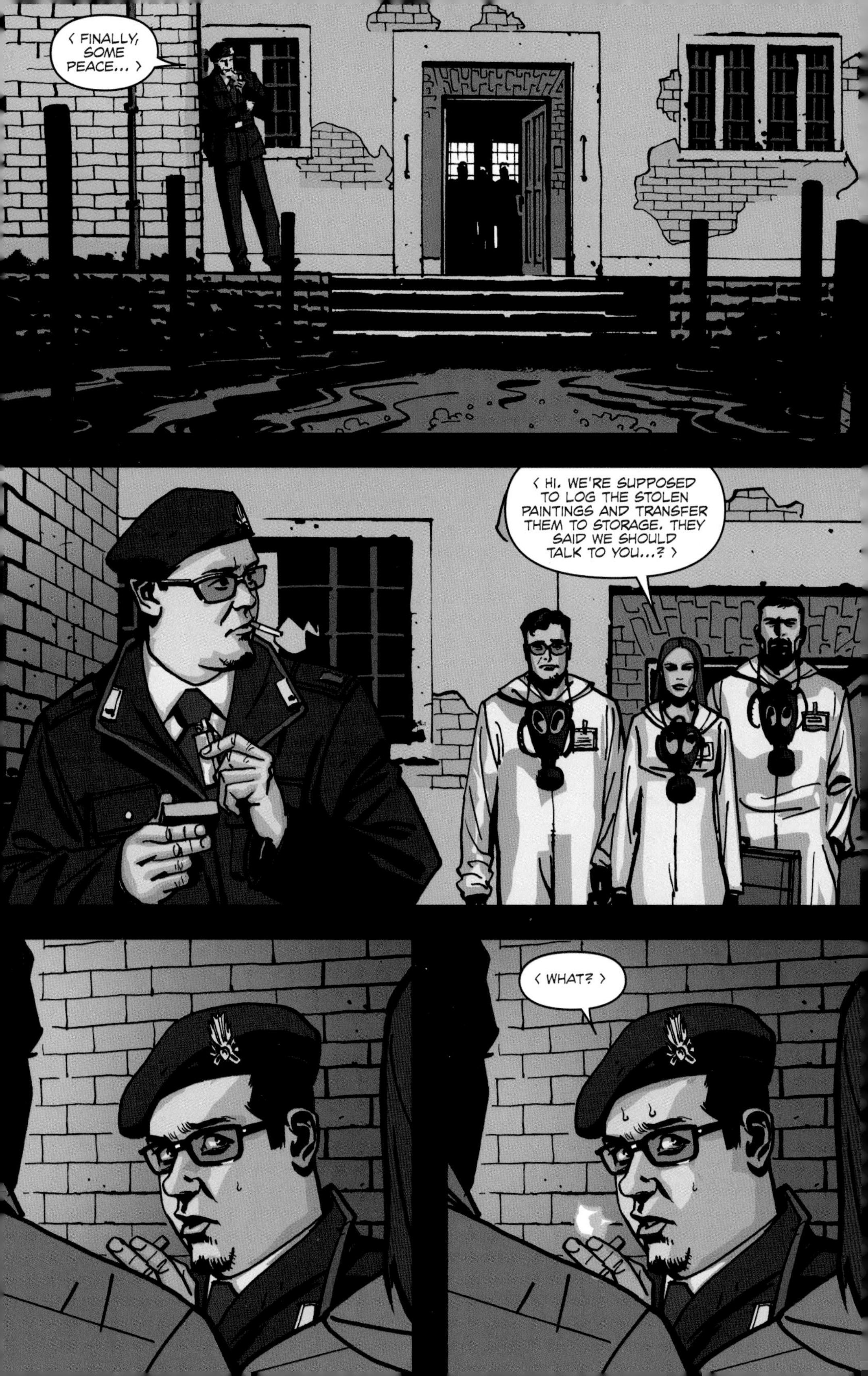
‹ FINALLY, SOME PEACE... ›
‹ HI. WE'RE SUPPOSED TO LOG THE STOLEN PAINTINGS AND TRANSFER THEM TO STORAGE. THEY SAID WE SHOULD TALK TO YOU...? ›
‹ WHAT? ›

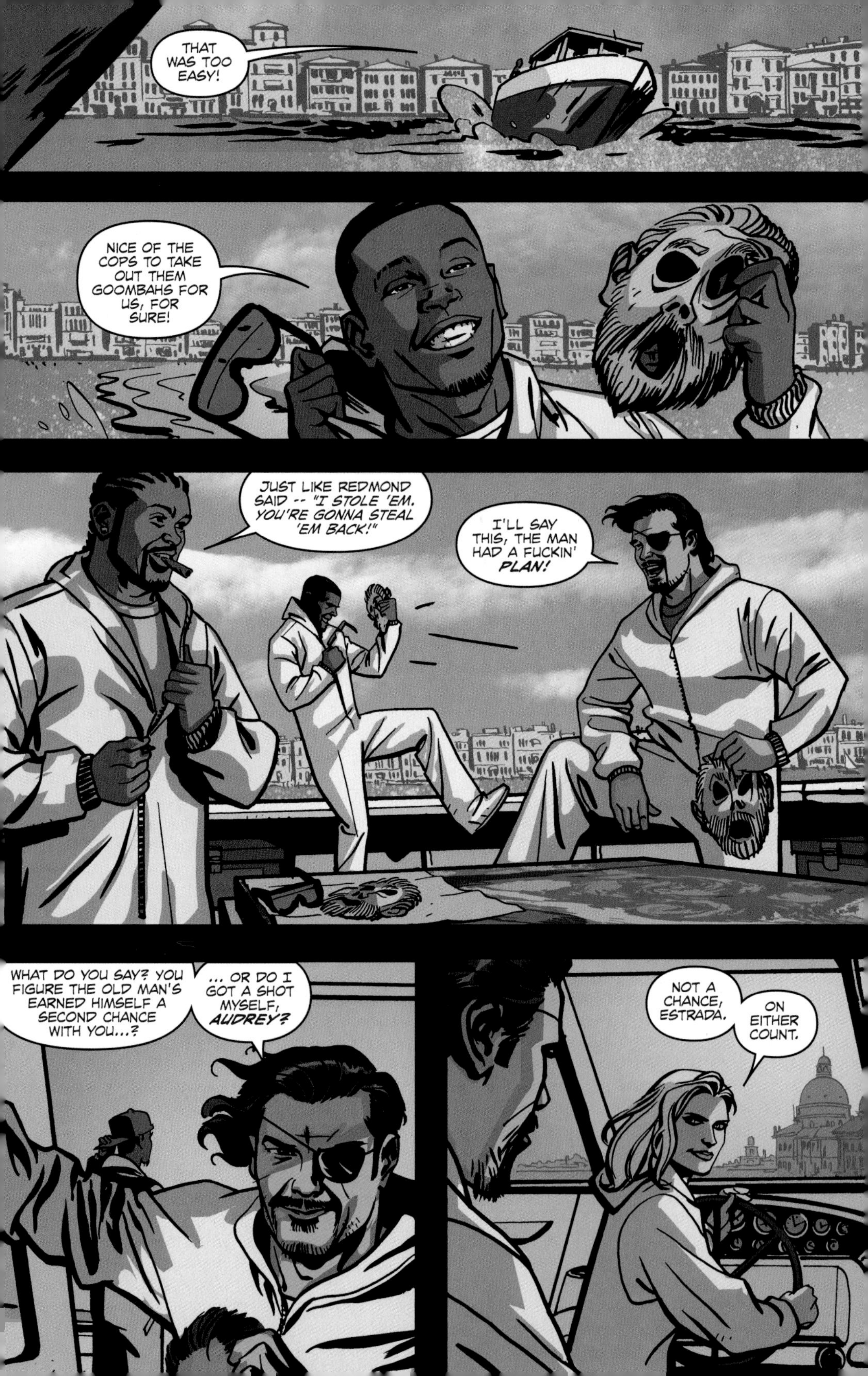
THAT WAS TOO EASY!
NICE OF THE COPS TO TAKE OUT THEM GOOMBAHS FOR US, FOR SURE!
JUST LIKE REDMOND SAID -- "I STOLE 'EM. YOU'RE GONNA STEAL 'EM BACK!"
I'LL SAY THIS, THE MAN HAD A FUCKIN' PLAN!
WHAT DO YOU SAY? YOU FIGURE THE OLD MAN'S EARNED HIMSELF A SECOND CHANCE WITH YOU...?
... OR DO I GOT A SHOT MYSELF, AUDREY?
NOT A CHANCE, ESTRADA.
ON EITHER COUNT.

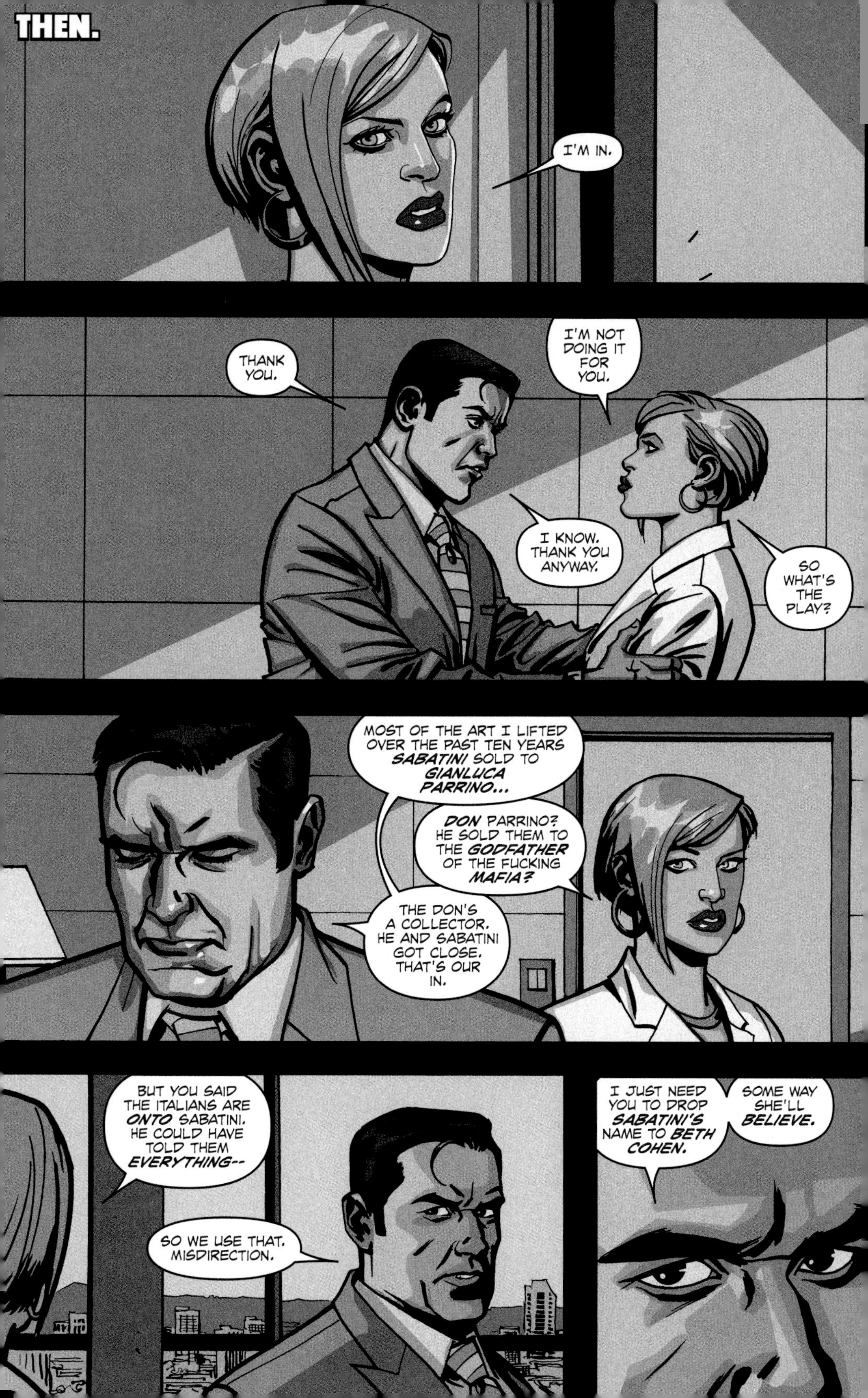
THEN.
I'M IN.
THANK YOU.
I'M NOT DOING IT FOR YOU.
I KNOW. THANK YOU ANYWAY.
SO WHAT'S THE PLAY?
MOST OF THE ART I LIFTED OVER THE PAST TEN YEARS SABATINI SOLD TO GIANLUCA PARRINO...
DON PARRINO? HE SOLD THEM TO THE GODFATHER OF THE FUCKING MAFIA?
THE DON'S A COLLECTOR. HE AND SABATINI GOT CLOSE. THAT'S OUR IN.
BUT YOU SAID THE ITALIANS ARE ONTO SABATINI. HE COULD HAVE TOLD THEM EVERYTHING--
SO WE USE THAT. MISDIRECTION.
I JUST NEED YOU TO DROP SABATINI'S NAME TO BETH COHEN.
SOME WAY SHE'LL BELIEVE.

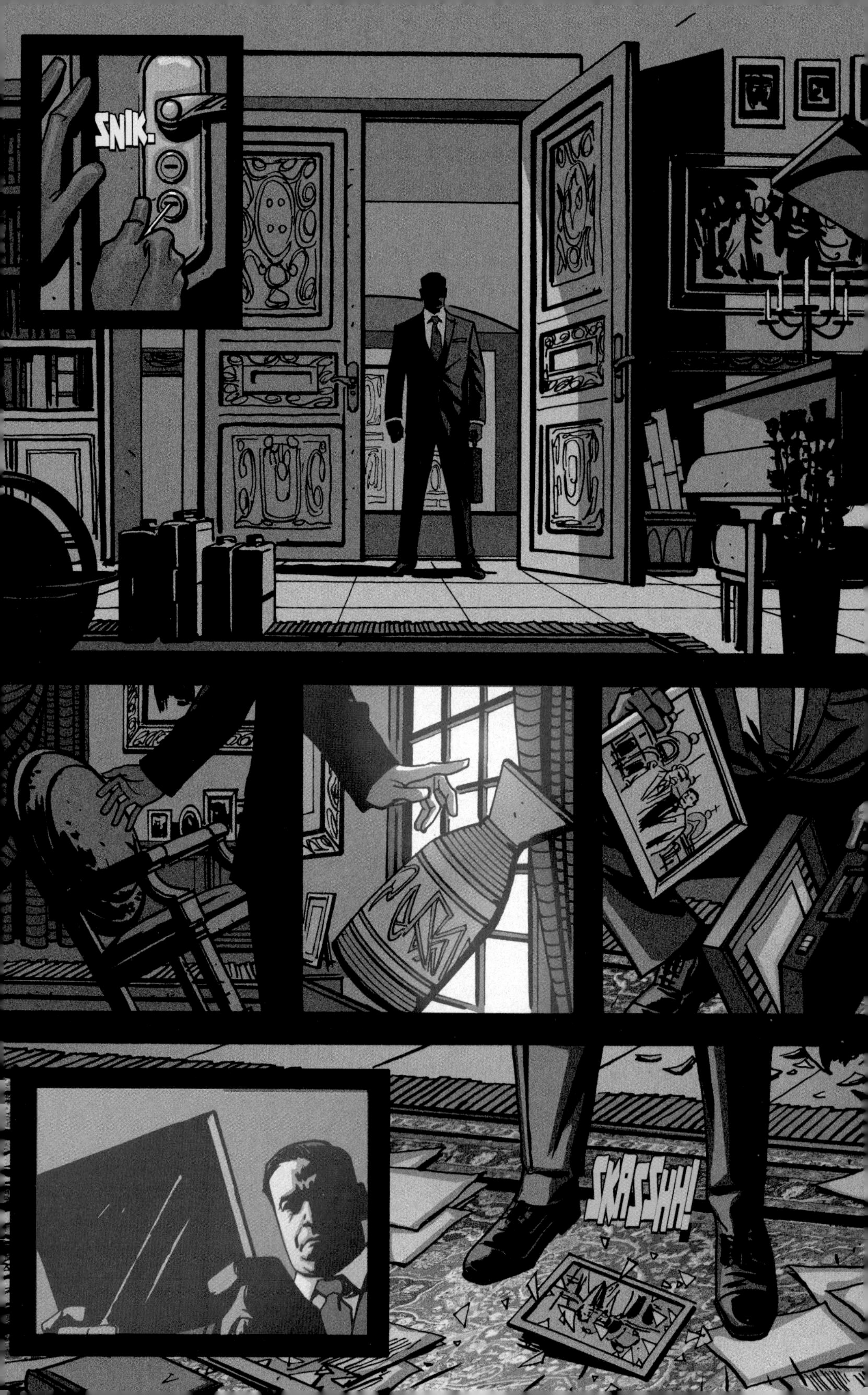
SNIK.
SKASSHH!

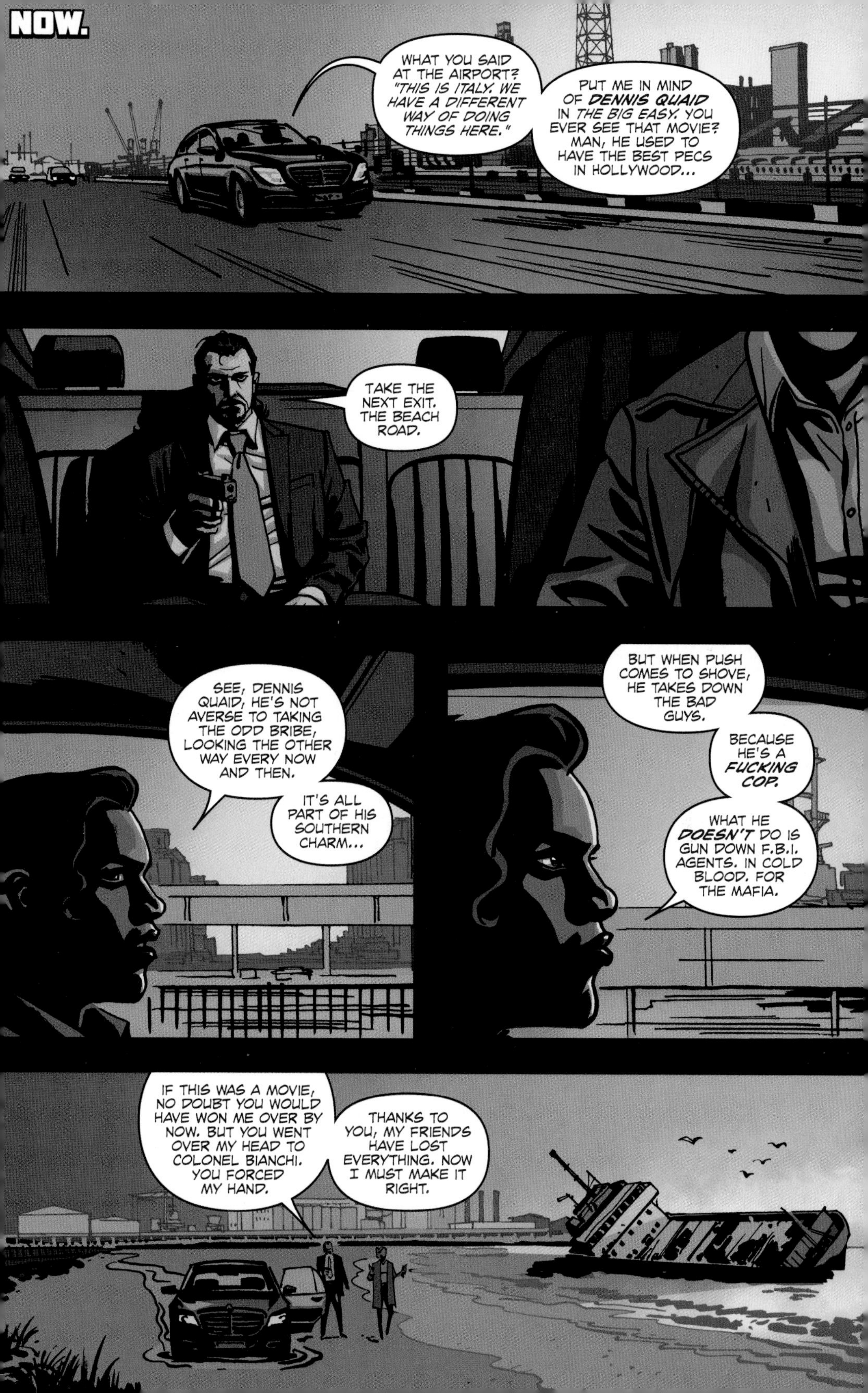
NOW.
WHAT YOU SAID AT THE AIRPORT? "THIS IS ITALY. WE HAVE A DIFFERENT WAY OF DOING THINGS HERE."
PUT ME IN MIND OF DENNIS QUAID IN THE BIG EASY. YOU EVER SEE THAT MOVIE? MAN, HE USED TO HAVE THE BEST PECS IN HOLLYWOOD...
TAKE THE NEXT EXIT. THE BEACH ROAD.
SEE, DENNIS QUAID, HE'S NOT AVERSE TO TAKING THE ODD BRIBE, LOOKING THE OTHER WAY EVERY NOW AND THEN.
IT'S ALL PART OF HIS SOUTHERN CHARM...
BUT WHEN PUSH COMES TO SHOVE, HE TAKES DOWN THE BAD GUYS.
BECAUSE HE'S A FUCKING COP.
WHAT HE DOESN'T DO IS GUN DOWN F.B.I. AGENTS. IN COLD BLOOD. FOR THE MAFIA.
IF THIS WAS A MOVIE, NO DOUBT YOU WOULD HAVE WON ME OVER BY NOW. BUT YOU WENT OVER MY HEAD TO COLONEL BIANCHI. YOU FORCED MY HAND.
THANKS TO YOU, MY FRIENDS HAVE LOST EVERYTHING. NOW I MUST MAKE IT RIGHT.

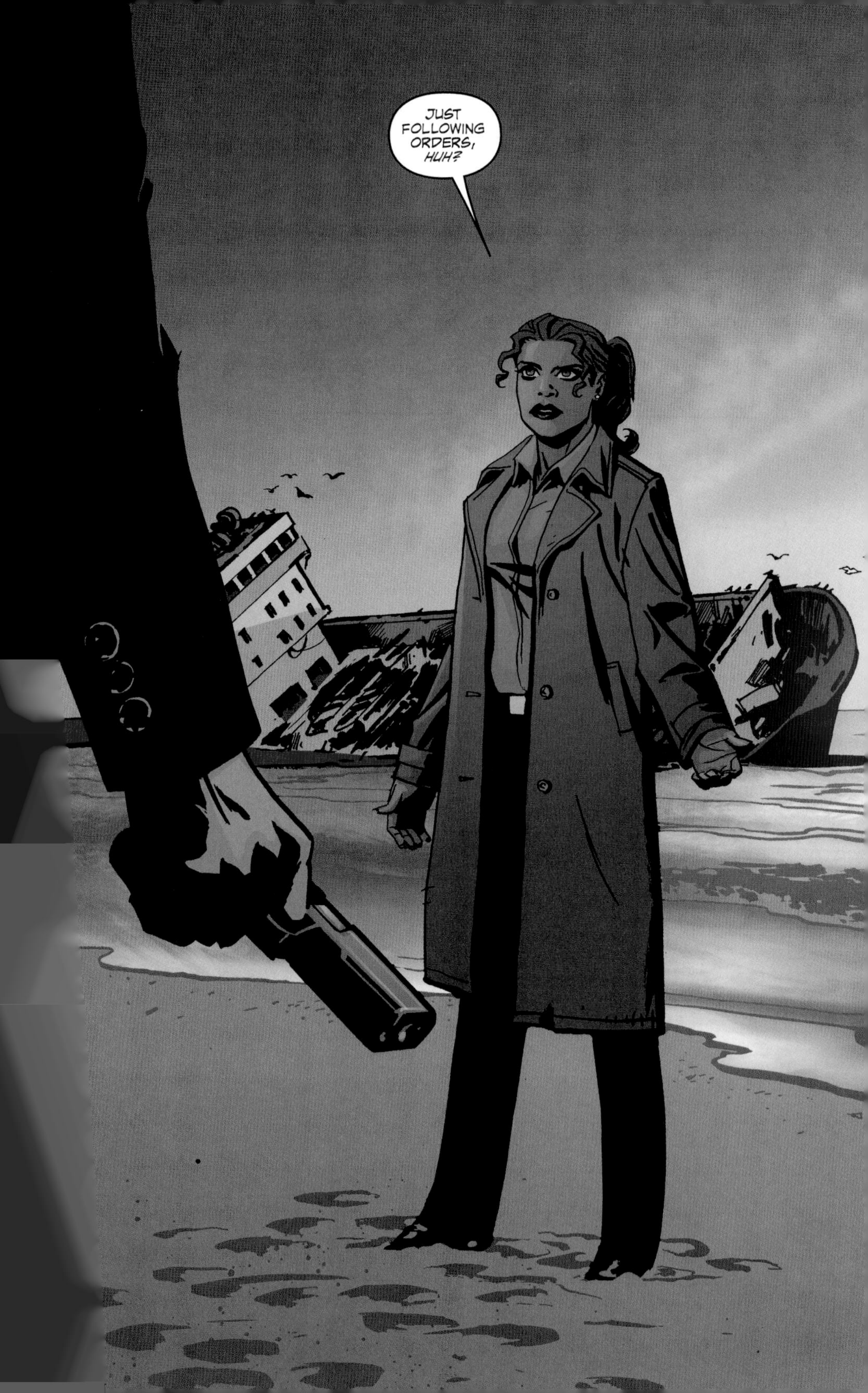
JUST FOLLOWING ORDERS, HUH?

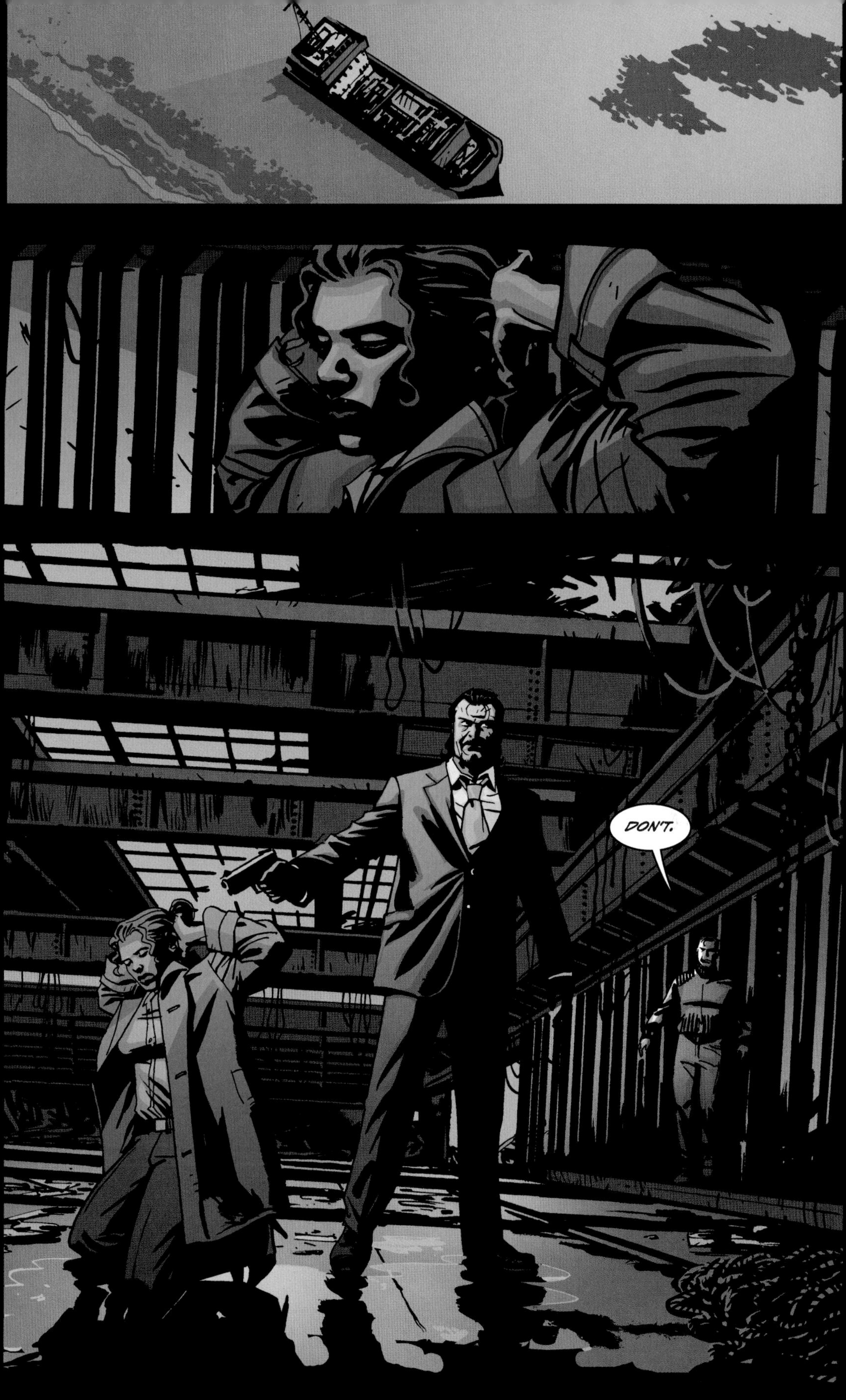
DON'T.

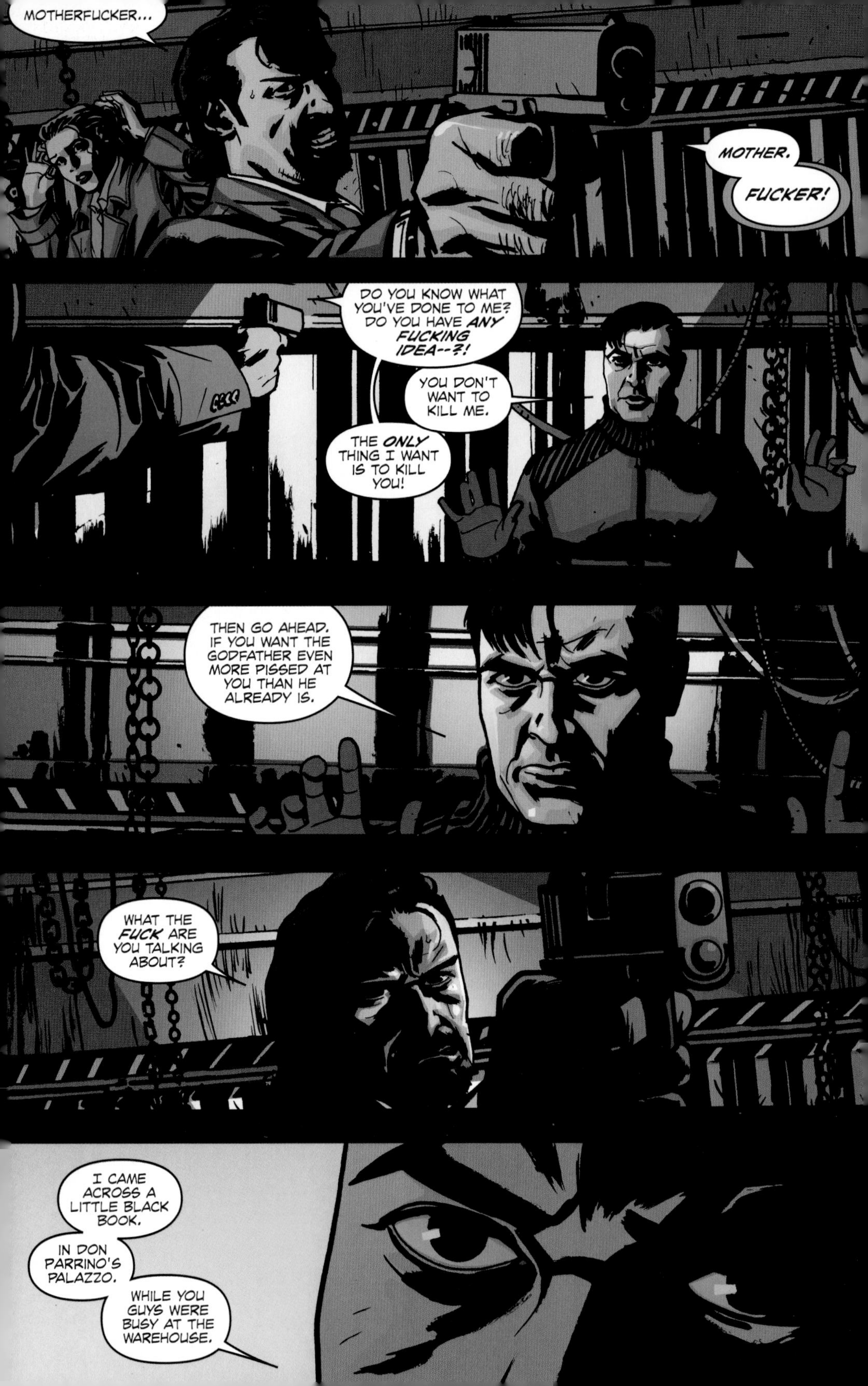
MOTHERFUCKER...
MOTHER.
FUCKER!
DO YOU KNOW WHAT YOU'VE DONE TO ME? DO YOU HAVE ANY FUCKING IDEA--?!
YOU DON'T WANT TO KILL ME.
THE ONLY THING I WANT IS TO KILL YOU!
THEN GO AHEAD. IF YOU WANT THE GODFATHER EVEN MORE PISSED AT YOU THAN HE ALREADY IS.
WHAT THE FUCK ARE YOU TALKING ABOUT?
I CAME ACROSS A LITTLE BLACK BOOK.
IN DON PARRINO'S PALAZZO.
WHILE YOU GUYS WERE BUSY AT THE WAREHOUSE.

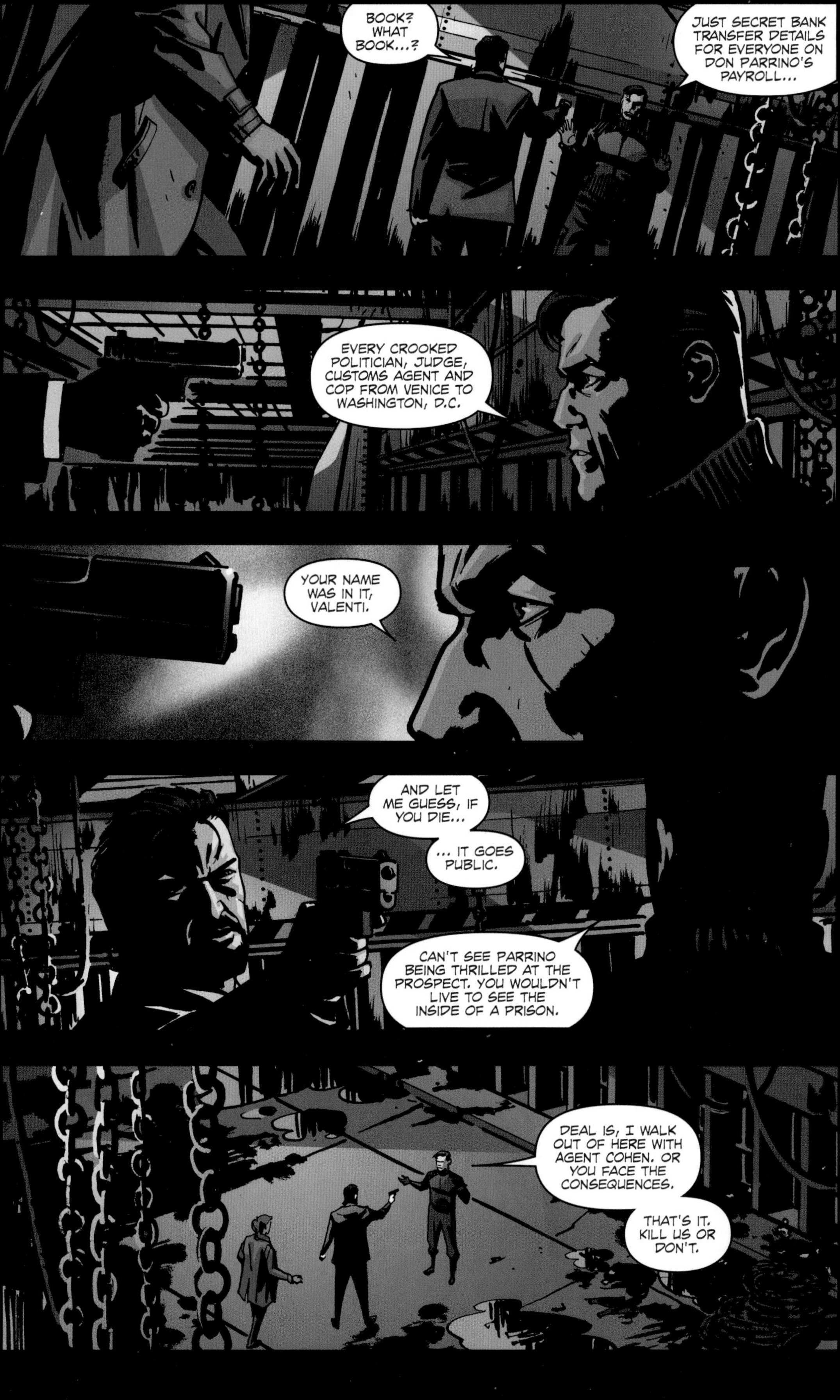
BOOK? WHAT BOOK...?
JUST SECRET BANK TRANSFER DETAILS FOR EVERYONE ON DON PARRINO'S PAYROLL...
EVERY CROOKED POLITICIAN, JUDGE, CUSTOMS AGENT AND COP FROM VENICE TO WASHINGTON, D.C.
YOUR NAME WAS IN IT, VALENTI.
AND LET ME GUESS, IF YOU DIE...
... IT GOES PUBLIC.
CAN'T SEE PARRINO BEING THRILLED AT THE PROSPECT. YOU WOULDN'T LIVE TO SEE THE INSIDE OF A PRISON.
DEAL IS, I WALK OUT OF HERE WITH AGENT COHEN. OR YOU FACE THE CONSEQUENCES.
THAT'S IT. KILL US OR DON'T.

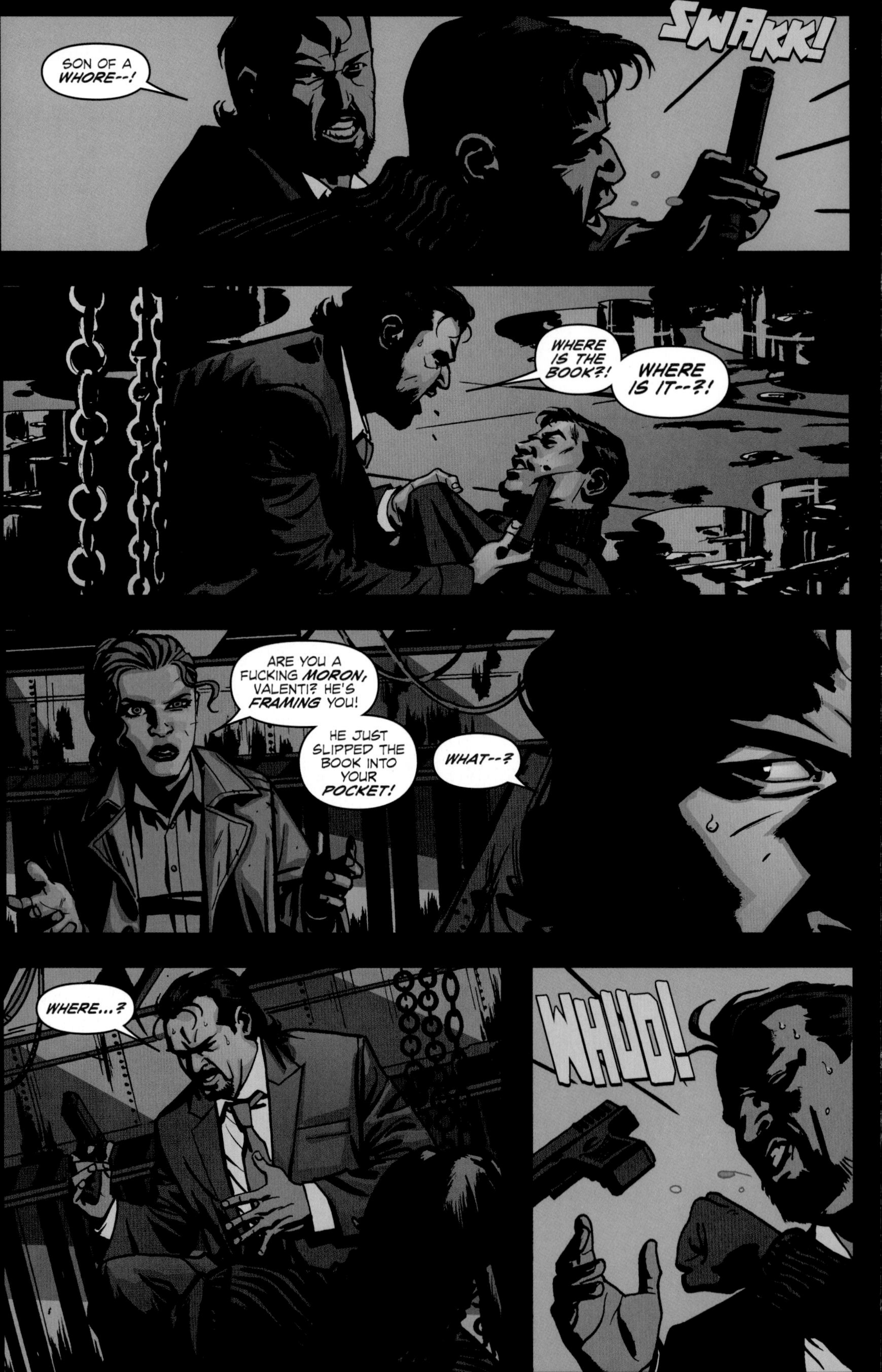
SWAKK!
SON OF A WHORE--!
WHERE IS THE BOOK?!
WHERE IS IT--?!
ARE YOU A FUCKING MORON, VALENTI? HE'S FRAMING YOU!
HE JUST SLIPPED THE BOOK INTO YOUR POCKET!
WHAT--?
WHERE...?
WHUD!

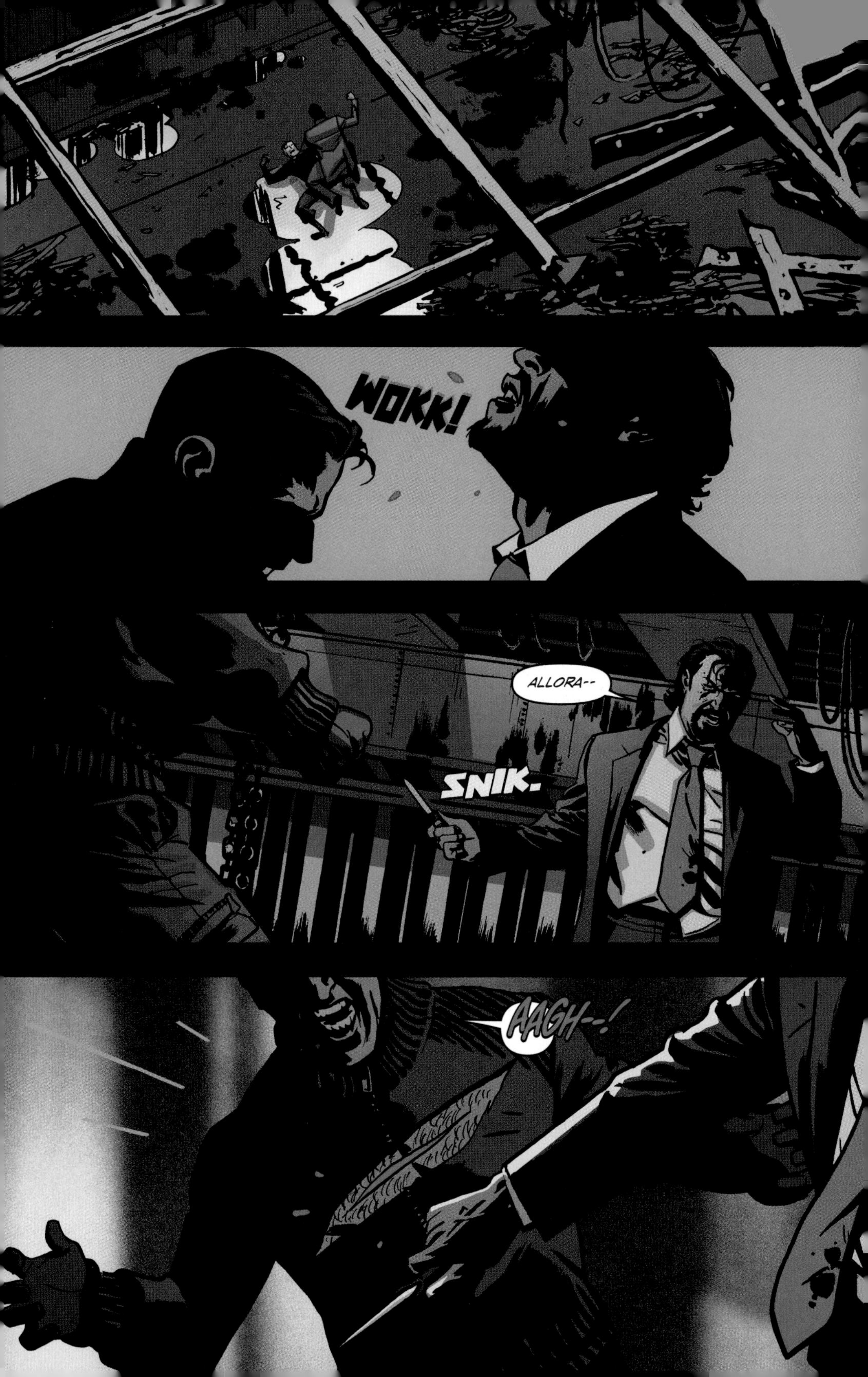
WOKK!
ALLORA--
SNIK.
AAGH--!

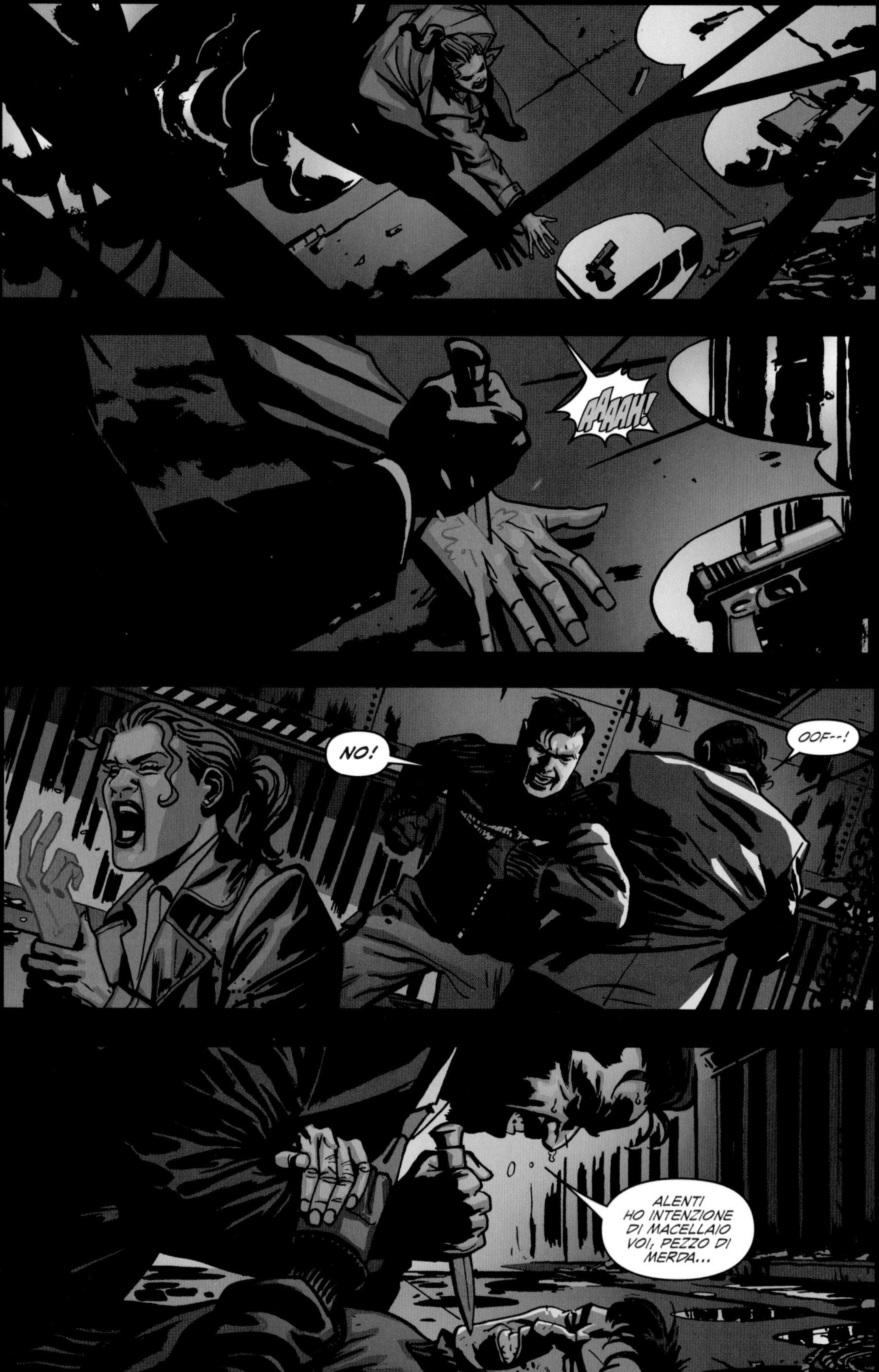
AAAAH!
NO!
OOF--!
ALENTI HO INTENZIONE DI MACELLAIO VOI, PEZZO DI MERDA...

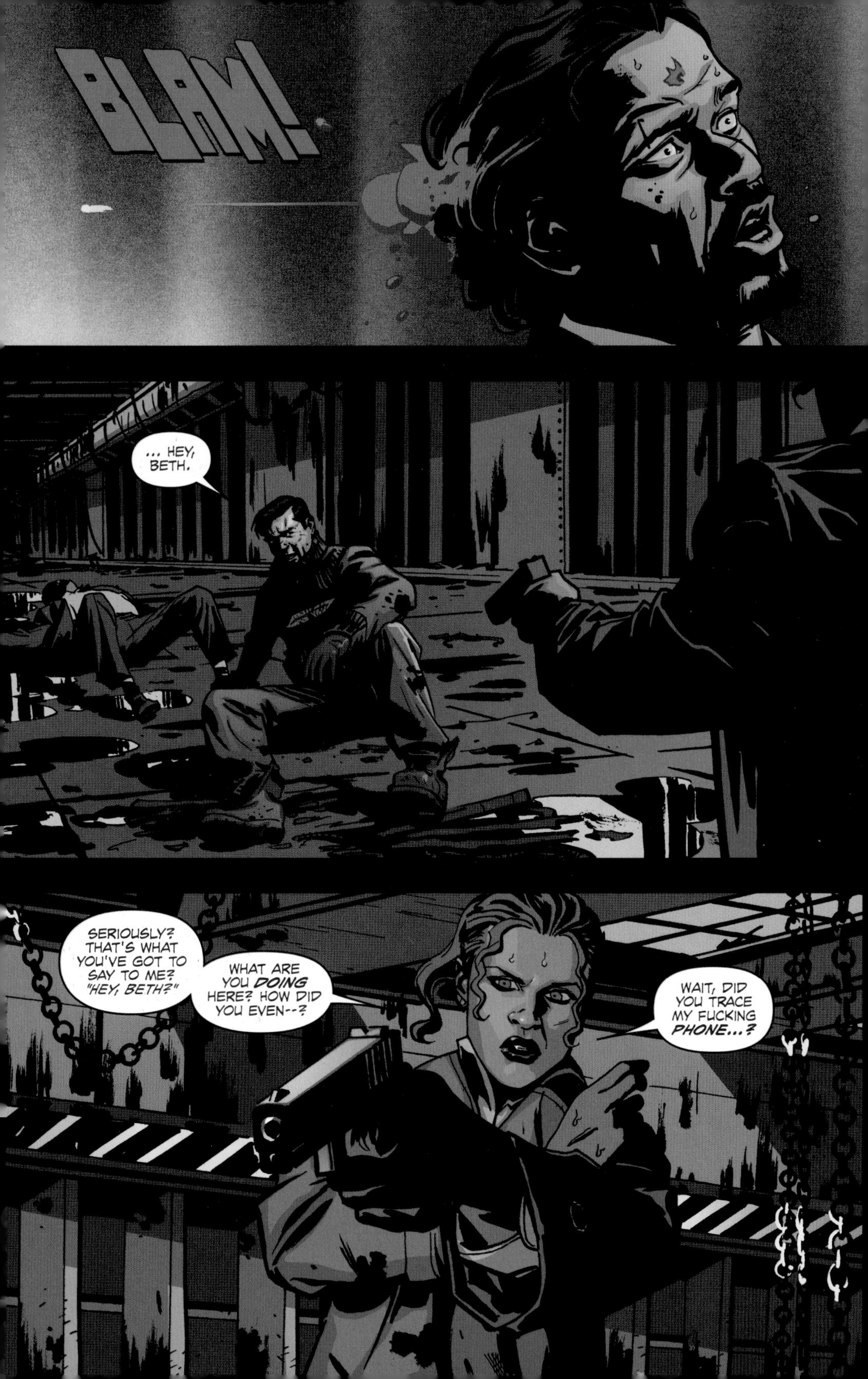
BLAM!
... HEY, BETH.
SERIOUSLY? THAT'S WHAT YOU'VE GOT TO SAY TO ME? "HEY, BETH?"
WHAT ARE YOU DOING HERE? HOW DID YOU EVEN--?
WAIT, DID YOU TRACE MY FUCKING PHONE...?

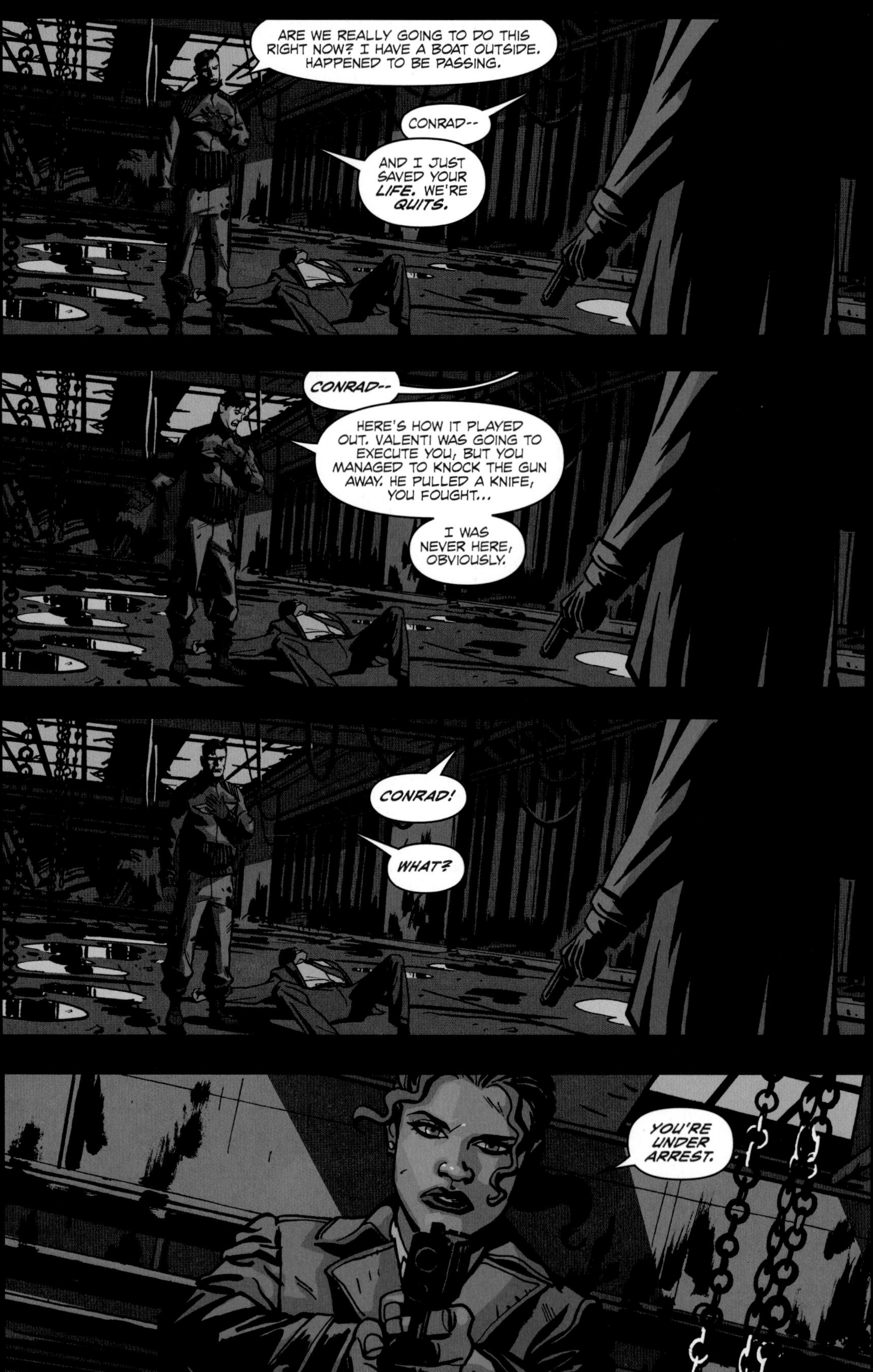
ARE WE REALLY GOING TO DO THIS RIGHT NOW? I HAVE A BOAT OUTSIDE. HAPPENED TO BE PASSING.
CONRAD--
AND I JUST SAVED YOUR *LIFE.* WE'RE *QUITS.*
CONRAD--
HERE'S HOW IT PLAYED OUT. VALENTI WAS GOING TO EXECUTE YOU, BUT YOU MANAGED TO KNOCK THE GUN AWAY. HE PULLED A KNIFE, YOU FOUGHT...
I WAS NEVER HERE, OBVIOUSLY.
CONRAD!
WHAT?
YOU'RE UNDER ARREST.

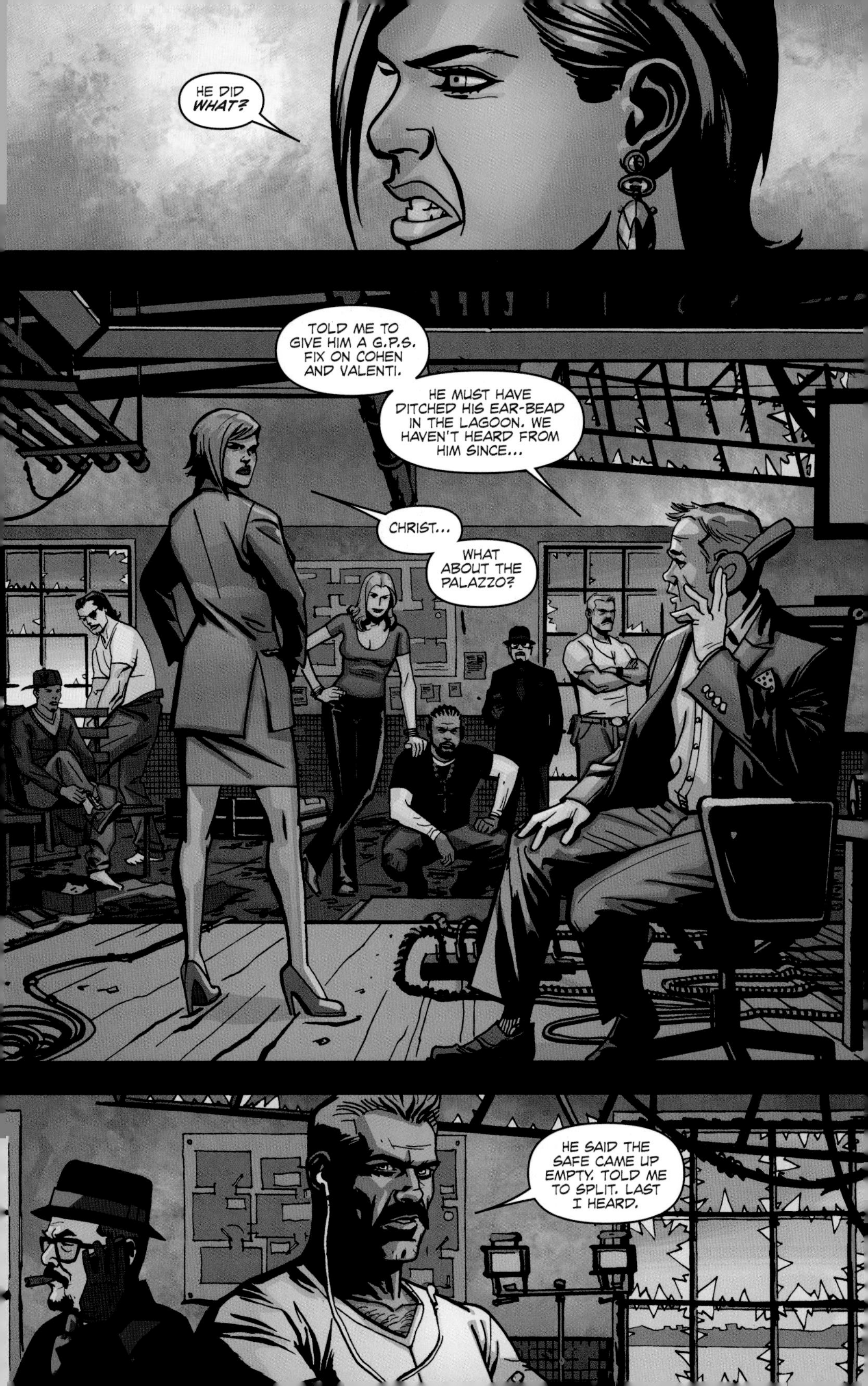
HE DID *WHAT?*
TOLD ME TO GIVE HIM A G.P.S. FIX ON COHEN AND VALENTI.
HE MUST HAVE DITCHED HIS EAR-BEAD IN THE LAGOON. WE HAVEN'T HEARD FROM HIM SINCE...
CHRIST...
WHAT ABOUT THE PALAZZO?
HE SAID THE SAFE CAME UP EMPTY. TOLD ME TO SPLIT. LAST I HEARD.

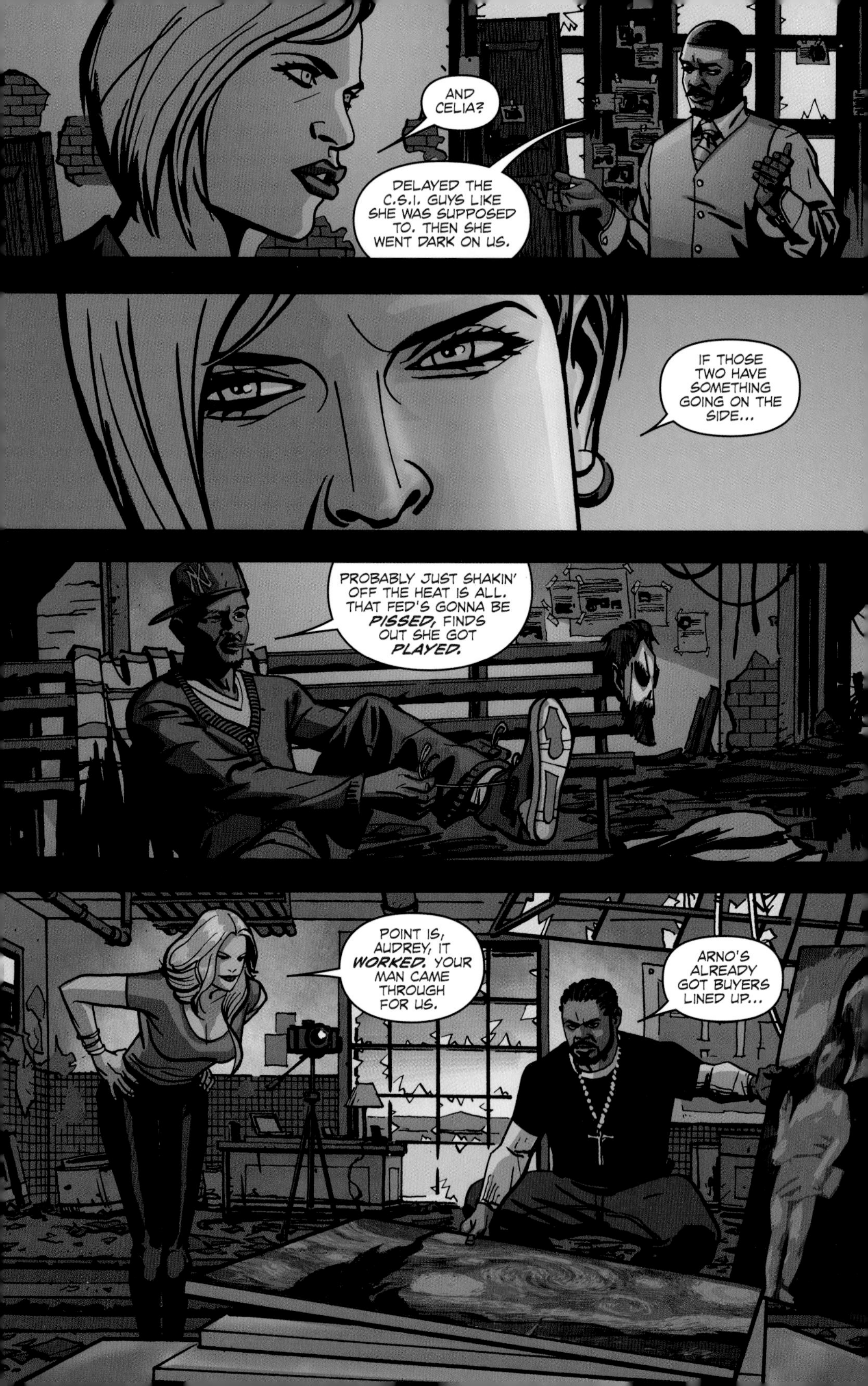
AND CELIA?
DELAYED THE C.S.I. GUYS LIKE SHE WAS SUPPOSED TO. THEN SHE WENT DARK ON US.
IF THOSE TWO HAVE SOMETHING GOING ON THE SIDE...
PROBABLY JUST SHAKIN' OFF THE HEAT IS ALL. THAT FED'S GONNA BE *PISSED,* FINDS OUT SHE GOT *PLAYED.*
POINT IS, AUDREY, IT *WORKED.* YOUR MAN CAME THROUGH FOR US.
ARNO'S ALREADY GOT BUYERS LINED UP...

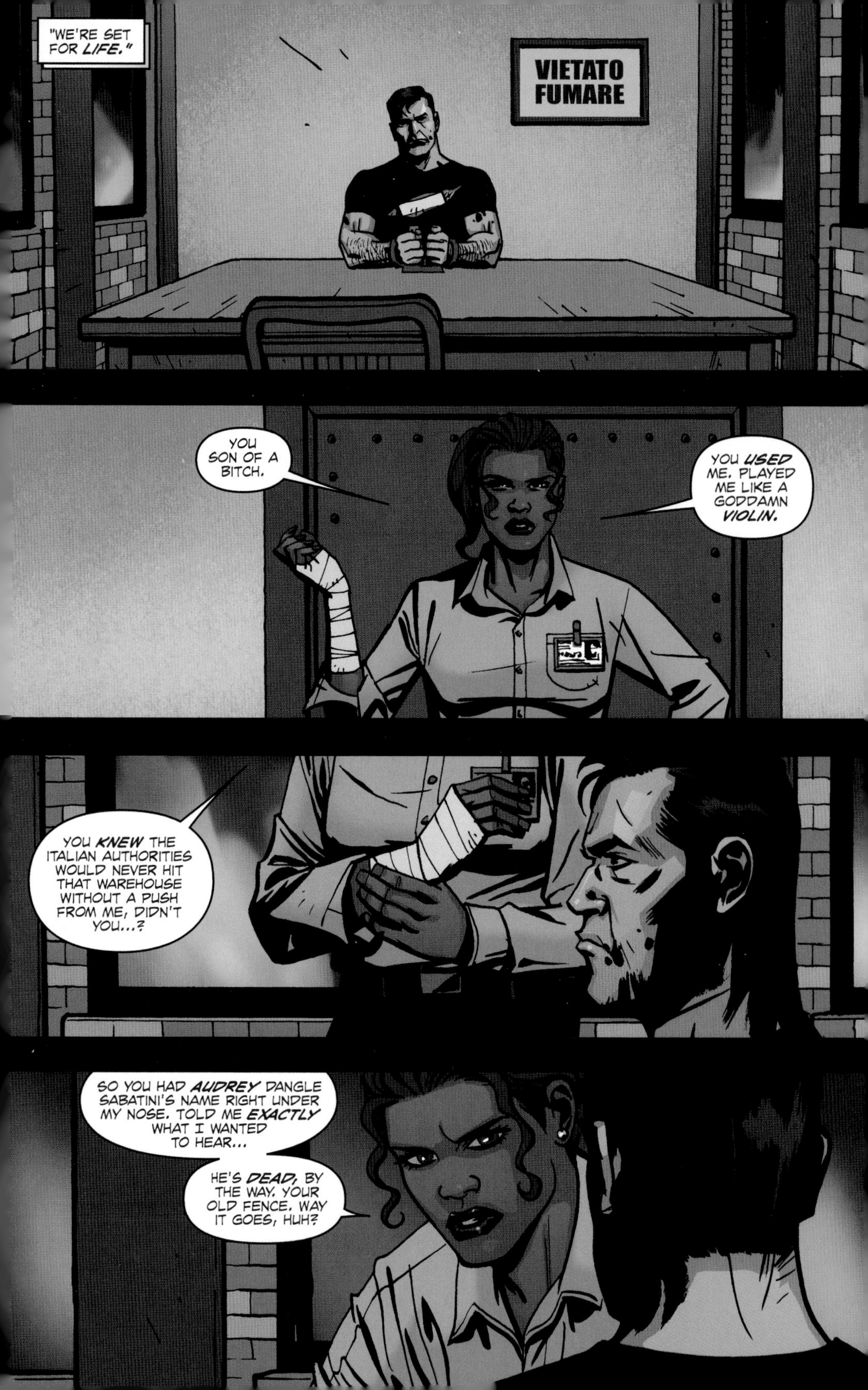
"WE'RE SET FOR LIFE."
VIETATO FUMARE
YOU SON OF A BITCH.
YOU USED ME. PLAYED ME LIKE A GODDAMN VIOLIN.
YOU KNEW THE ITALIAN AUTHORITIES WOULD NEVER HIT THAT WAREHOUSE WITHOUT A PUSH FROM ME, DIDN'T YOU...?
SO YOU HAD AUDREY DANGLE SABATINI'S NAME RIGHT UNDER MY NOSE. TOLD ME EXACTLY WHAT I WANTED TO HEAR...
HE'S DEAD, BY THE WAY. YOUR OLD FENCE. WAY IT GOES, HUH?

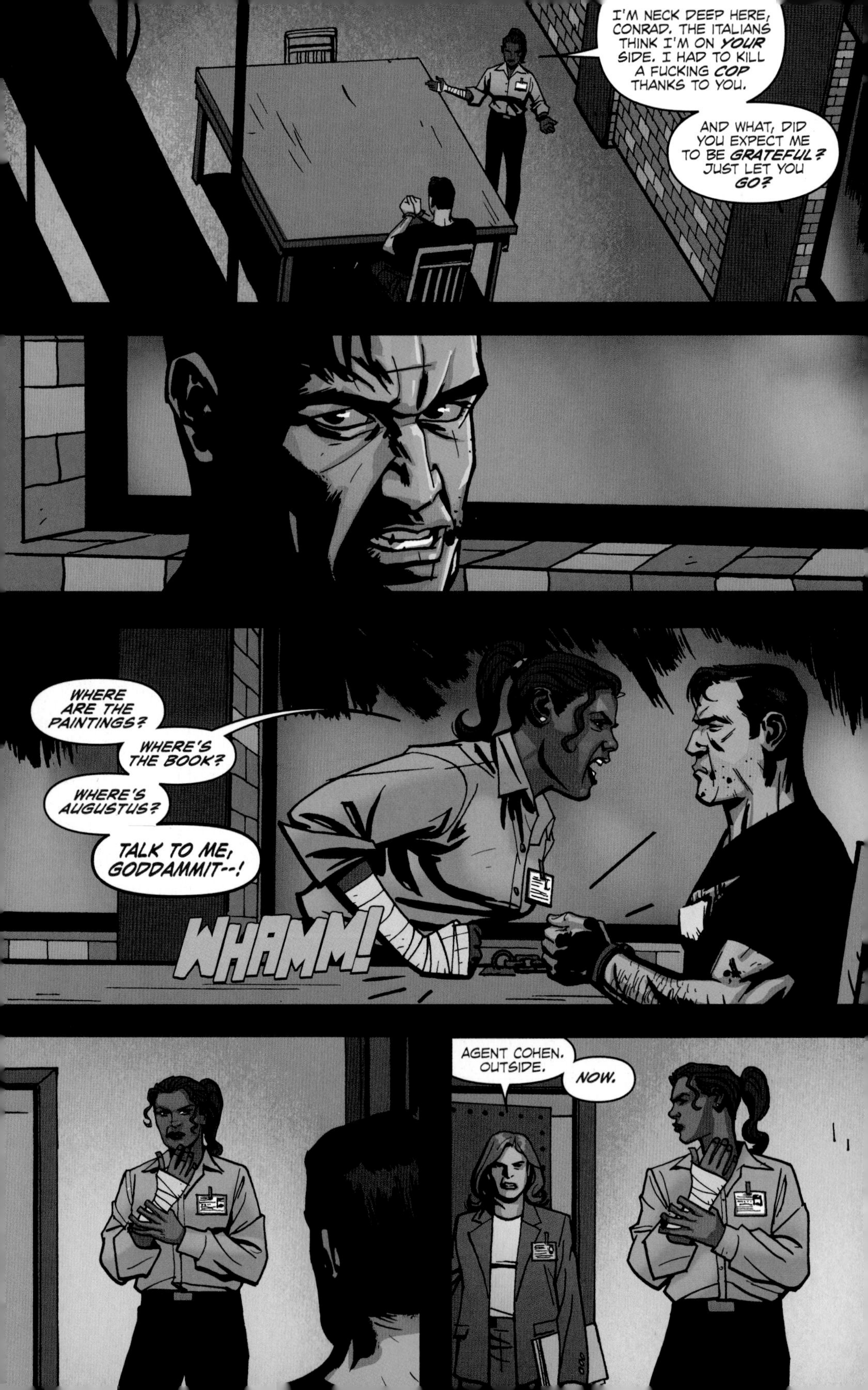

I'M NECK DEEP HERE, CONRAD. THE ITALIANS THINK I'M ON YOUR SIDE. I HAD TO KILL A FUCKING COP THANKS TO YOU.
AND WHAT, DID YOU EXPECT ME TO BE GRATEFUL? JUST LET YOU GO?
WHERE ARE THE PAINTINGS?
WHERE'S THE BOOK?
WHERE'S AUGUSTUS?
TALK TO ME, GODDAMMIT--!
WHAMM!
AGENT COHEN. OUTSIDE.
NOW.

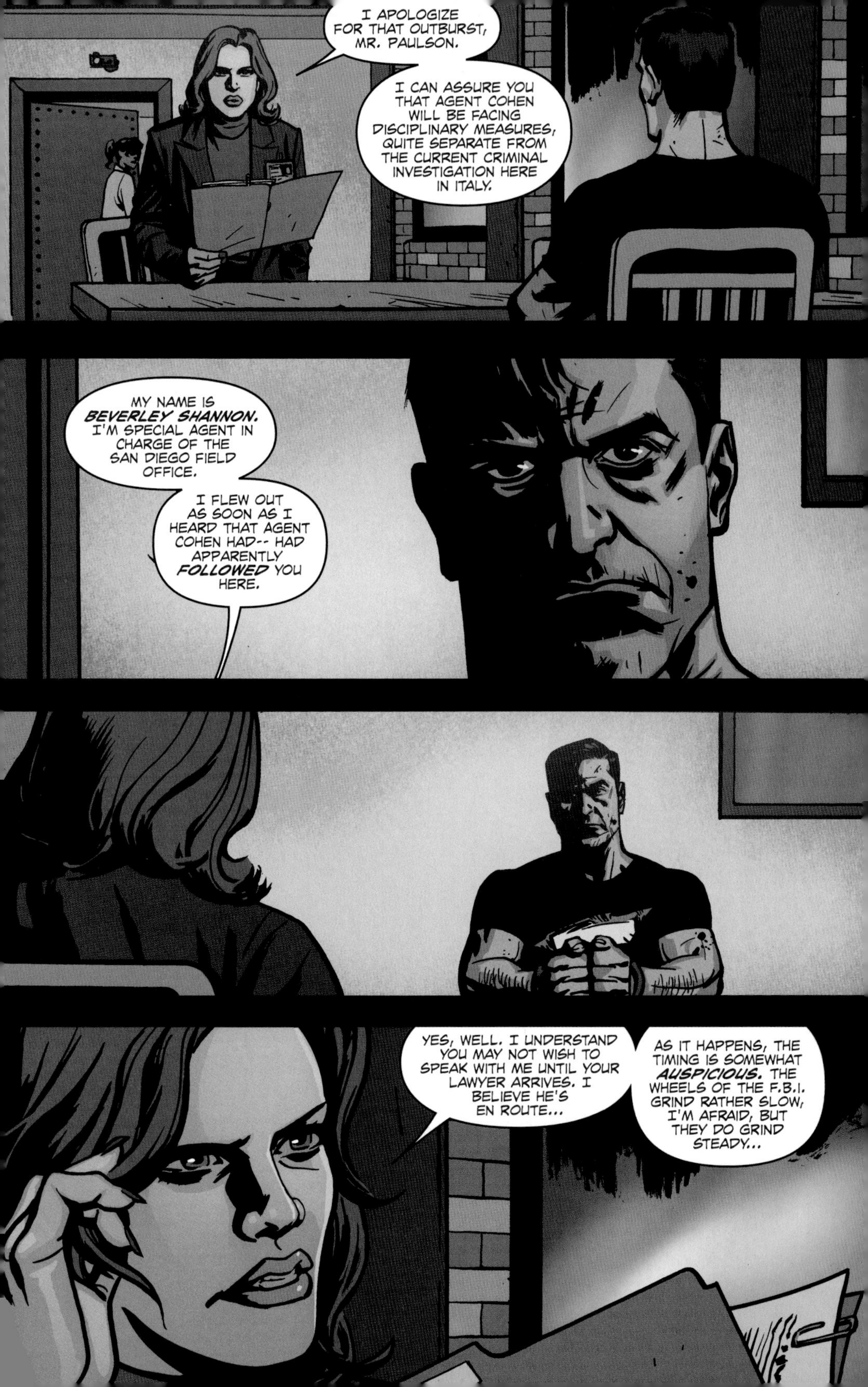
I APOLOGIZE FOR THAT OUTBURST, MR. PAULSON.
I CAN ASSURE YOU THAT AGENT COHEN WILL BE FACING DISCIPLINARY MEASURES, QUITE SEPARATE FROM THE CURRENT CRIMINAL INVESTIGATION HERE IN ITALY.
MY NAME IS BEVERLEY SHANNON. I'M SPECIAL AGENT IN CHARGE OF THE SAN DIEGO FIELD OFFICE.
I FLEW OUT AS SOON AS I HEARD THAT AGENT COHEN HAD-- HAD APPARENTLY FOLLOWED YOU HERE.
YES, WELL. I UNDERSTAND YOU MAY NOT WISH TO SPEAK WITH ME UNTIL YOUR LAWYER ARRIVES. I BELIEVE HE'S EN ROUTE...
AS IT HAPPENS, THE TIMING IS SOMEWHAT AUSPICIOUS. THE WHEELS OF THE F.B.I. GRIND RATHER SLOW, I'M AFRAID, BUT THEY DO GRIND STEADY...

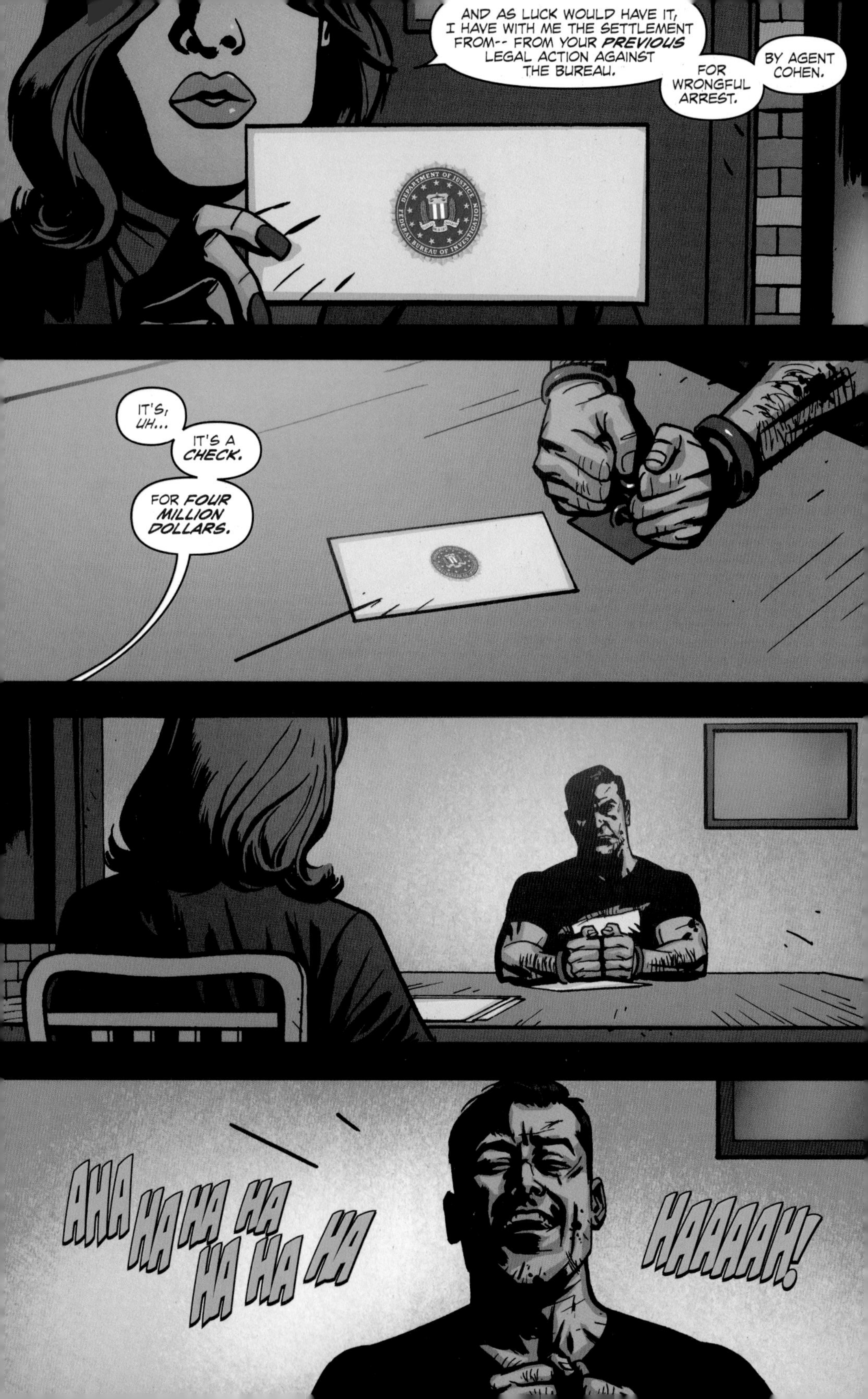
AND AS LUCK WOULD HAVE IT, I HAVE WITH ME THE SETTLEMENT FROM-- FROM YOUR PREVIOUS LEGAL ACTION AGAINST THE BUREAU.
FOR WRONGFUL ARREST.
BY AGENT COHEN.
IT'S, UH...
IT'S A CHECK.
FOR FOUR MILLION DOLLARS.
AHAHAHAHA HA HA HA HA HA
HAAAAH!

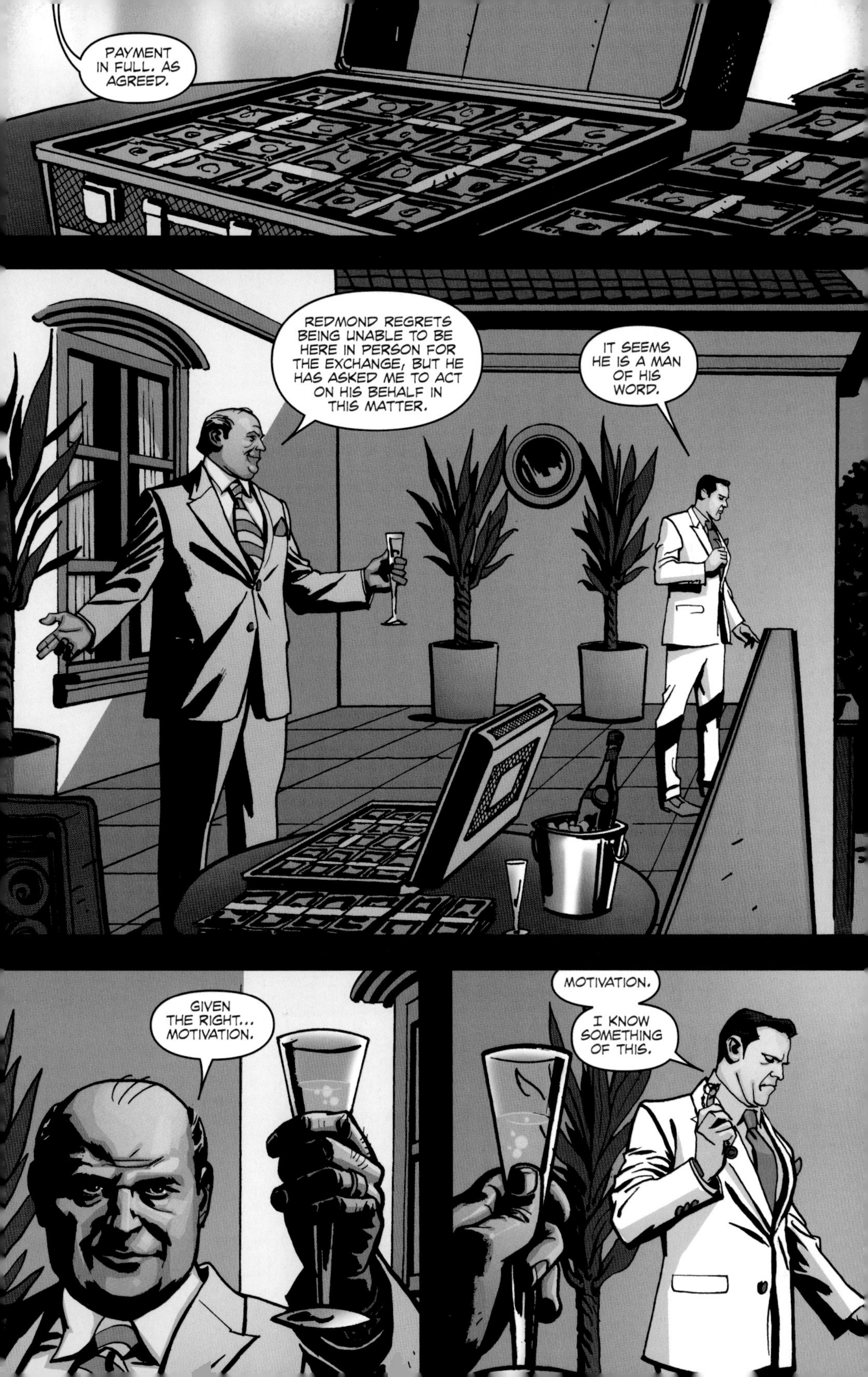
PAYMENT IN FULL. AS AGREED.
REDMOND REGRETS BEING UNABLE TO BE HERE IN PERSON FOR THE EXCHANGE, BUT HE HAS ASKED ME TO ACT ON HIS BEHALF IN THIS MATTER.
IT SEEMS HE IS A MAN OF HIS WORD.
GIVEN THE RIGHT... MOTIVATION.
MOTIVATION.
I KNOW SOMETHING OF THIS.

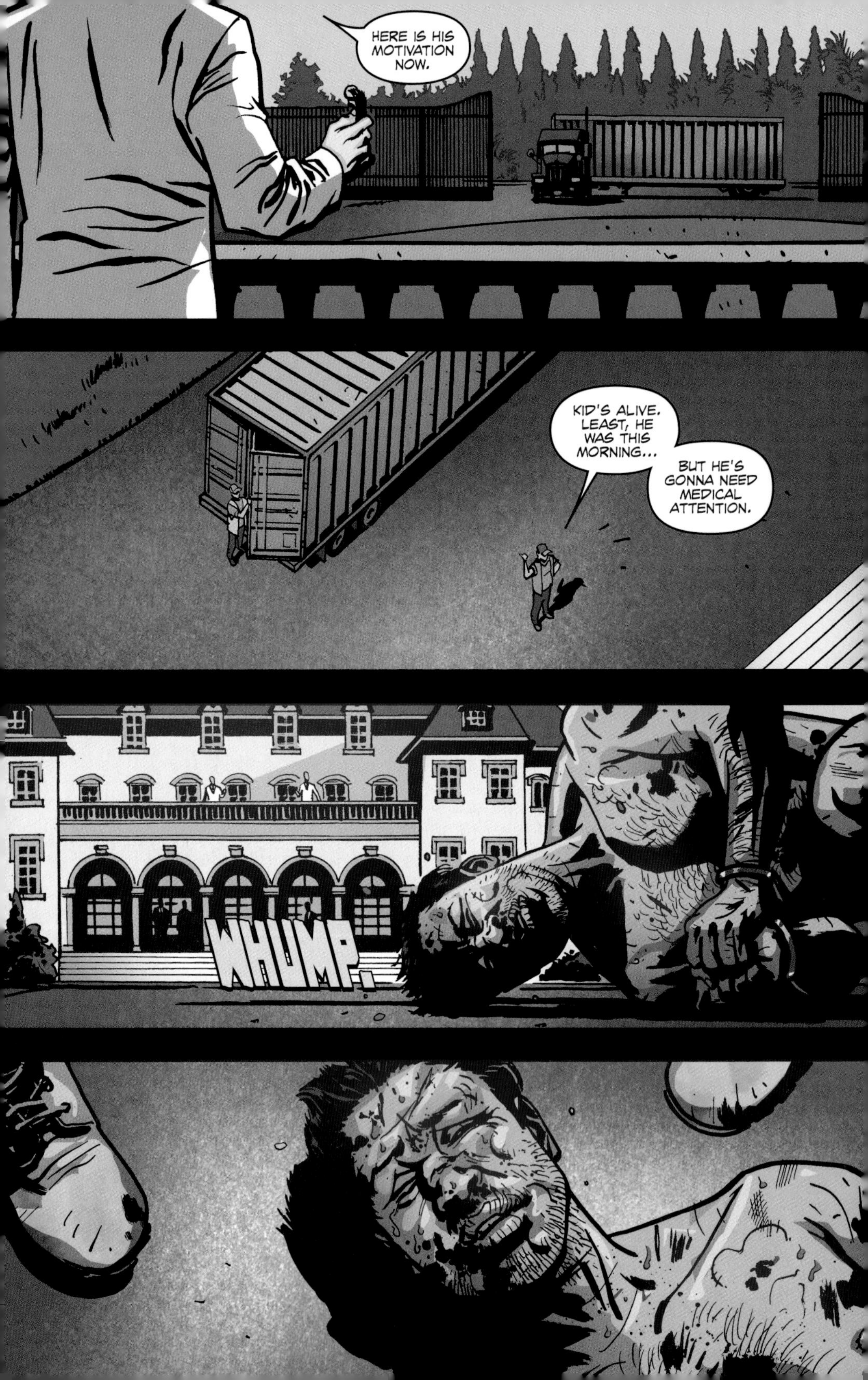
HERE IS HIS MOTIVATION NOW.
KID'S ALIVE. LEAST, HE WAS THIS MORNING...
BUT HE'S GONNA NEED MEDICAL ATTENTION.
WHUMP.

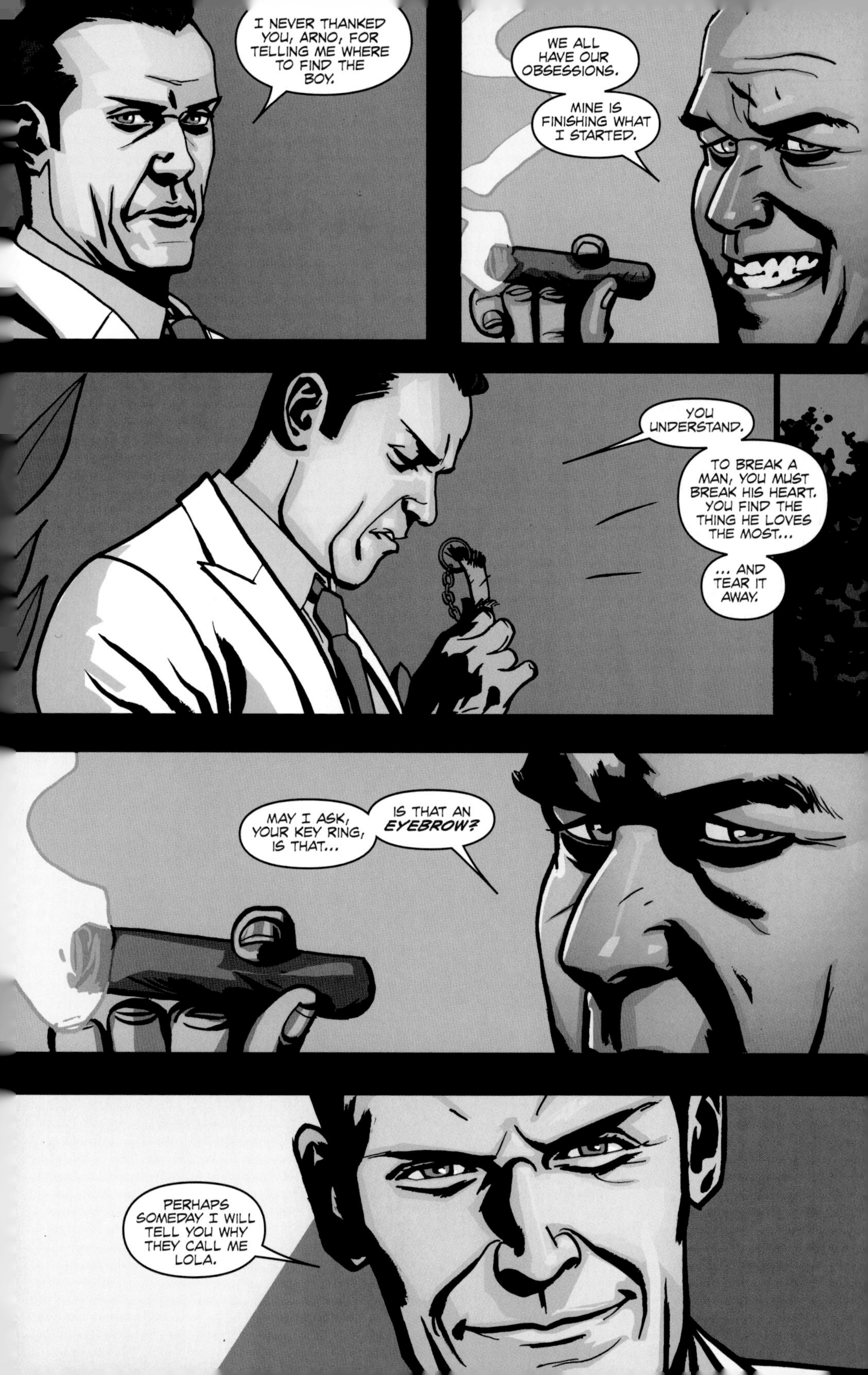
I NEVER THANKED YOU, ARNO, FOR TELLING ME WHERE TO FIND THE BOY.
WE ALL HAVE OUR OBSESSIONS.
MINE IS FINISHING WHAT I STARTED.
YOU UNDERSTAND.
TO BREAK A MAN, YOU MUST BREAK HIS HEART. YOU FIND THE THING HE LOVES THE MOST...
... AND TEAR IT AWAY.
MAY I ASK, YOUR KEY RING, IS THAT...
IS THAT AN *EYEBROW?*
PERHAPS SOMEDAY I WILL TELL YOU WHY THEY CALL ME LOLA.

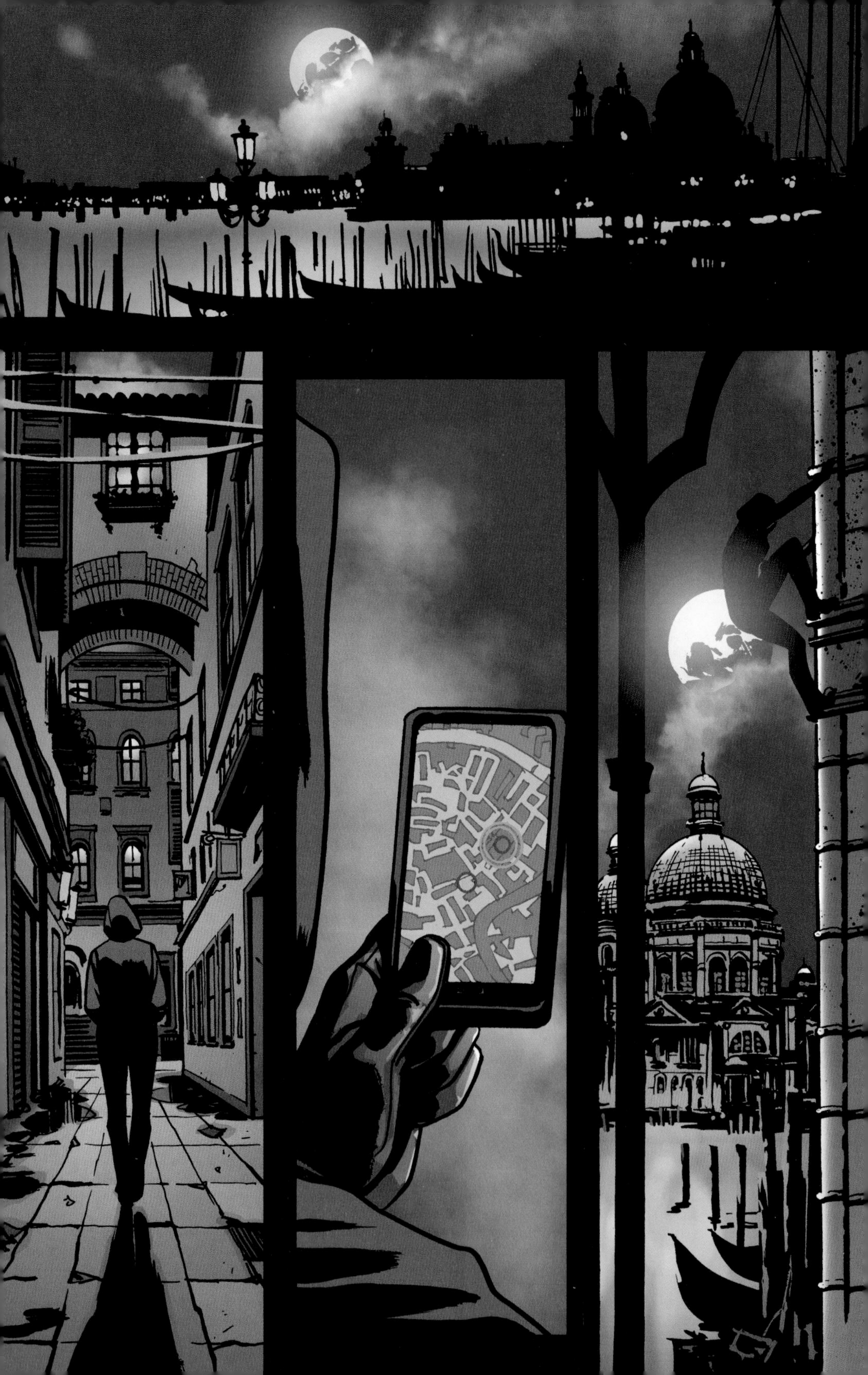

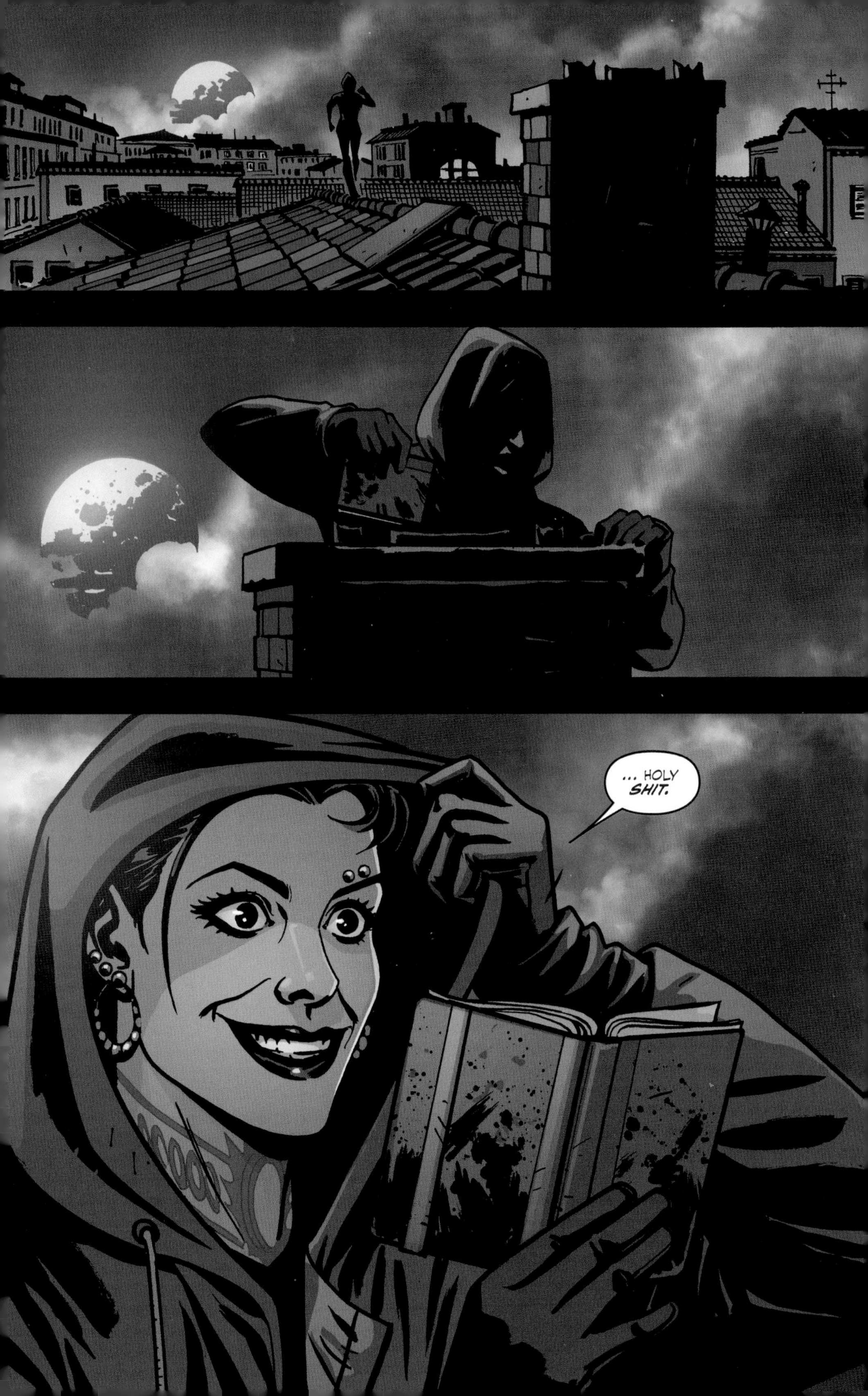
... HOLY SHIT.

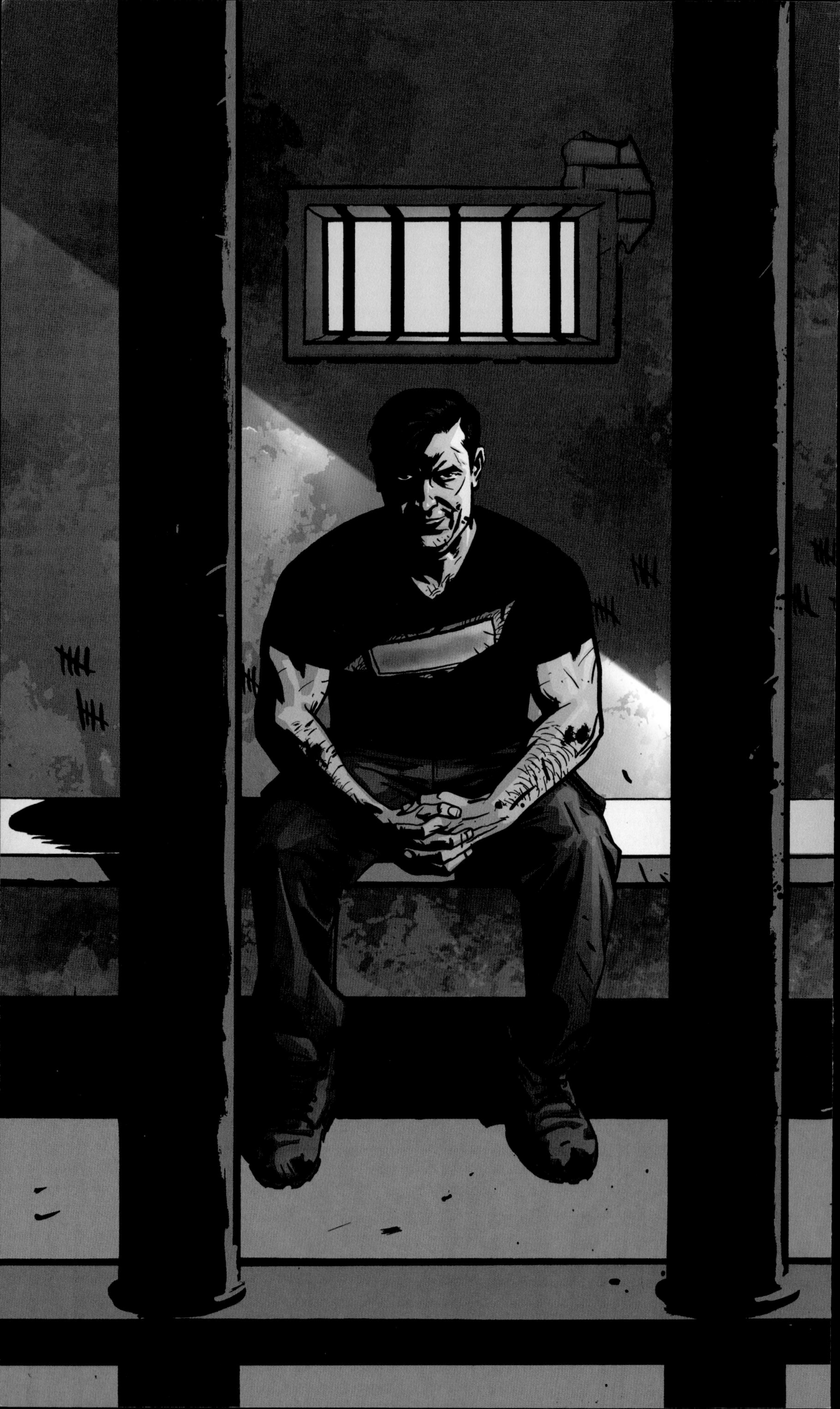

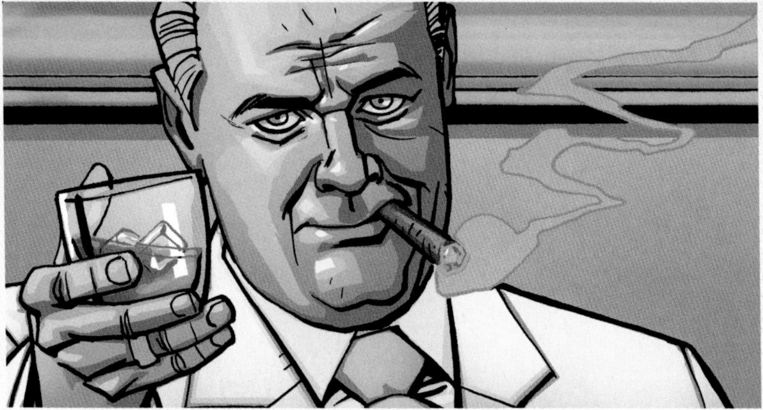

TO BE CONTINUED...

MORE BOOKS FROM

ROBERT KIRKMAN

AND SKYBOUND!

THIEF OF THIEVES

THIEF OF THIEVES
VOL. 1: "I QUIT."
ISBN: 978-1-60706-592-0
$14.99
VOL. 2: "HELP ME."
ISBN: 978-1-60706-676-7
$14.99
VOL. 3: "VENICE."
ISBN: 978-1-60706-844-0
$14.99

BRANDON SEIFERT
LUKAS KETNER
ANDY TROY
WITCH DOCTOR
MAL PRACTICE

WITCH DOCTOR
VOL. 1: UNDER THE KNIFE TP
ISBN: 978-1-60706-441-1
$12.99
VOL. 2: MAL PRACTICE TP
ISBN: 978-1-60706-693-4
$14.99

KIRKMAN · CERENO · GETTY · ANKA
GUARDING THE GLOBE
VOLUME ONE
UNDER SIEGE

GUARDING THE GLOBE
VOL. 1: UNDER SIEGE TP
ISBN: 978-1-60706-356-8
$16.99
VOL. 2: HARD TO KILL TP
ISBN: 978-1-60706-673-6
$16.99

TO FIND YOUR NEAREST COMIC BOOK STORE, CALL:
1-888-COMIC-BOOK

KIRKMAN · OTTLEY · RATHBURN · RAUCH
INVINCIBLE
VOLUME EIGHTEEN
THE DEATH OF EVERYONE

INVINCIBLE
VOL. 1: FAMILY MATTERS TP
ISBN: 978-1-58240-711-1
$12.99
VOL. 2: EIGHT IS ENOUGH TP
ISBN: 978-1-58240-347-2
$12.99
VOL. 3: PERFECT STRANGERS TP
ISBN: 978-1-58240-793-7
$12.99
VOL. 4: HEAD OF THE CLASS TP
ISBN: 978-1-58240-440-2
$14.95
VOL. 5: THE FACTS OF LIFE TP
ISBN: 978-1-58240-554-4
$14.99
VOL. 6: A DIFFERENT WORLD TP
ISBN: 978-1-58240-579-7
$14.99
VOL. 7: THREE'S COMPANY TP
ISBN: 978-1-58240-656-5
$14.99
VOL. 8: MY FAVORITE MARTIAN TP
ISBN: 978-1-58240-683-1
$14.99
VOL. 9: OUT OF THIS WORLD TP
ISBN: 978-1-58240-827-9
$14.99
VOL. 10: WHO'S THE BOSS TP
ISBN: 978-1-60706-013-0
$16.99
VOL. 11: HAPPY DAYS TP
ISBN: 978-1-60706-062-8
$16.99
VOL. 12: STILL STANDING TP
ISBN: 978-1-60706-166-3
$16.99
VOL. 13: GROWING PAINS TP
ISBN: 978-1-60706-251-6
$16.99
VOL. 14: THE VILTRUMITE WAR TP
ISBN: 978-1-60706-367-4
$19.99
VOL. 15: GET SMART TP
ISBN: 978-1-60706-498-5
$16.99
VOL. 16: FAMILY TIES TP
ISBN: 978-1-60706-579-1
$16.99
VOL. 17: WHAT'S HAPPENING TP
ISBN: 978-1-60706-662-0
$16.99
VOL. 18: DEATH OF EVERYONE TP
ISBN: 978-1-60706-762-7
$16.99
ULTIMATE COLLECTION, VOL. 1 HC
ISBN 978-1-58240-500-1
$34.95
ULTIMATE COLLECTION, VOL. 2 HC
ISBN: 978-1-58240-594-0
$34.99
ULTIMATE COLLECTION, VOL. 3 HC
ISBN: 978-1-58240-763-0
$34.99
ULTIMATE COLLECTION, VOL. 4 HC
ISBN: 978-1-58240-989-4
$34.99
ULTIMATE COLLECTION, VOL. 5 HC
ISBN: 978-1-60706-116-8
$34.99
ULTIMATE COLLECTION, VOL. 6 HC
ISBN: 978-1-60706-360-5
$34.99
ULTIMATE COLLECTION, VOL. 7 HC
ISBN: 978-1-60706-509-8
$39.99
ULTIMATE COLLECTION, VOL. 8 HC
ISBN: 978-1-60706-680-4
$39.99
COMPENDIUM VOL. 1
ISBN: 978-1-60706-411-4
$64.99
THE COMPLETE INVINCIBLE LIBRARY, VOL. 2 HC
ISBN: 978-1-60706-112-0
$125.00
THE COMPLETE INVINCIBLE LIBRARY, VOL. 3 HC
ISBN: 978-1-60706-421-3
$125.00
THE OFFICIAL HANDBOOK OF THE INVINCIBLE UNIVERSE TP
ISBN: 978-1-58240-831-6
$12.99
INVINCIBLE PRESENTS, VOL. 1: ATOM EVE & REX SPLODE TP
ISBN: 978-1-60706-255-4
$14.99

SUPER DINOSAUR 3

SUPER DINOSAUR
VOL. 1
ISBN: 978-1-60706-420-6
$9.99
VOL. 2
ISBN: 978-1-60706-568-5
$12.99
VOL. 3
ISBN: 978-1-60706-667-5
$12.99
DELUXE COLORING BOOK
ISBN: 978-1-60706-481-7
$4.99

THE ASTOUNDING WOLF-MAN
VOL. 1 TP
ISBN: 978-1-58240-862-0
$14.99
VOL. 2 TP
ISBN: 978-1-60706-007-9
$14.99
VOL. 3 TP
ISBN: 978-1-60706-111-3
$16.99
VOL. 4 TP
ISBN: 978-1-60706-249-3
$16.99

BATTLE POPE
VOL. 1: GENESIS TP
ISBN: 978-1-58240-572-8
$14.99
VOL. 2: MAYHEM TP
ISBN: 978-1-58240-529-2
$12.99
VOL. 3: PILLOW TALK TP
ISBN: 978-1-58240-677-0
$12.99
VOL. 4: WRATH OF GOD TP
ISBN: 978-1-58240-751-7
$9.99

BRIT
VOL. 1: OLD SOLDIER TP
ISBN: 978-1-58240-678-7
$14.99
VOL. 2: AWOL
ISBN: 978-1-58240-864-4
$14.99
VOL. 3: FUBAR
ISBN: 978-1-60706-061-1
$16.99

CAPES
VOL. 1: PUNCHING THE CLOCK TP
ISBN: 978-1-58240-756-2
$17.99

HAUNT
VOL. 1 TP
ISBN: 978-1-60706-154-0
$9.99
VOL. 2 TP
ISBN: 978-1-60706-229-5
$16.99
VOL. 3 TP
ISBN: 978-1-60706-552-4
$14.99
THE IMMORTAL EDITION, VOL. 1 HC
ISBN: 978-1-60706-241-7
$34.99

THE INFINITE
VOL. 1 TP
ISBN: 978-1-60706-475-6
$9.99

SUPERPATRIOT
AMERICA'S FIGHTING FORCE
ISBN: 978-1-58240-355-1
$14.99

TALES OF THE REALM
HARDCOVER
ISBN: 978-1-58240-426-0
$34.95
TRADE PAPERBACK
ISBN: 978-1-58240-394-6
$14.95

TECH JACKET
VOL. 1: THE BOY FROM EARTH TP
ISBN: 978-1-58240-771-5
$14.99

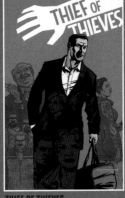

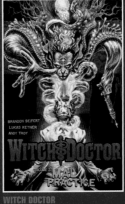

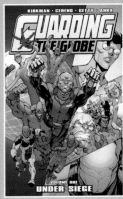

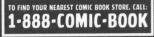

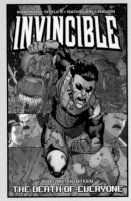

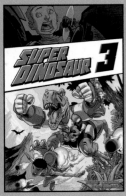

FOR MORE OF THE WALKING DEA

TRADEPAPERBACKS

ROBERT KIRKMAN TONY MOORE
THE WALKING DEAD
VOLUME 1
DAYS GONE BYE

VOL. 1: DAYS GONE BYE TP
ISBN: 978-1-58240-672-5
$14.99
VOL. 2: MILES BEHIND US TP
ISBN: 978-1-58240-775-3
$14.99
VOL. 3: SAFETY BEHIND BARS TP
ISBN: 978-1-58240-805-7
$14.99
VOL. 4: THE HEART'S DESIRE TP
ISBN: 978-1-58240-530-8
$14.99
VOL. 5: THE BEST DEFENSE TP
ISBN: 978-1-58240-612-1
$14.99
VOL. 6: THIS SORROWFUL LIFE TP
ISBN: 978-1-58240-684-8
$14.99
VOL. 7: THE CALM BEFORE TP
ISBN: 978-1-58240-828-6
$14.99
VOL. 8: MADE TO SUFFER TP
ISBN: 978-1-58240-883-5
$14.99

VOL. 9: HERE WE REMAIN TP
ISBN: 978-1-60706-022-2
$14.99
VOL. 10: WHAT WE BECOME TP
ISBN: 978-1-60706-075-8
$14.99
VOL. 11: FEAR THE HUNTERS TP
ISBN: 978-1-60706-181-6
$14.99
VOL. 12: LIFE AMONG THEM TP
ISBN: 978-1-60706-254-7
$14.99
VOL. 13: TOO FAR GONE TP
ISBN: 978-1-60706-329-2
$14.99
VOL. 14: NO WAY OUT TP
ISBN: 978-1-60706-392-6
$14.99
VOL. 15: WE FIND OURSELVES TP
ISBN: 978-1-60706-440-4
$14.99
VOL. 16: A LARGER WORLD TP
ISBN: 978-1-60706-559-3
$14.99

VOL. 17: SOMETHING TO FEAR TP
ISBN: 978-1-60706-615-
$14.99
VOL. 18: WHAT COMES AFTER TP
ISBN: 978-1-60706-687-
$14.99
VOL. 19: MARCH TO WAR TP
ISBN: 978-1-60706-818-
$14.99
VOL. 12: ALL OUT WAR TP
ISBN: 978-1-60706-882-
$14.99
VOL. 1: SPANISH EDITION TP
ISBN: 978-1-60706-797-
$14.99
VOL. 2: SPANISH EDITION TP
ISBN: 978-1-60706-845-
$14.99

HARDCOVERS

THE WALKING DEAD
BOOK ONE
a continuing story of survival horror.

BOOK ONE HC
ISBN: 978-1-58240-619-0
$34.99
BOOK TWO HC
ISBN: 978-1-58240-698-5
$34.99
BOOK THREE HC
ISBN: 978-1-58240-825-5
$34.99
BOOK FOUR HC
ISBN: 978-1-60706-000-0
$34.99
BOOK FIVE HC
ISBN: 978-1-60706-171-7
$34.99
BOOK SIX HC
ISBN: 978-1-60706-327-8
$34.99
BOOK SEVEN HC
ISBN: 978-1-60706-439-8
$34.99
BOOK EIGHT HC
ISBN: 978-1-60706-593-7
$34.99
BOOK NINE HC
ISBN: 978-1-60706-798-6
$34.99

COMPENDIUMS

The ultimate edition of The New York Times bestseller!
THE WALKING DEAD
COMPENDIUM ONE
Robert Kirkman • Charlie Adlard • Tony Moore • Cliff Rathburn

COMPENDIUM TP, VOL. 1
ISBN: 978-1-60706-076-5
$59.99
COMPENDIUM TP, VOL. 2
ISBN: 978-1-60706-596-8
$59.99

THE WALKING DEAD
THE COVERS

THE WALKING DEAD: THE COVERS, VOL. 1 HC
ISBN: 978-1-60706-002-4
$24.99
THE WALKING DEAD SURVIVORS' GUIDE
ISBN: 978-1-60706-458-9
$12.99

OMNIBUS

THE WALKING DEAD

OMNIBUS, VOL. 1
ISBN: 978-1-60706-503-6
$100.00
OMNIBUS, VOL. 2
ISBN: 978-1-60706-515-9
$100.00
OMNIBUS, VOL. 3
ISBN: 978-1-60706-330-8
$100.00
OMNIBUS, VOL. 4
ISBN: 978-1-60706-616-3
$100.00

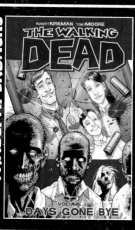

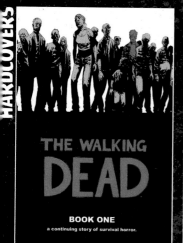

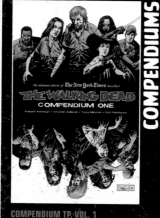

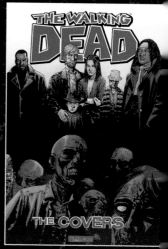

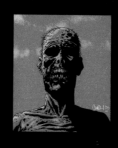

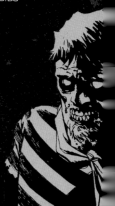

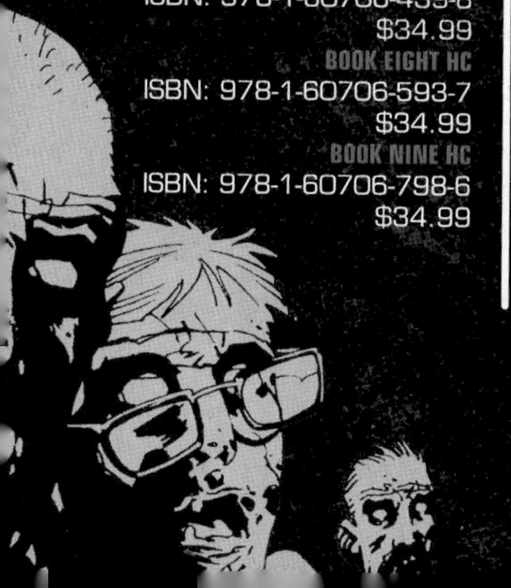

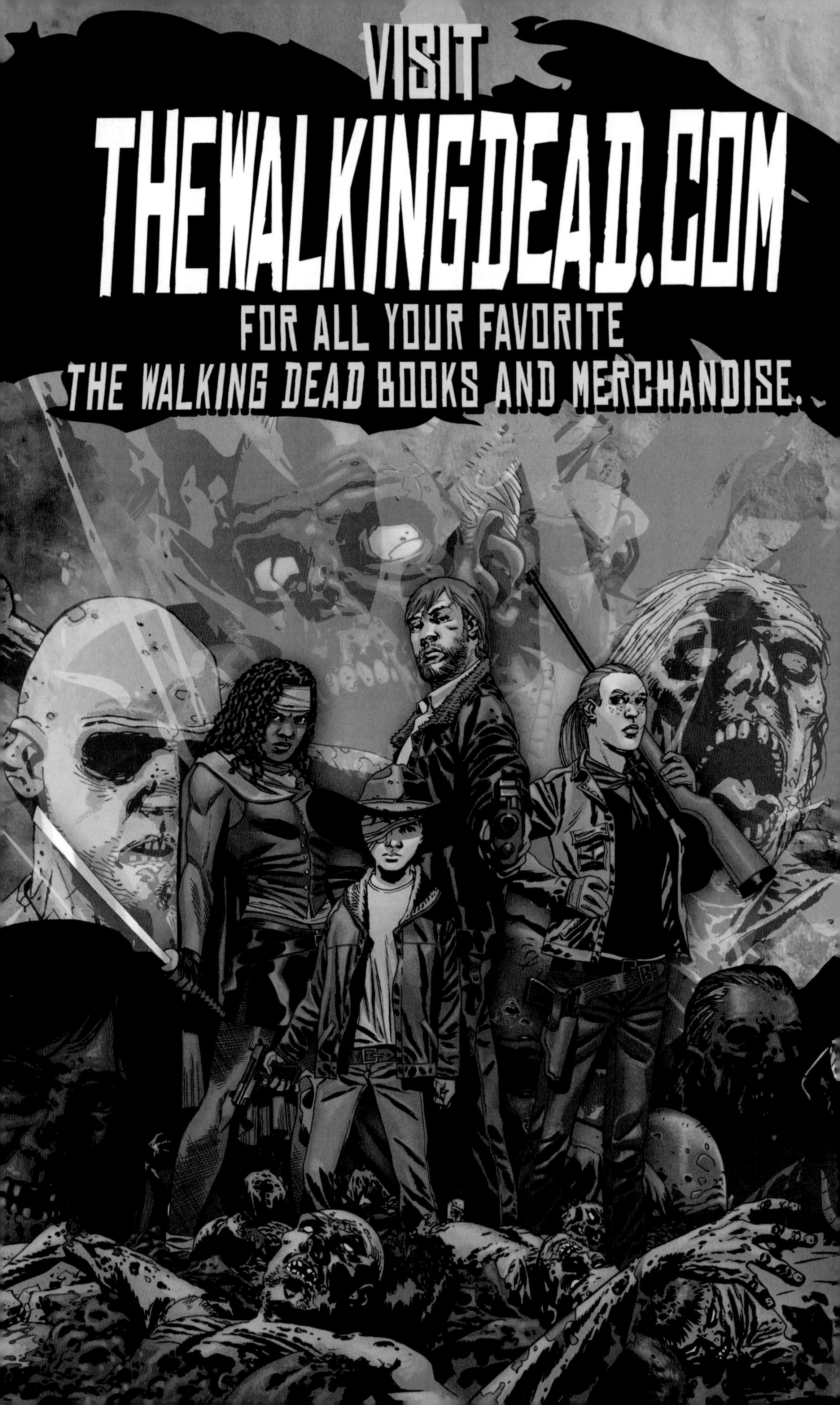
VISIT
THEWALKINGDEAD.COM
FOR ALL YOUR FAVORITE
THE WALKING DEAD BOOKS AND MERCHANDISE.

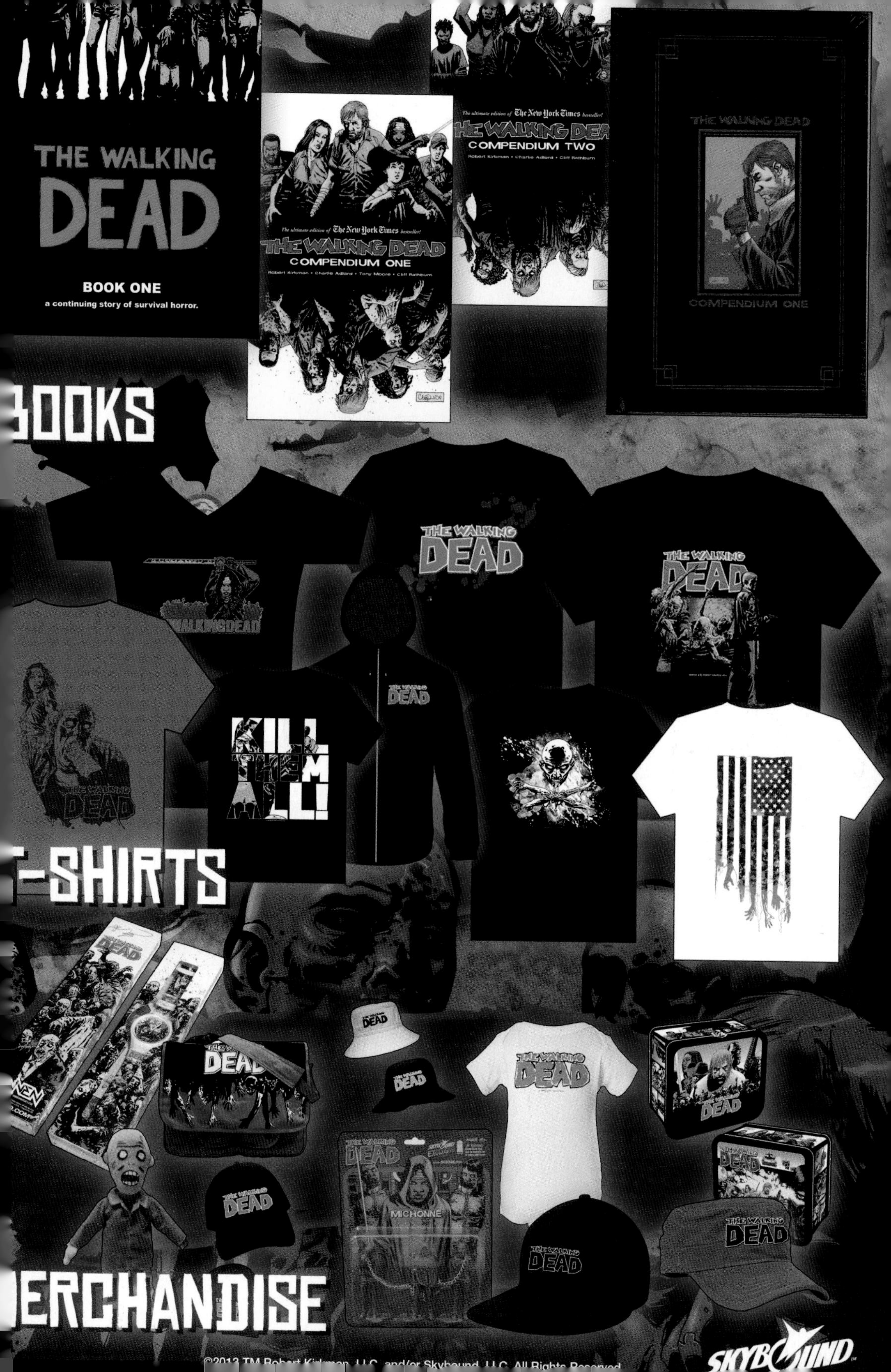
THE WALKING DEAD
BOOK ONE
a continuing story of survival horror.
The ultimate edition of The New York Times bestseller!
THE WALKING DEAD
COMPENDIUM ONE
Robert Kirkman • Charlie Adlard • Tony Moore • Cliff Rathburn
The ultimate edition of The New York Times bestseller!
THE WALKING DEAD
COMPENDIUM TWO
Robert Kirkman • Charlie Adlard • Cliff Rathburn
THE WALKING DEAD
COMPENDIUM ONE
BOOKS
-SHIRTS
ERCHANDISE
MICHONNE
SKYBOUND

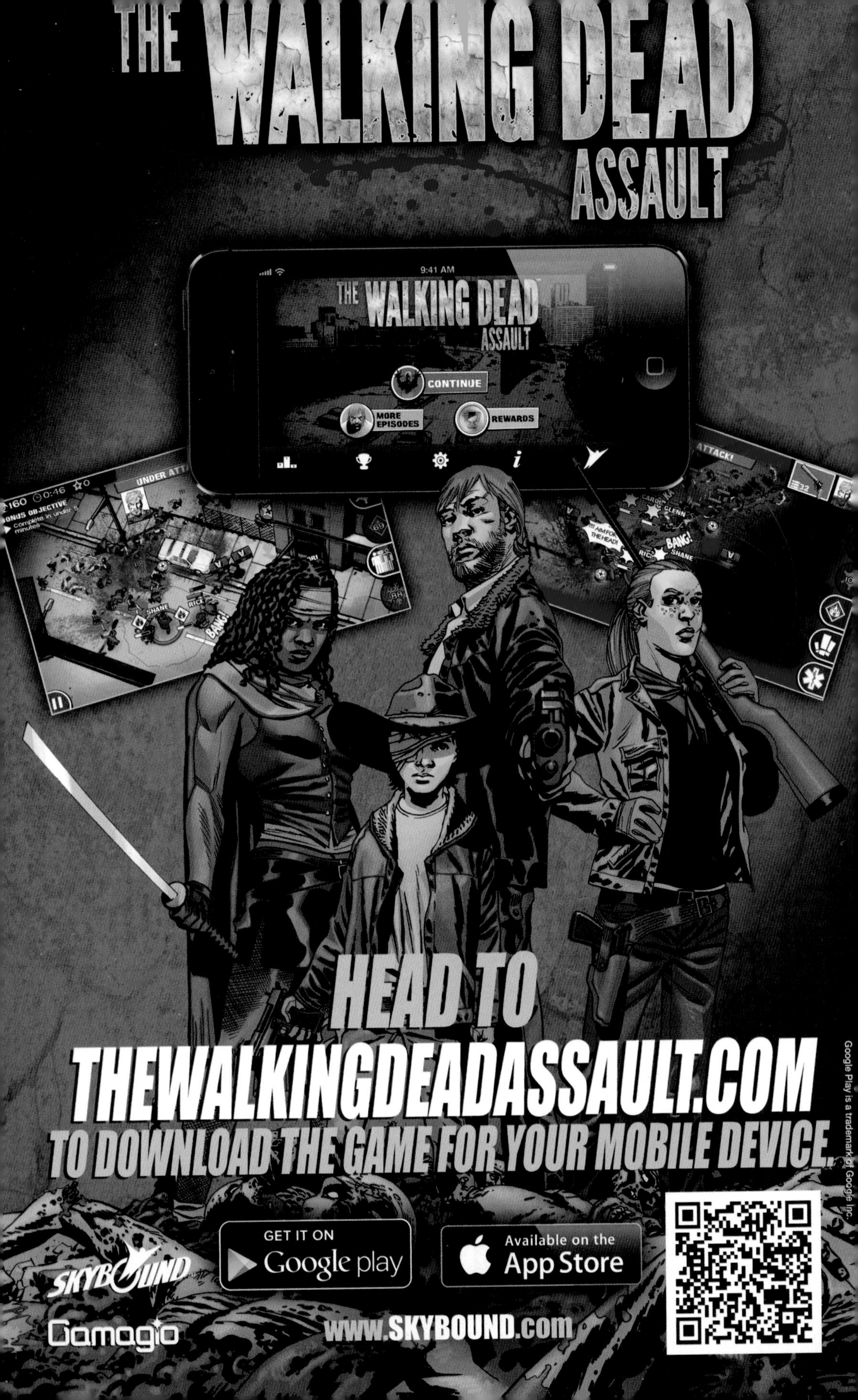
THE WALKING DEAD
ASSAULT
9:41 AM
THE WALKING DEAD
ASSAULT
CONTINUE
MORE EPISODES
REWARDS
HEAD TO
THEWALKINGDEADASSAULT.COM
TO DOWNLOAD THE GAME FOR YOUR MOBILE DEVICE.
GET IT ON
Google play
Available on the
App Store
SKYBOUND
Gamagio
www.SKYBOUND.com
Google Play is a trademark of Google Inc.